Cooperative Education
in a New Era

Kenneth G. Ryder
James W. Wilson
and Associates

Foreword by Ralph W. Tyler

Cooperative Education in a New Era

Understanding and Strengthening the Links Between College and the Workplace

Jossey-Bass Publishers

San Francisco   •   London   •   1987

COOPERATIVE EDUCATION IN A NEW ERA
Understanding and Strengthening the Links Between College and the Workplace
 by Kenneth G. Ryder, James W. Wilson, and Associates

Copyright © 1987 by: Jossey-Bass Inc., Publishers
433 California Street
San Francisco, California 94104
&
Jossey-Bass Limited
28 Banner Street
London EC1Y 8QE

Library of Congress Cataloging-in-Publication Data

Ryder, Kenneth G., date.
  Cooperative education in a new era.

  (The Jossey-Bass higher education series)
  Includes bibliographies and index.
  1. Education, Cooperative—United States.
2. College students—Employment—United States.
I. Wilson, James Warner, date. II. Title.
III. Series.
LB1029.C6R93   1987   378'.103   87-45500
ISBN 1-55542-072-9 (alk. paper)

Manufactured in the United States of America

The paper in this book meets the guidelines for permanence and durability of the Committee on Production Guidelines for Book Longevity of the Council on Library Resources.

JACKET DESIGN BY WILLI BAUM

FIRST EDITION

Code 8742

The Jossey-Bass
Higher Education Series

Contents

Foreword

In a scant eighty years, cooperative education has been accepted, greatly expanded, and strengthened. Instituted in 1906 at the University of Cincinnati as an effective way to help engineering students connect theory and practice, cooperative education is now used by a wide range of educational institutions for a number of additional purposes. Arthur Morgan, then president of Antioch College, was the first to extend it to the liberal arts program in 1921. He had learned of the cooperative education program in engineering and saw the promise this kind of program held for the liberal arts. Thus began an effort to adapt cooperative education to a new set of conditions while preserving the principles of learning that were essential to the program's educational success.

In these early days several other colleges adapted cooperative education to the particular circumstances of their institutions. For example, in 1922 Carnegie Institute of Technology developed a program in retailing to train students for the retail institutions in the Pittsburgh area.

My first direct contact with cooperative education was in 1929 in Rochester, New York. The civic and industrial leaders of that city realized that industries in Rochester were shifting their primary dependence from skilled workmen (for example, lens grinders for the optical industry) to technicans (for example, engineering technicians for the photographic industry). The training of the needed technicians involved postsecondary education. But the potential students were generally the children of skilled workmen who viewed book learning as unnecessary and distasteful. Not very successful in their high school courses, they now merely wanted jobs. They could see little connection between jobs and college courses.

The University of Rochester had an excellent engineering school, but it required advanced high school mathematics for admission. These prospective students did not take advanced mathematics in high school and believed they would have failed the courses if they had taken them. Moreover, most of these young people considered mathematics unrelated to the real world of work in which they wished to be engaged.

A special committee formed by the Rochester community leaders to seek a solution to this problem recommended establishing a new postsecondary institution that would take over two earlier charters—those of the Rochester Athenaeum, chartered to offer courses in liberal education to adults, and of the Mechanics Institute, chartered to furnish continuing education to mechanics. The president of this new Rochester Athenaeum and Mechanics Institute invited W. W. Charters, director of the Bureau of Educational Research at Ohio State University, to guide the faculty in developing an effective curriculum. I was a research associate in the bureau, and Charters asked me to assist him in this project.

Charters recognized the value of cooperative education in attracting students who were leery of a college curriculum. While pursuing their studies, they would actually be engaged in work in the industrial sector. To help the students gain confidence and relate their work to their studies, we designed what was then called "an upside-down curriculum." In the freshman year, the students operated the machines, and their college engineering courses helped them understand the engineering principles on which the machines operated. In their second year, as their work became more complex, their courses in physics helped to explain the engineering principles with which they had been working in the first year. In the third and last year, their courses in mathematics helped them to understand more precisely how these operations could be measured and controlled. The curricular sequence was thus engineering, physics, and mathematics, whereas the conventional curriculum teaches these subjects in reverse order. Hence the upside-down curriculum.

This cooperative education program was highly effective in attracting the kinds of students for which the Rochester Athenaeum and Mechanics Institute was established. The Institute, later renamed the Rochester Institute of Technology, became the primary and chief source of technicians for industry in Rochester. I continued as consultant to the Institute from 1929 until 1979 and was able to see the variety of ways in which cooperative education assisted students in their education.

With the founding of the National Commission for Cooperative Education and the publication of the Wilson-Lyons Study in 1961, which provided research support for the educational values of cooperative education, the number of colleges and universities adopting this type of educational program increased rapidly. In many cases, the adoption of cooperative education programs seemed to be based on their reputation rather than on a clear understanding of the conditions required for an effective program. To meet the need for a better understanding, the *Handbook of Cooperative Education* was published in 1972.

Since that time, the number of institutions that have established cooperative education programs has continued to increase. In many cases, no modifications were made in the plan to adapt it to local conditions. In other cases, modifications appear to have been made without considering whether these adjustments would be in harmony with the basic principles of an effective program. Thus, there is a clear and pressing need for a publication that will clarify the basic principles of cooperative education and explicate more fully the possibilities and the problems involved in extensive modifications. This book, *Cooperative Education in a New Era,* is being published at a time when colleges and universities are being questioned about their mission, their adherence to their mission, their effectiveness, and their responsiveness to problems and inadequacies. Institutions of higher learning are often accused of being ivory towers in which little attention is paid to the problems and needs of the real world outside academe. The chapters in this book will help stimulate the reader's thinking about the possibilities and problems involved in using cooperative education as a major means by which an educational institution can meet the responsibilities entrusted to it by the public.

Milpitas, California   Ralph W. Tyler
September 1987   *President*
                              Systems Development Corporation
                              Director Emeritus
                              Center for Advanced Study
                              in the Behavioral Sciences

Preface

Cooperative education is an instructional method that links classroom instruction and work for the purpose of enhancing the total educational program of students. Over the past twenty-five years we have seen dramatic growth in the number of institutions of higher education making cooperative education available to their students and the number of students and employers participating. Current estimates indicate that more than 1,000 colleges and universities offer programs of cooperative education, more than 200,000 students participate, and between 75,000 and 85,000 businesses, industries, and service and governmental agencies employ these students. Students have been attracted to these programs because they provide practical experience in their chosen fields and because they can ease the burden of educational costs; institutions have seen cooperative education as an effective means of strengthening their educational programs by providing a dimension of relevant, "hands-on" experience; and employers have become involved because cooperative education students are an important resource for immediate employment needs and a source of candidates for future full-time employment.

Cooperative education could not have expanded as it has and become an important educational strategy among U.S. colleges and universities had it not proved its considerable merit. Neither could it have expanded so rapidly without the effective advocacy of individuals, professional societies, and specialized

xvii

groups committed to its soundness or without the support of the federal government, which came to view cooperative education as a singularly effective means of strengthening the nation's postsecondary education.

The confluence of increasing competitiveness for students because of changing demographics, rising costs of education, decreasing availability of financial aid, growing concern of students about viable careers, and increasing desire of employers to find more reliable and cost-effective means for recruiting graduates has led administrators to search for ways of making their institutions more attractive and affordable for students and their graduates more appealing to employers. Cooperative education appears to be a viable solution, and hence it appears that cooperative education may experience another period of dramatic growth.

During this same twenty-five year period, and particularly during the fifteen years since the publication of Asa S. Knowles's *Handbook of Cooperative Education,* our knowledge of cooperative education has expanded through research and experimentation: we have learned more about its impact on the student and graduate, on the employer, and on the institution. We have increased our understanding of the processes of planning, implementing, and nurturing an effective program.

Both new and experienced practitioners need authoritative information about the nature, status, and benefits of cooperative education and about the processes and means of strengthening cooperative education programs. Filling this need is the principal intent of this book. We seek to provide the newcomer to cooperative education—from both the academy and the workplace—with a sound introduction to this instructional methodology. The experienced cooperative education professional will find in this book authoritative information on numerous issues relating to program operation and continued growth.

Cooperative Education in a New Era has a second purpose: to provide curriculum planners, educational administrators, and educators interested in experience-based education in its various forms with an insightful description of cooperative education. As an instructional methodology, cooperative educa-

tion touches on numerous areas of interest in higher education—
educational philosophy, social foundations of education, curriculum planning, outcome assessment, institutional innovation
and change, organizational behavior, and program evaluation.
This book clarifies the relevance and application of cooperative
education to each of these areas of concern. Thus, for those interested in comparative strategies of education, this book delineates the place of cooperative education within the field of
higher education.

Overview of the Contents

The chapters of *Cooperative Education in a New Era*
were expressly commissioned to achieve the purposes of the
book. This work may be read straight through to attain a thorough description of contemporary cooperative education, or
one or more chapters may be consulted to glean advice and
practical ideas on particular topics from authorities in the field.

Part One serves as an introduction to postsecondary cooperative education. Chapter One outlines the educational and
social forces that gave rise to cooperative education in the
United States. Chapter Two continues with a discussion of
events that affected the growth of cooperative education in
America over the past thirty years. Chapters Three and Four
present first a detailed examination of cooperative education in
the United States today and then a look at this movement in
other countries.

Part Two focuses on topics and issues vital to the development, operation, and enhancement of cooperative education
programs. Chapter Five delineates the process of establishing a
cooperative program, including planning, implementing, marketing, and assessing the program. Then, Chapter Six explores the
potential benefits that can accrue to institutions through cooperative education and suggests strategies for achieving them.
Chapter Seven analyzes the institutional cost of cooperative programs and offers approaches for achieving cost efficiency while
ensuring program effectiveness. Chapter Eight discusses the
need for information, as well as techniques for systematically

collecting, storing, and analyzing this information, from the perspectives of both day-to-day operations and general program assessment. Chapter Nine examines legal responsibilities and liabilities that affect the principal participants in a cooperative program. Chapter Ten presents practical ideas and suggestions concerning the development of cooperative education from the employer's perspective. Chapter Eleven discusses the means of enhancing the cooperative experience for the student. Chapter Twelve examines the assignment of foreign nationals to cooperative education positions and the international placement of American students.

Part Three examines the potential benefits cooperative education offers students, graduates, and employers. With respect to the students, Chapter Thirteen looks at both how cooperative education enhances the educational process and how it provides practical support. The contributions cooperative education makes to the career paths of graduates are presented in Chapter Fourteen, as are the human resource benefits to employers. Chapter Fifteen reviews the past accomplishments of cooperative education, explores current conditions in America and the world, and speculates on their implications for higher education and the future of cooperative education. Listed in the resource are organizations and agencies that can provide additional information on experiential and cooperative education.

The 1960s saw the publication of the first national study of cooperative education, *Work-Study College Programs: Appraisal and Report of the Study of Cooperative Education*. This important document detailed the values of cooperative education and stimulated interest in program initiation. In the 1970s, Knowles's *Handbook of Cooperative Education* became the reference work used by those seeking to explore the possibilities of cooperative education for their institutions and by those needing expert advice on program implementation and operation. We hope that *Cooperative Education in a New Era* will serve as an authoritative text for those in the higher education community who are seeking a greater understanding of the nature, scope, and potential values of cooperative education and of the means to develop significant and effective programs in the late 1980s and beyond.

Acknowledgments

To all the authors who contributed chapters, we wish to express our deepest thanks. We are extremely grateful for their generosity in sharing their special knowledge and insights about cooperative education and for their diligence in writing, modifying, and rewriting their contributions.

With affection and sincere appreciation we acknowledge the contribution of Asa S. Knowles, chancellor of Northeastern University, to the publication of this book. He encouraged us and gave generously of his time and wisdom as we developed its nature and scope and selected authors. His assistance was invaluable.

We extend special thanks to Judi Carson and Kelly Dolan, both of Northeastern University's Cooperative Education Research Center, for their efforts in preparing the manuscript for publication. They entered the entire manuscript into a word processor, edited it to ensure that both the text and the reference citations conformed to the publisher's style, and proofread everything. Theirs was a vital element in the preparation of this book, and we greatly appreciate their contribution.

Boston, Massachusetts   Kenneth G. Ryder
September 1987   James W. Wilson

The Authors

Kenneth G. Ryder is president of Northeastern University in Boston, a position he has held since 1975. Ryder first came to Northeastern in 1949 as a member of the history faculty. He taught until the mid-1950s, when he was appointed dean of administration. He was later named vice-president for university administration (1967) and then executive vice-president (1971).

Ryder holds a B.A. degree (1946) in history from Boston University and an M.A. degree (1947) in history from Harvard University. He has received honorary degrees from Nasson College, Northeastern University, and the University of Massachusetts, Amherst. Ryder is an internationally known spokesman for cooperative education and higher education. He is a trustee of the National Commission for Cooperative Education and, in 1983, became the first president of the World Council for Cooperative Education. He is a former chairman of the National Association of Independent Colleges and Universities and serves on the National Commission for Student Financial Assistance.

James W. Wilson is the Asa S. Knowles Professor of Cooperative Education at Northeastern University and director of Northeastern's Cooperative Education Research Center. He received his B.S. degree (1944) in psychology from St. Lawrence University, his M.A. degree (1947) in psychology from the University of Rochester, and his Ph.D. (1954) in education from the University of Chicago.

xxiii

Wilson's academic career has included graduate and undergraduate teaching, college administration, and educational research. He was the executive director of the National Study of Cooperative Education (1959-1960) and senior author of the resulting report, *Work-Study College Programs.* Since joining Northeastern University, he has conducted considerable research into cooperative education and has published extensively on that subject.

Sylvia J. Brown is an educational research consultant to universities and public school systems and was formerly a research associate with the Cooperative Education Research Center, Northeastern University.

Paul E. Dubé is director of the Center for Cooperative Education, Northeastern University.

Bruce T. Evans is professor of field service, Division of Professional Practice, University of Cincinnati. For several years he has directed workshops for employers of cooperative education students.

Antoinette Frederick is assistant vice-president, Shawmut Corporation, Boston.

Michael B. Goldstein is a partner in the firm of Dow, Lohnes & Albertson, Washington, D.C., where he heads the firm's higher education practice. He is co-chair of the Education Law Committee of the Federal Bar Association.

Harry N. Heinemann is dean of international education, Fiorello H. LaGuardia Community College, City University of New York, Long Island City, and has served as dean of cooperative education at that institution.

Alice F. Korngold is university director of cooperative education, Pace University, New York.

Robert R. Tillman is assistant professor and coordinator of civil engineering students, Northeastern University.

Solveig M. Turner is director of the Center for International Higher Education, Boston, and was formerly director of Northeastern University's Center for Educational Documentation.

James W. Varty is associate dean for alternative education, Macomb Community College, Warren, Michigan.

Patricia T. van der Vorm is executive director of the American University Career Center, Washington, D.C., and a past president of the Cooperative Education Association, Inc.

Robert E. Vozzella is director of international cooperative education, Northeastern University.

Peter C. Wolk is an associate in the firm of Dow, Lohnes & Albertson, Washington, D.C., and was formerly director of the legal reference service of the National Association of College and University Attorneys.

Roy L. Wooldridge is vice-president for cooperative education, Northeastern University, and vice-chairman of the National Commission for Cooperative Education.

Cooperative Education
in a New Era

One

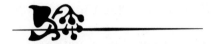

Social and Educational Roots

Kenneth G. Ryder

Cooperative education is in its ninth decade as an instructional methodology in American higher education. It has evolved from the experimental idea of one man, implemented in a single university, into a well-tested and well-regarded approach to education, adopted by one-third of this nation's institutions of postsecondary education. The intent of this chapter is threefold: to clarify the nature of cooperative education; to examine the backdrop of educational thought that both spawned and permitted it to grow; and to describe several broad models of cooperative education that function consistently within the basic concept of this complex and important instructional methodology.

The Nature of Cooperative Education

Over the years, numerous definitions of what constitutes cooperative education have been advanced, often reflecting the programmatic bias of the authors (Armsby, 1954; National Commission for Cooperative Education, 1978; Wilson, 1970; World Council for Cooperative Education, 1985). It is not the intent here to propose a formal definition of cooperative education. Experience has shown that this exercise almost always leads to heat and polarization of thought, while supplying limited enlightenment. Rather, a description of what appear to be

the most basic elements of cooperative education will be specified. The objective is to provide a generic description of cooperative education which will have appropriate application to the
variety of implementations found throughout the United States
and, perhaps, to programs worldwide.

To set the context it is best to think of cooperative education as a specific example or application of what has come to
be called "experiential learning." According to the definition advanced by Keeton and Tate (1978), "experiential learning refers
to learning in which the learner is directly in touch with the
realities being studied" (p. 2). Clearly, this is at the heart of cooperative education, which puts the student "in touch with the
realities being studied" by integrating academic study and work
into a single unified curriculum plan.

The procedural intent of cooperative education is to involve students in planned, productive work, which typically is
related to the academic program being pursued and/or the career goals of the students. An essential ingredient of cooperative
education is that the institution sponsoring this work-education
effort assume programmatic responsibility for the work opportunities provided the student. It must, for example, build work
opportunities into the curriculum that make it possible for students to leave the campus to work and to return to the campus
to study. The institution also assumes responsibility to provide
students with appropriate guidance and assistance in preparing
for work, job seeking and selection, and integrating the work
experience and academic pursuits.

In summary, cooperative education is a particular application of the concept of experiential learning in which productive
work performed by students is integrated into the curriculum
and for which the institution assumes primary responsibility.

It is not at all unusual for persons, when first introduced
to the notion of cooperative education, to ask in what way it
differs from another well-known form of experiential education, the internship. It must be said that there are no hard and
fast distinctions between the two and often they look very
much alike. The differences tend to be ones of statistical frequency. For example, internships are most often single experi-

ences not exceeding a single academic term and frequently less than one term. In contrast, most cooperative education experiences involve multiple terms of work. Although most internships have students engaged in productive work, there are many instances in which the student's primary function is to observe or "shadow" professionals at work. One of the defining characteristics of cooperative education is that students are engaged in productive work. Most often, internships are part of a specific course of study and are supervised by a faculty member. More often, cooperative programs are offered throughout the institution or at least in several divisions of an institution, and the principal responsibility for administering the program belongs to a professional staff. Co-op students are almost always compensated for their work, whereas interns often are not.

Finally, internships are most often capstone experiences within the curriculum. In contrast, the cooperative experience begins much earlier in the student's curriculum, often during the first year in junior and community colleges and during the second year in senior institutions. It should also be understood that these differences are not absolute; it is entirely possible that on a single campus one may find a listing for both cooperative education and internships and hardly recognize the difference between the two. In general, however, they are different in the ways outlined above.

Social Roots of Cooperative Education

Innovation in higher education requires both inspiration and energetic advocacy. Cooperative education was provided with both attributes by Herman Schneider. Schneider was a civil engineer who earned his degree from Lehigh University in 1894 and became an instructor there in 1899. In 1903, he moved to the University of Cincinnati as a professor of civil engineering. Later, he became Dean of Engineering and, still later, he served briefly as the president of the University. Schneider was a dedicated teacher, a good administrator, and an educator who concerned himself deeply about the adequacy and relevancy of higher education. He was an academician, but he had a very practical side as well.

As a small boy, he worked for his father in the family store. After the death of his father, he went to work in the coal mines of Pennsylvania, before entering Lehigh University. As a student he worked for an architect part-time, thereby learning the practical side of engineering. Following his graduation, he established his own engineering practice in Cumberland, Maryland. Before returning to Lehigh to teach, he moved to Oregon to build bridges for the Shortline Railroad. Precisely when his conception of cooperative education took shape, and what the causes behind it were, is not known. It seems clear, however, that it was the confluence of his earlier practical experience and his astuteness as a teacher that gave rise to the idea. His idea was really based on two observations. First, most college students worked at least part-time, and usually the work they performed had no relationship at all to their fields of study or to their future careers. Second, there were a number of elements in the teaching of engineering that simply could not be adequately conveyed in the classroom or the laboratory. They had to be learned in the shops and foundries.

His conception of having students leave the campus to go to work and then return to the campus took root while he was still on the faculty of Lehigh University. Initially, it was his plan to have the university create and operate shops that would be manned by a skeleton force of trained workers. Because of the obvious cost of the proposal, the faculty of the university rejected the plan. Schneider, however, did not let this disappointment deter him from his conviction that practical application of classroom study would substantially strengthen engineering education.

This conviction was further reinforced by an extensive series of interviews with practicing engineers, during which he found that most of them worked either while attending college or during their vacations, or they stayed out of college for some period of time to work before returning to the campus to complete their studies. Although convinced more than ever of the efficacy of relating work and study, he still did not know how to go about it. We are told that the idea came to him almost by surprise. Clyde W. Park (1943), who has written the definitive biography of Schneider, describes the event as follows: "One evening, after teaching hours, Herman Schneider was pondering this question while he walked across the Lehigh University campus. Suddenly, he was startled out of his reverie by the blast of a Bessemer converter at a nearby steel plant. In that moment, an idea came to him that offered a possible solution to his problem. Here was a huge modern industry existing side by side with a university—a vast industrial laboratory filled with the latest, the most expensive equipment, made to order for his scheme of training" (p. 44). Thus, the concept of cooperative education came into being.

Lehigh University, however, turned down Schneider's plan for "hitching the school and shop abreast, rather than in tandem; combining theory and practice" (1910, p. 148). He thereupon accepted an appointment to teach civil engineering at the University of Cincinnati, arriving there in 1903. He began at once to try to stimulate interest in his scheme. Although he met with considerable indifference and opposition, by 1906 he was given permission to begin a voluntary program that formally linked work and education. This one person, concerned, perceptive, creative, and persistent, founded cooperative education in the United States.

When or whether cooperative education would have been initiated had it not been for Herman Schneider is a moot point. As is the case with any innovation, though, it is unlikely that it could have happened in the absence of influences in the environment. Changes in U.S. higher education had been occurring in the United States for half a century, rendering higher education in the beginning of the twentieth century a very different enterprise from that which existed prior to the Civil War.

American higher education began in 1636 with the founding of Harvard, an institution designed to educate the ministry and meet the educational needs of the aristocracy of an agrarian society. Two forces began to bring about changes in this traditional and classic form of education. The first influence was Jeffersonian democracy. It was Jefferson who first set forth the premise that any country affirming government by its citizenry can endure and prosper only if that citizenry be educated. In response to this interpretation of the nation's democratic ideals, admission to higher education began slowly to shift from a base of aristocracy to one of meritocracy. The base from which the future citizens of this country would be educated was being substantially broadened.

The second force exerting an influence on higher education was the industrialization of America. By the mid-nineteenth century, the industrial revolution was well under way. With it came new inventions, new technologies, and new demands for specialized knowledge and training. The nation's colleges and universities began to respond to the demand for new courses of study that would prepare people for effective participation in a rapidly changing society. Certainly one, if not the greatest, impetus to the changes in higher education was the Morrill Act, which President Lincoln signed in 1861. Known popularly as the Land Grant Act, it provided states with money to establish colleges devoted to agriculture and the mechanic arts. Every state in the union responded, providing institutions that could offer a practical education to their middle-class citizens.

By the beginning of the twentieth century, numerous professional curricula had developed in our nation's colleges and universities, and the idea of education for a specific professional career had become acceptable. Even prior to Schneider's first program in 1906, there were advocates for an education that would be related to work. One proposal was for educational institutions to operate their own shops and, insofar as possible, duplicate the work and conditions of the factory. Another approach was to encourage students to seek summer employment related to their course of study. Clearly, by the turn of the century, education for doing had achieved near parity with education for knowing. It was within this milieu of a changing society, changing knowledge, and changing perceptions of educational function that Herman Schneider conceived and finally implemented his idea of cooperative education.

Philosophic Foundations of Cooperative Education

Integral to the vast changes occurring in nineteenth-century America was the scientific revolution taking place throughout the civilized world. In 1859, Darwin published his revolutionary *On the Origin of Species;* between 1857 and 1866, Pasteur proved that fermentation demanded the presence of living organisms, thus disproving the long-held doctrine of spontaneous generation; in 1866, Gregor Mendel discovered the basic laws of heredity; in 1869, Mendeleev developed the periodic table of the elements and was able to predict the characteristics of as yet undiscovered elements; and in 1887, Michelson measured the speed of light. Discoveries and scientific advances were being made in such diverse areas as sound, electromagnetism, astronomy, and optics.

Science was flourishing and its impact was immense. First in significance, of course, were the implications of the scientific breakthroughs themselves. Second, and equally important, however, was the growing idea that the methods used by scientists had applicability in all spheres of life. Thus it was that persons outside the scientific community sought to emulate the scientific method of inquiry. Philosophers of the day began to articulate a new philosophy that considered truth to be something other than absolute; they thought of knowledge as something to be acquired from experimentation and saw purpose in means-to-an-end relationships. They began to speak of "workable," "useful," and "practical" outcomes. In America the chief proponents of this new philosophy, "pragmatism," were William James, Charles Peirce, and John Dewey.

Inevitably, pragmatism—more a philosophy of method and strategy than one of content and substance—affected education in America. Dewey, in particular, had great influence upon educational thought and practice. One of his central beliefs was that people learn from experience and from doing. Commitment to this philosophy allowed Herman Schneider to believe that if you want to educate a student to become an engineer, then you should provide that student with the opportunity to practice being an engineer. Furthermore, a general acceptance of such philosophy created an environment in which cooperative education could take root in the institutions of higher education in this country.

Cooperative education is a particular expression of educational pragmatism. Its advocates believe with the pragmatists that education is not an end in itself. Rather, it is a means to some other end, to some other goal or purpose. For Dewey, that purpose and hence the function of education was to help prepare students for effective and satisfying citizenship. In like fashion, the proponents of cooperative education provide students with work experience not for its own sake but because they believe it is a sound way to help students achieve important learning, which in turn will contribute to their effective citizenship.

Pragmatists think that all education is grounded in experience. For example, Dewey (1949) said, "... there is an intimate and necessary relation between the processes of actual experience and education" (p. 7). The essence of cooperative education is that it is a strategy to provide students with experiences that are applicable to their future working lives and to their roles as informed, responsible citizens.

Models of Cooperative Education

The first program of cooperative education in the United States was initiated in early September 1906. Dean Schneider had, with some difficulty, recruited twenty-seven engineering students to participate in his new program. The essential plan was that they would be divided into two groups, with one group studying on campus when the other group was at work in local factories. After one week, the two groups would exchange places. Initially, participation in the program delayed graduation for two years. Later, however, the extension was reduced to one year.

Early cooperative education programs adopted the major characteristics of the Cincinnati plan. Like it, these programs were designed for engineering students, operated on an alternating pattern of study and work, and required an additional year for graduation. This mode of cooperative education is sometimes referred to today as the classical model of cooperative education. Since those very early years, additional characteristics have been attached to this classical model. Foremost among those characteristics is having the programs centrally administered by a director and a staff of professional coordinators who develop work assignments for the students, give advice, and monitor work experience. Many institutions that adhere to this model also require their students to participate in the cooperative plan. For example, in 1909 when Northeastern University in Boston established a new college of engineering, it was modeled after the Cincinnati plan and cooperative work was compulsory for all students.

There were three deviations from the initial pattern of cooperative education, which, while they did not change the model itself, were nevertheless important to both the future development of cooperative education and the full spectrum of cooperative education programs that exists today. In 1917, again at the University of Cincinnati, the program was extended from engineering to business administration. Three years later, and once again at the University of Cincinnati, the first female students participated in cooperative education.

In 1921, a very important addition to the cooperative education community occurred. Antioch College, a liberal arts institution, adopted the plan. President Arthur Morgan of Antioch was convinced that it was important for students to have real-life experience outside a sheltered campus and that a liberal education would be more meaningful to students who had a clear understanding of contemporary society. Antioch hired Philip C. Nash, who had been supervising cooperative work placements for engineering students at Northeastern University. He brought to Yellow Springs, Ohio, knowledge of how best to administer a cooperative education program for students seeking diverse experiences.

Thus, within the first fifteen years of cooperative education, the basic pattern of operation had been established. By 1921, this new educational model had been accepted by eleven universities and higher education institutions. It had been demonstrated that cooperative education had applicability to fields of study other than engineering, including the liberal arts, and it had been found applicable to female as well as male students. This was significant because it paved the way for the very broad application of the cooperative education plan that exists today.

Until the 1960s, there were very few changes in the way cooperative education was run. In that decade two modifications were made that have considerable significance today. First, concomitant with the rise of the community college and the adoption by those community colleges of cooperative education was the so-called parallel plan of operation. The parallel plan may be thought of as a kind of half-day alternation. Typically, students attend classes in the morning and work part-time, fifteen to twenty-five hours per week, in the afternoons and evenings. The plan was important because a large portion of the student body was older than traditional students and had different financial requirements. In many instances, had the community colleges insisted upon the traditional alternating plan, they simply would not have gotten students to participate.

The second significant innovation was the introduction of academic credit for students undertaking cooperative work experience. To the extent that early programs had required students to participate in cooperative work to earn a degree, it can be said that they gave credit for cooperative experience. The specific academic credits, however, were only awarded for the traditional classroom study portion of the program. Now students could earn credit while working. There is little question that the change was instituted in public institutions for economic reasons. These institutions found their cash flow was disrupted when students left the campus for cooperative work experiences and could not be counted as students for fiscal purposes. The only way they could be counted as students would be if they earned academic credits. This is not to say that there was no pedagogical justification for students' earning academic credit based on their cooperative work experience, but the reason for the wide adoption of the practice was probably economic.

The practice of awarding credit led to other necessary

changes in the operation of cooperative education. The award of credit is the province of teaching faculty, so teachers had to be brought into the cooperative education process, to assess student learning and to determine the appropriateness of credit.

A single program of cooperative education poses a host of difficult questions. For example, should students' participation be optional or required? What pattern of work and study should be followed—alternating or parallel? How should the program be organized—centralized or decentralized? How should it be administered—with a professional staff or with a professional staff and teaching faculty? Should credit be awarded or not? Taking all of these questions and potential answers into consideration, one recognizes that a good many models of cooperative education are possible.

In fact, two models exist, with obvious flexibility within each. The first is the classic model which has already been described: it is alternating, highly centralized, does not award credit, and has little direct involvement of the teaching faculty. Additionally, it tends to function most effectively in professional areas of study and in fields involving large numbers of students. In contrast is the model that awards credit and usually comprises smaller programs, and in which the active involvement of teaching faculty is encouraged. This model is found most often in the liberal arts areas—the social sciences and humanities.

What is important about these two models is not that they are substantially different but that they both fit very well within the broad concept of cooperative education, and both serve their students.

In summary, cooperative education is the legacy of the genius and persistence of one man, of a changing society that required an educated citizenry, and of a changing system of higher education that became involved in the affairs of the community about it. It started as a single program at the beginning of this century and has grown both in number and in application, in fields of study, and in constituency. Its mode of operation has been modified to meet the particular needs and conditions of the institutions that have adopted it.

References

Armsby, H. H. *Cooperative Education in the United States.* Bulletin no. 11. Washington, D.C.: U.S. Department of Health, Education and Welfare, 1954.

Dewey, J. *Experience and Education.* New York: Macmillan, 1949.

Keeton, M. T., and Tate, P. J. "The Boom in Experiential Learning." In M. T. Keeton and P. J. Tate (eds.), *Learning by Experience—What, Why, How.* New Directions in Experiential Learning, no. 1. San Francisco: Jossey-Bass, 1978.

National Commission for Cooperative Education. "Definition of Cooperative Education." Unpublished paper, National Commission for Cooperative Education, Boston, Mass., 1978.

Park, C. W. *Ambassador to Industry.* Indianapolis, Ind.: Bobbs-Merrill, 1943.

Schneider, H. "Notes on the Cooperative System." *Proceedings of the Society for the Promotion of Engineering Education,* 1910, *18,* 147-387.

Wilson, J. W. "On the Nature of Cooperative Education." *Journal of Cooperative Education,* 1970, *6* (2), 1-10.

World Council for Cooperative Education. "Definition of Cooperative Education." *Global Newslink,* 1985, *1* (1), 7.

Two

Factors Influencing
Recent Growth and Expansion

Roy L. Wooldridge

This chapter will portray the modern growth of cooperative education, an era that began in the late 1950s. For the purpose of clarity, each decade will be presented separately: Occurrences in the Late Fifties, Evolving Sequences Through the Sixties, Emerging Patterns of the Seventies, and Current Status and Outlook in the Eighties.

Occurrences in the Late Fifties

It is often surprising how one individual with power and influence can profoundly change the flow of an idea or concept. This was certainly the case for cooperative education when, in 1956, Charles F. Kettering decided that something should be done to encourage more widespread use and understanding of the co-op concept.

At that time, exactly fifty years after its founding, cooperative education had been adopted by approximately sixty colleges and universities in a very limited variety of academic programs. Occurring predominantly in engineering or technology, most programs were elective. Only a few were mandatory. From its beginning at the University of Cincinnati in 1906, cooperative education had a dual thrust—to provide educational

enrichment through career-related work experience and to provide financial aid through paid employment. In 1956, all of the
schools with co-op programs embodied both objectives.

The directors of most of these co-op programs met twice
a year to exchange information and to discuss recent developments in the field. The meetings were held under the auspices
of the only professional association available to co-op personnel—the Cooperative Education Division of the American Society for Engineering Education. The June meeting was always
held as a subset of the larger annual meeting of the parent society. The mid-winter meeting, usually held in January, was sponsored solely by the Cooperative Education Division. In reality,
this meeting was the most meaningful to the majority of co-op
directors.

The professional society did a great deal to hold the community together as a loose confederation. However, it did not
see itself as a "missionary" body, seeking neither to win new
converts nor to encourage innovative programming. One of the
society's major contributions had been the 1946 publication,
Cooperative Education: A Manifesto (Freund and others, 1946)
which, in effect, established a solid definition of cooperative
education. Some schools with primarily engineering co-op programs still regard it today as the only valid definition.

This, then, was the status of cooperative education at the
time of Charles Kettering's most fortunate intervention. A
trustee and benefactor of Antioch College and Research Director of the General Motors Corporation, Kettering had nourished
an admiration for cooperative education for a long time. Disap-
pointed with the nation's lack of attention to co-op's fiftieth
anniversary, he decided to do something about it. Also Chairman of the Thomas Alva Edison Foundation, he charged its
Executive Director, George E. Probst, with the responsibility of
focusing appropriate attention on co-op. The modern era for
cooperative education had been born.

The Edison Foundation organized a conference entitled
"Cooperative Education and the Impending Educational Crisis," held in 1957 in Dayton, Ohio. The purpose was to bring
together experienced supporters of co-op and leaders of tradi-

tional education unexperienced in co-op. This group examined the role co-op might play in helping higher education meet the tidal wave of students then advancing through the primary and secondary schools.

As a result of the conference, it was decided that the increased use of faculties and facilities provided by cooperative education's unique alternating calendar indeed offered potential relief for the coming crisis. Even so, many of the traditional educators were reluctant to initiate co-op because there was no documentation of its claimed educational values. While co-op proponents demonstrated a missionary zeal about the program, their conviction was built on experience rather than evidence. It was clear that in order for cooperative education to be more widely accepted at colleges and universities across the country, substantial proof of its educational value would have to be documented in an acceptable, scientific manner.

Ordinarily it would not have been an easy task to obtain funding to launch such a study. However, due to a network of friends from his days at the University of Chicago, George Probst had brought the significant influence of Ralph W. Tyler to the Dayton conference. Together, Probst and Tyler convinced their former colleague, Clarence Faust of the Ford Foundation's Fund for the Advancement of Education, of the need for such a study. The Ford Foundation agreed to fund the study and Tyler was named Chairman of the newly formed Study Committee. James W. Wilson of Rochester Institute of Technology, another former University of Chicago colleague, and Edward H. Lyons of the University of Detroit were engaged to undertake the study under Tyler's leadership.

From 1958 to 1960, students, graduates, faculty, and administrators of both co-op and conventional schools were interviewed, studied, and categorized. As a result of this massive collection and analysis of data, Wilson and Lyons were able to put before the Study Committee a persuasive rationalization of the claimed advantages of cooperative education. A book entitled *Work-Study College Programs* (Wilson and Lyons, 1961) was compiled, along with a summary of the findings. Thus the decade of the fifties closed with influential people, armed with significant data, poised to launch an expansion of the nationwide use of cooperative education.

Evolving Sequences Through the Sixties

The first public announcement of the study results was made in 1960 in the city where the idea of a national study was conceived, Dayton, Ohio. Princeton, however, was the site of a second announcement and workshop on initiating co-op programs. A "handout" at that conference was a summary of findings and recommendations from the study (Tyler and Mills, 1961). Although the visionary educators assembled recognized the value of both the study and the book, that was not enough for Chairman Tyler. He raised a pertinent question. How could the committee prevent the Wilson-Lyons study from the fate shared by most studies of this type—merely collecting dust on bookshelves?

One suggestion was to form a national organization with a board of trustees—real human beings who could breathe life into the concept of cooperative education. The board would launch a nationwide campaign to promote co-op and to raise funds in its behalf. Those at the Princeton conference enthusiastically endorsed the idea, and the National Commission for Cooperative Education was launched. Tyler, who had so adeptly steered the Wilson-Lyons study, was named chairman of the board. The board itself was composed of college presidents. The Edison Foundation contributed some of its prime office space in Manhattan, and in 1962 the National Commission was incorporated.

The new board officially named George Probst as part-time executive director of the new National Commission, giving him responsibility for its success. Even in its fledgling days, the National Commission wielded influence. Through his commitment as chairman, Tyler brought international prestige and renown to the organization.

Two "loaned executives," J. Dudley Dawson from Antioch College and Roy L. Wooldridge from Northeastern University, were asked to give the National Commission half of their professional time and energies. Their role was to take the Wilson-Lyons study all over the country, to speak up for cooperative education, and to win "converts" among leading colleges and universities. The board had given them very clear objectives. Within ten years, they were to double the number of students in co-op programs to 60,000 or more. Also within ten years, they were to double the number of schools offering co-op to 120.

Among the National Commission's first tasks was the gathering of data concerning co-op programs already in operation around the country. Wooldridge (1964) compiled the findings into the National Commission's first publication, *Student Employment and Cooperative Education: Its Growth and Stability*. It was important because it quieted the fears of some educators that the usefulness and practicality of cooperative education rises and falls with the economy. The publication compared the history of co-op with that of the American economy and demonstrated that co-op was drastically affected only by World War II. It proved that co-op was healthy, that it survived hard times such as the Depression, and that it actually helped to fend off unemployment.

Reaching the masses was crucial to the National Commission during its first decade. George Probst, having hosted the "Chicago Roundtable" radio program for years, was instrumental in opening up the media to its message. While J. Dudley Dawson focused his efforts on the receptivity of the burgeoning California educational system, Roy Wooldridge hosted a television show on co-op, originating from New York and broadcast biweekly for a period of two years. Feature stories in national magazines like *Time* and *Parents* also helped to position co-op in the minds of parents and students as a practical alternative to traditional higher education.

Mostly, the media reflected the anxieties of the time, and for the United States the sixties were indeed a troubled time. Ironically, there were four major occurrences during that period that worked to the distinct advantage of the National Commission and its message of cooperative education. Each was a result of outside forces, all beyond the organization's control. Each was an expression of a long-overdue change in American thinking.

First was President Lyndon Johnson's "War on Poverty," and the related Higher Education Act of 1965. In essence, the act increased the availability of higher education, the generally recognized ticket to upward mobility. Cooperative education not only offered the education but the money to pay for it along the way. For hard-pressed families understandably more concerned about youths contributing to the family income than pursuing academics, co-op was a promising compromise.

Second was the focusing of the American conscience on racial equality through the efforts and dreams of its prime mover, Martin Luther King, Jr. Words were spoken, bills passed into law, and still discriminatory practices continued at colleges and universities across the country. Recognizing that black colleges were still the choice for many minority students, the Ford Foundation generously supported them through grants. Primarily because it offered a way to pay for college, a number of these schools looked into initiating programs of cooperative education.

Third was the escalating cost of higher education at all schools, public and private. While the "War on Poverty" was providing financial aid to many who desperately needed assistance, it did little to ease the burden for middle-class families. They made too much money to qualify for federal aid, but not enough to pay tuition, room, and board. Again, the financial rewards of cooperative education opened the doors for many who could not otherwise afford higher education.

Fourth was the war in Vietnam, and the national outrage it ignited. College students were the first to attack the integrity of a federal government that was sending thousands of their friends to die in Southeast Asia. Their indignation inflamed college campuses and spread throughout the country. Distrust of government became distrust of "the establishment" and anything connected to it. The relevance of a college education was questioned, and schools responded with a new emphasis on service and commitment to society. Conventional courses gave way to volunteer work at social agencies, for example, for academic credit. Society began to see that indeed something could be learned outside the classroom, off campus, "out there." The public was more prepared now to consider cooperative education and the real-world experience it provided than ever before.

During the sixties, the National Commission's ten-year goals came within reach. There were several developments in co-op itself which gave the movement special impetus. In 1963, the Cooperative Education Association (CEA) was formed as a professional society for the many academic fields beyond engineering that had embraced co-op. Until then, the only professional society for co-op had been the division of the American Society for Engineering Education. Although it initially met with some resistance from engineers, the CEA flourished. It offered services such as a professional journal and annual conferences. It was initially housed in the National Commission's New York offices. Today, the CEA has more than 1,000 members and is headquartered in Washington, D.C.

Largely due to the country's changing mood and the National Commission's constant crusade, Washington became increasingly receptive to the notion of funding cooperative education. While Congress was debating what was to become of the Higher Education Act, members of the National Commission were asked to testify on the need for funding to both House and Senate committees. They had little trouble convincing politicians of the virtues of co-op because it was so inherently part of "the American way." Students could actually earn a significant portion of their college expenses through their co-op assignments. In the end, Title III of the Higher Education Act of 1965 provided funding for the development of co-op programs.

By the time the Higher Education Act came up for reauthorization in 1968, the National Commission expressed its concern that the Title III co-op funding for "developing institutions" only was too restrictive. Legislators listened and in 1968 co-op funding was moved to Title IV D. The move meant that any postsecondary institution, "developing" or not, could now apply for funding to support co-op programs.

While the National Commission was approaching the federal government for funding, colleges and universities were approaching private foundations with similar intentions. The Ford

Foundation agreed to fund co-op programs in six schools, if Northeastern University would provide consulting services to them. Northeastern responded with a three-year proposal to create a co-op consulting center for all schools, with the understanding that the Foundation's original six schools would continue to receive the attention and service the Foundation was seeking for them. The six schools were Wilberforce University, Alabama Agricultural and Mechanical University, Hampton Institute, Golden Gate College, New York Institute of Technology, and the certificate program of the Water and Sewage Technical Institute in Neosho, Missouri.

In 1965, with this Ford Foundation consulting grant, the Center for Cooperative Education was born. A year later, the Ford Foundation sent consultants to evaluate it and was so impressed with the Center's work that it gave another round of grants to six additional schools and to the Center's host, Northeastern. In 1968, the Foundation funded the university's first endowed chair, the Asa S. Knowles Research Professorship. Named as first incumbent was James Wilson, senior author of the earlier Wilson-Lyons Study.

The year 1965 was also the year the National Commission launched a television show, "New Dimensions," hosted by George Probst and Roy Wooldridge and featuring at least two guests who discussed cooperative education from various viewpoints. Assisted by the Broadcasting Foundation of America (BFA), the show was aired on the educational, municipally operated channel in New York City for two years. Although it was broadcast live, it was taped and then shown twice again. In addition, the BFA distributed the audiotapes of the show free to radio stations across the country. The result was that the advantages of cooperative education—to students, parents, employers, and communities—were being heard nationwide. The mail poured into the National Commission from everywhere.

Washington continued to react to the concern constituents voiced regarding the high cost of college, and, in the Higher Education Act of 1965, Congress created the College Work/Study Program as a form of financial aid. In 1967, the National Commission urged that federal monies designated for work/

study be applied to cooperative education programs as well. The positive ruling gave co-op a substantial boost, broadening opportunities in the nonprofit sector for possible work assignments, and enabling more co-op students to work in agencies, hospitals, and other social programs.

The influence of federally funded training programs in the growth and development of cooperative education was important and substantial. Three centers are particularly noted because of their scope and the number of years they provided training to the co-op community. (Two continue today.) George Miller directed the Southeastern Center out of the University of South Florida from 1973 until 1980; Donald Hunt of the University of Detroit directed, until his retirement in 1987, the Midwest Training Center; and Paul Dubé, succeeding Charles Seaverns, continues to direct the Center for Cooperative Education at Northeastern University. For many persons entering co-op professionally, their first introduction was through a workshop offered by one of these federally supported training centers. Hence, training centers became an influential communications network for the concept of cooperative education and its practices and innovations.

Another means of communication was also becoming increasingly influential—professional societies. The Cooperative Education Division of the American Society for Engineering Education continued as articulate spokesperson for co-op programs in engineering. The Cooperative Education Association was growing rapidly because of the great expansion of programs in fields other than engineering. To facilitate communication, both organizations began to publish newsletters on a regular basis for their members. To respond to more local needs, regional and state associations began to emerge. These groups not only served to meet the need for communication but, in a number of instances, influenced state legislators to support cooperative education.

Finally, Northeastern University's Cooperative Education Research Center provided another communication link. Through its Clearinghouse of Cooperative Education Information, it made articles and reports available; and through its annual survey of cooperative education, it was able to respond to many queries concerning cooperative education practices.

Emerging Patterns of the Seventies

The 1970s saw the relevance of cooperative education recognized and, ironically, its need for funding questioned. During this decade, three major reports analyzed the relationship between education and work, and all extolled the virtues of co-op. First was the *Report on Higher Education* by Frank Newman (1971) for the U.S. Department of Health, Education and Welfare. Second was *Less Time, More Options,* which came to be known simply as the "Carnegie Commission Report," by Clark Kerr (Carnegie Commission on Higher Education, 1971). Third was *A First Report: The Assembly on University Goals and Governance* by Martin Meyerson for The American Academy of Arts and Sciences (1971).

Reflecting the still supportive mood of the country, co-op received significant appropriations under federal legislation. In 1971, HEW decreed that a percentage of work/study funds be used for cooperative education. Under this directive, co-op received nearly $4.5 million annually during the next two years. In 1972, the National Commission requested that co-op funding be a line item under Title IV D of the Higher Education Act, rather than a percentage of the work/study monies. A year later, Congress appropriated co-op funding as a separate line item, at about $10 million. These and subsequent appropriations made training, research, and evaluation programs possible, while significantly raising co-op's stature in higher education. Federal funding for co-op stood at about $14 million in 1985, having peaked at $23 million.

As a consequence of strong individual and group advocacy, existing social conditions, and especially federal encouragement and support, co-op expanded considerably during the early years of the 1970s. In 1970 there were approximately 190 programs throughout the United States and by 1975 there were over 1,000. With program expansion and increasing federal funding, the National Commission's concern shifted to the need for more co-op employers. In 1973, the National Commission, with federal funding, initiated a series of workshops for chief executive officers and presidents of businesses in major cities across the United States. Also sponsored by local chambers of commerce, these Employer Institutes effectively communicated the benefits of cooperative education to executives searching for ways to bring a youthful spirit of inquiry and creativity into their enterprises.

When the Higher Education Act came up for reauthorization in 1976, federal funding for cooperative education was moved out from under financial aid in order to give it more stature and visibility in its own right. It became the new Title VIII, making all co-op funding a separate line item but also making it more susceptible to the Congressional budget axe. It dropped the stipulation that co-op programs be full-time in order to be federally funded, and enabled college students to work and study on the same day. One of the effects of this change was to encourage community colleges to set up parallel co-op programs, wherein students would attend classes in the morning and work part-time in the afternoon, opening new possibilities of interaction between students and communities.

Having focused earlier on federal funding for co-op and on co-op employers, the National Commission now turned its attention to students. The Employer Institutes had been so successful that there were now too few students to meet co-op employers' requests. In 1977, Presidents and Chancellors Seminars were introduced. Knowles of Northeastern and other co-op university presidents visited postsecondary schools across the country, sharing their conviction that cooperative education brings vitality and reality to traditional higher education. The seminars continued for two years.

As the seventies continued, cooperative education's own success began to work against it. More and more schools adopted it, but in an increasingly limited fashion. Public colleges and universities depended on registered full-time equivalents (FTEs) to justify maximum state appropriations. FTEs required academic credit to be earned, and academic credit required instruction by faculty. These factors worked against the development of large-scale co-op programs. Instead, they resulted in a growing number of small, highly supervised co-op programs for what were viewed as privileged, high-achieving students. One hundred million dollars had been spent by the federal government in supporting cooperative education. The Carter Administration proposed a phase-out of federal funding for this rather selective type of education, and a task force was assembled in Washington, D.C., to develop a counterproposal.

The task force recommended that multiyear federal funding in the form of demonstration grants be directed to only those schools undertaking the development of comprehensive cooperative education programs. In 1980, the regulations for the administration of Title VIII of the Higher Education Act were comprehensive programs. *Comprehensive* was taken to mean that at least one academic unit or department within a school would have at least 50 percent of its students enrolled in co-op programs.

Current Status and Outlook in the Eighties

Fortunately, President Carter's attempt to phase out federal funding for cooperative education was averted. Prior to the 1980 amendments to the Higher Education Act, federal funding for co-op was limited to five years per college or university. The 1980 amendments allowed each department or unit within a college or university to apply for its own five-year funding. Now there was a wider range to the amount of federal funding a school could receive for cooperative education. In addition, the amendments provided for three-year federal funding for large-scale, comprehensive co-op programs.

The National Commission continued its efforts to increase and strengthen comprehensive programs. For example, it produced monographs and guides for those considering cooperative education based on a two-year study of relevant issues and strategies. It initiated self-focusing training programs for chancellors, presidents, and deans deliberating the possibilities of co-op. Many times, these top administrators screened their institutions out, once they became aware of the university-wide commitment and adjustment necessary for a successful co-op program.

Although it was careful not to "lobby" in Washington on behalf of cooperative education, the National Commission took advantage of every opportunity to speak, at the request of legislative committees, as expert witnesses on co-op. Its efforts were rewarded in 1981 in two ways. First was the reversal of an earlier U.S. Department of Education ruling that identified co-op earnings as income in calculating financial need. Second was legislation allowing 50 percent of unspent monies from the federal College Work/Study Program to be returned to co-op schools. Previously, when colleges and universities had overestimated their work/study needs, the unused funds were simply returned to the federal government.

Recognizing the need for more public awareness of co-op, the National Commission began to seek the attention and support of the Advertising Council, Inc. The Ad Council is a private, nonprofit organization in New York City that conducts nationwide public service advertising campaigns, such as those featuring "Smokey the Bear" and "McGruff the Crime Dog." Advertisers, media, and business volunteered expertise and media time and space for radio, television, newspapers, consumer magazines, mass transit, billboards, special educational materials, direct mail items, business press, and company employee publications.

In 1981, the National Task Force on Cooperative Education was formed, and a year later it recommended the establishment of a National Employer Advisory Council. Loaned executives from IBM, Xerox, Burroughs corporations, and Oakland Community College went to work promoting cooperative education as the perfect subject of an Ad Council campaign. Presenting co-op as a strategy to help meet the need to restore the American work ethic culminated in the Ad Council's official acceptance of cooperative education for a national campaign.

Valued at more than $30 million of advertising exposure per year, the campaign was released in late 1985. It was expected to reach almost everyone in the United States but was aimed especially at the 37 million youths between the ages of sixteen and twenty-four, parents, older students, and 4.5 million employers. It was hoped that the campaign would double co-op enrollment to 350,000 nationwide within five years.

State councils were established in Michigan and Connecticut in 1984 and others are currently being developed. Through these councils, local groups promoted cooperative education in their areas and helped coordinate procedures for responding to the Ad Council campaign. Michigan was chosen as a test site in order to see what impact its high rate of unemployment might have on its citizens' acceptance of co-op.

During the 1980s the Cooperative Education Association has matured and become a truly influential force in the co-op community. Through its system of regional representatives it has rooted a national organization in its "grass roots" membership, and, through its Legislative Affairs Committee, it has had strong impact on continued federal support of cooperative education.

Concluding Remarks

These past decades have seen cooperative education both questioned and exalted—in Washington, D.C., in corporate boardrooms, on campuses, around kitchen tables. It has survived, flexed its muscles, and now with the Ad Council campaign is prepared for even more success. The numbers, however, tell a somewhat different story. Only about one-third of the nearly 3,000 colleges and universities nationwide have co-op programs at all. Only a handful have comprehensive, large-scale programs. Why, in spite of the work and advocacy of individuals and groups and the general support of the federal government, does co-op not flourish at far more schools?

There have been several deterrents to more nationwide acceptance. First, the faculty usually resist cooperative education. It is an unconventional system of learning, implying that learning can take place outside of the classroom, outside of the traditional course structure, and, perhaps most threatening, outside of the professor's reach. It also undermines the flexibility of teaching schedules, altering academic calendars and most likely requiring summer instruction. Faculty commitment to co-op is crucial to its success at any school.

Second, cooperative education is sometimes viewed as anti-intellectual by faculty, but also by families. Its alternating pattern of work and study is seen as "corrupting education with the realities of life." It is outside the realm of classical education and breaks up the community of scholars that traditionalists strive to protect.

Third, institutional inertia often delays any kind of change with endless committee discussion and debate. The academic and administrative changes necessary for the introduction of a comprehensive co-op program are monumental. They overwhelm all but the most committed.

Fourth, there is the related need for status quo at colleges and universities. Ralph Tyler has pointed out that schools are similar to professional societies. Both discourage innovation and guard their membership and accreditation criteria fiercely.

Fifth, there is a fear of the administrative costs of implementing cooperative education. Large numbers of students on co-op work assignments can be translated into a substantial loss of registered full-time equivalents, the accepted justification for regional and state funding. Also in co-op, there is usually a need to supplement faculty with coordinators who oversee students on co-op jobs.

It is clear that for co-op to be successful on a campus, there must be a demonstrable and profound belief that cooperative education offers distinct advantages, to students and their families, to employers, and to communities. There are certainly reasons for optimism concerning co-op's future. Demography predicts that during the next ten years, there will be a tremendous decrease in the number of youths in school or in jobs. Because of their growing scarcity, there will be more competition by employers to hire the very best among them. That competition could result in more co-op jobs, as employers try to hire the most talented at the earliest point in their professional development.

The escalating costs of higher education are prompting more parents and students to consider co-op as a means of financial aid. Today, the cost of a degree from an independent college or university is in the neighborhood of $40,000–$50,000. Cuts in financial aid to college students make the price tag even more out of reach. However, annual co-op earnings can soften the financial blow.

Employers are expecting more from graduates now than ever before. The competition is keen, and prospective employees know that a degree is no longer sufficient to obtain a job. Employers' perceptions and expectations are sharper now and they want energetic employees with experience as well as a degree. They want employees who have worked in the professional setting before, who can make an immediate contribution to their operation. They are updating their recruitment patterns, searching for that invaluable combination of experience and education.

Thanks to the work of many individuals and such organizations as the National Commission for Cooperative Education, the Cooperative Education Association, regional and state associations and councils, training programs, and the Department of Education, more and more people will know that there is indeed such a combination: cooperative education.

References

American Academy of Arts and Sciences. *A First Report: The Assembly on University Goals and Governance.* Cambridge, Mass.: Assembly on University Goals and Governance, 1971.

Carnegie Commission on Higher Education. *Less Time, More Options.* New York: McGraw-Hill, 1971.

Freund, C. J., and others. "Cooperative Education: A Manifesto." *Journal of Engineering Education,* 1946, *37* (2), 117–134.

Newman, F. *Report on Higher Education.* Department of Health, Education and Welfare. Washington, D.C.: U.S. Government Printing Office, 1971.

Tyler, R., and Mills, A. *Report on Cooperative Education: Summary of the National Study.* New York: Thomas Alva Edison Foundation, 1961.

Wilson, J. W., and Lyons, E. H. *Work-Study College Programs.* New York: Harper & Row, 1961.

Wooldridge, R. L. *Student Employment and Cooperative Education: Its Growth and Stability.* New York: National Commission for Cooperative Education, 1964.

Three

Contemporary Trends in the United States

James W. Wilson

The intent of this chapter is to provide a view of postsecondary cooperative education in the United States today. To do so, three kinds of information will be presented. First, data about programs—demographic, administrative, and operational—will be examined. Second, information about student participation—curriculum areas and numbers—will be presented. Finally, major issues facing cooperative education today will be noted and described. The statistical data presented throughout this chapter come from the program census database of the Cooperative Education Research Center of Northeastern University, Boston, Massachusetts.

Programs

Demographics. There are currently 1,012 known postsecondary cooperative education programs in the United States. They are to be found in all fifty states, the District of Columbia, and Puerto Rico. As the data in Table 3-1 show, however, nearly 50 percent of all programs are located in just eleven states.

Three-quarters of these programs have been initiated since 1970. The data in Table 3-2 show that the decade of the 1970s was the most active in terms of program expansion. While

Table 3-1. Eleven States with Largest Number of
Cooperative Education Programs.

State	Number of Programs
California	82
New York	56
Texas	56
Michigan	49
Pennsylvania	44
North Carolina	42
Florida	38
Ohio	36
Illinois	35
New Jersey	30
Massachusetts	26

Table 3-2. Percentage of U.S. Cooperative Education Programs
by Year Started.

Year Started	Percent	Cumulative Percent
1981–1985	15.6	100.0
1976–1980	27.7	84.4
1971–1975	32.9	56.7
1966–1970	13.0	23.8
1961–1965	3.4	10.8
1956–1960	2.2	7.4
1906–1955	5.2	5.2

new programs are still being implemented, the frequency of new starts has slowed substantially. Further, for several years, the number of programs that were discontinued each year more than matched the number initiated. This is demonstrated by the fairly steady decline in the total number of programs from 1981 through 1984. It would appear that the number discontinuing has slowed during the past two years and hence, the total number of programs is increasing.

1981	998
1982	994
1983	927
1984	895
1985	930
1986	1,012

The majority (56 percent) of all U.S. co-op programs are located within senior colleges and universities. In 1969, when data began to be collected annually, 82 percent of all co-op programs were in baccalaureate institutions. The 1970s, however, experienced the creation of a great many community colleges throughout the country, and substantial numbers of these initiated cooperative education. The greatest proportion of two-year programs was reached in 1975, when they accounted for 46 percent of all U.S. co-op programs. About 1980 their proportion of the total began to decline slightly and for the past several years has held steady at 43 percent. Seventy-two percent of all programs are in public institutions. Ninety-three percent of the associate degree programs are in public community colleges, and 56 percent of the baccalaureate programs are in public institutions. These percentages have held constant for the past several years.

Programs may be found in all sizes and complexities of institutions. Colleges with fewer than 100 students operate co-op programs and so does one university with 55,000 students. The arithmetic average is 6,000 students, but this is heavily weighted by a relatively few very large institutions with co-op programs. The median is 2,800 students.

Finally, although a few of the relatively old programs and even fewer that were initiated at the birth of the institution have designed institution calendars to facilitate the cooperative program, the vast majority have developed within the context of whatever calendar the institution was using. Hence, most (69 percent) co-op programs function on a semester calendar with one or two summer sessions. Twenty-five percent operate with a quarter plan and 5 percent with a trimester calendar.

Administration. Before the great growth of cooperative education during the 1970s, the majority of programs were either centralized, with a full-time staff responsible for all phases of the co-op experience, or they were decentralized within specific academic units of the institutions, for example, business or engineering. Today, however, 62 percent of all U.S. programs are organized on a combined centralized/decentralized basis. They have a centralized co-op department with coordinators and/or job developers who have the responsibility of finding appropriate work assignments, counseling students with regard to assignment possibilities, making sure students have jobs, visiting students at the job sites, and other related tasks. However, they also use teaching faculty on a part-time basis to provide students with academic advisement in relation to co-op and award academic credit. Specific responsibilities of central staff and faculty may differ from program to program, but this is a typical division of labor. This shift in the administrative organization of programs paralleled and was in fact a consequence of the movement to award credit for the co-op experience.

All but 7 percent of U.S. programs have a director of cooperative education, and all that do not are programs housed within a specific academic unit. Of those programs with directors, 44 percent report to the chief academic officer of the institution—the academic vice-president, provost, or dean of instruction. Seventeen percent of the directors report to the chief student affairs officer and 22 percent, where the program is located within an academic area, report to a dean or department head. In relatively few instances the director reports to the president, the dean of continuing education, or the director of career planning and placement.

Within departments of cooperative education, full-time staff are sometimes classified as administrators or faculty. In 34 percent of the programs, staff hold academic rank. In an additional 12 percent, some portion of the staff are classified as faculty and some as administrators.

Operation. There are a number of different objectives that guide cooperative education programs in the United States. These include objectives aimed at student learning, student support, and institutional support. However, the two objectives that are particularly important to 92 percent of the programs are that the cooperative experience should enhance the total academic program of students and that it should contribute to their career development.

In 86 percent of all U.S. programs, co-op is offered to students on some sort of elective basis. Eleven percent require student participation and the remaining have variable arrangements. The 86 percent elective programs are not all freely elective from the students' standpoint, although 41 percent are. The other 45 percent are so-called selective programs, in that to participate the student must maintain an academic average greater than that necessary to be a student in good standing at the institution.

The co-op experience in most institutions begins either during a student's second year (45 percent) or third year (29 percent). A fair number (18 percent), however, start co-oping students during the freshman year. All but a small number of these are two-year institutions. The typical (78 percent) work period is one term, either a semester or a quarter, although a small percentage operate with a work period less than one term in length, and another small percentage employ two consecutive terms. There is a wide range of maximum work terms possible, but three quarters of all programs have from one to five possible terms of work. The average is three terms. Thirty-eight percent of the programs require a minimum number of co-op work terms, for graduation if mandatory or for diploma recognition if elective. The number required ranges from one to six, with the average being two.

Cooperative education was first initiated using an alternating scheme, in which students rotated between periods of full-time, on-campus study and full-time work. Until 1970, alternating co-op was virtually the only operating mode, but with the growth of the community colleges and their adoption of cooperative education came the parallel scheme, in which students typically attend classes full-time in the morning and work part-time (fifteen to twenty-five hours per week) in the afternoon. This operating mode was adopted by community colleges because it better suits the needs of older students, which they particularly attract. Today, these two schedules, as the sole schedule, account for three-quarters of all programs, with more (43 percent) using the parallel than the alternating scheme (32 percent). A majority (67 percent) of two-year programs and a substantial number (25 percent) of senior programs use the parallel schedule. The remaining 25 percent of all programs use other schedules, such as field (a single work experience) or extended day (evening classes and full-time work during the day), which account for 10 percent, or combinations of schedules, mostly alternating and parallel, which account for 15 percent.

One of the principal characteristics of cooperative education is that students are paid for their work. All or most co-op students are paid for their work in nearly 90 percent of all programs. In only 3 percent is voluntary work typical. During the total co-op experience, students work, on the average, for one and a half different employers, ranging from only one employer to as many as six different ones. The number of employers students work for is, at least partly, a function of their majors. Students in professional fields such as nursing, engineering, or accounting are more apt to work for a single employer; whereas students in less specifically directed career fields are far more likely to work for a different employer each work term.

One of the most pervasive trends in cooperative education during the 1970s was the linking of degree credit to cooperative education. In 1969, only 18 percent of 127 programs awarded credit for co-op that replaced credits earned through classroom courses (Wilson, 1973). In 1975, when the rapid expansion of co-op plateaued, 70 percent of about 1,000 programs awarded degree credit for co-op. That proportion has held fairly constant to the present.

Like many educational practices, the reasons for awarding co-op credit preceded the rationale. The reasons were largely economic and first emerged in public institutions, in which operating income is directly tied to the total student count (tabulated from course registrations and average daily attendance). Students on co-op were not being counted because they did not meet the operational definition of student and hence, academic departments were not receiving tuition allocations for their co-ops during their work periods. This, of course, upset their budget forecasts and cash flow, even though in the long run there was no tuition deficiency. Nonetheless, it became a source of irritation and an issue that impacted adversely on faculty support for co-op. The solution was to ensure student status for co-ops during their work terms. The most direct means was to award credit. The educational rationale, which came as a means of enacting the practice, was argued and implemented.

The rationale is simply that as educators our concern is focused on the learning that accrues to students and not on whether it is achieved in the traditional classroom setting or in the workplace.

The number of credits awarded students per work term varies widely, from as few as one in some engineering programs to as many as eighteen in a very few liberal arts programs. The mean, however, is four credits, and the median, three credits. There have been several consequences of the practice of awarding credit for co-op: attraction of students to the program; reduction of graduation delay caused by addition of work terms to academic terms; institution assertion that co-op is a "mainstream" program because it awards the "coin of the realm." A particularly significant outcome of giving credit has been the direct involvement of teaching faculty in the co-op process. It is teachers, consistent with their traditional responsibility, who award the credit. During the first few years of the movement toward awarding credit, it was not uncommon for the cooperative education staff to be empowered to give credit. This, however, raised considerable concern and discontent among faculty and hence for the most part was quickly abandoned in favor of involving faculty directly in the process.

Credit was also introduced to provide a solution to another problem. Early programs, such as at the University of Cincinnati, Northeastern University, and Drexel University, extended their undergraduate programs to five years to accommodate cooperative education. For the majority of programs started since 1970, this was not acceptable and they sought programming means to avoid it. Awarding credit was one approach. Currently, 64 percent of all U.S. programs are designed so that no additional time is required. Of the 36 percent that do require additional time for their co-ops, 60 percent require less than one full academic year and 40 percent require a full year.

Participation

Examples of cooperative education can be found in virtually all undergraduate programs of study offered by U.S. institutions of higher education. The annual census of cooperative education programs conducted by the Cooperative Education Research Center, however, records them in fifteen broad curriculum areas. These and the current number of participating students are presented in Table 3-3. Majors within the broad cate-

Table 3-3. Co-op Students by Undergraduate Curriculum Areas.

Curriculum Area	Number of Students
Agriculture and Natural Resources	3,242
Applied Art	6,277
Business	68,961
Computer Science	16,086
Education	6,341
Engineering	38,931
Health Professions	8,265
Home Economics	1,437
Humanities	8,607
Natural Sciences	5,199
Social and Behavioral Sciences	13,665
Technologies	13,520
Vocational Arts	9,308

gory of business studies account for the greatest number of co-op students, while those within engineering curricula make up the second largest group. In fact, these two curriculum areas account for nearly half (47 percent) of the total 191,000 U.S. co-op students. Another 30 percent of U.S. participation, however, is found in traditional liberal arts fields—natural sciences, social sciences, and humanities. Business, engineering, and liberal arts, then, constitute three-quarters of the U.S. co-op population.

The average size of co-op programs throughout the United States is 205 students. This figure is distorted, however, by a few very large programs. A more accurate picture of a typical program is obtained by reference to the median program participation, which is 105 students. Thus, the typical program in the United States is quite small. In fact, 75 percent of all programs have 205 or fewer student participants. Nationally, approximately one-third of all postsecondary institutions have programs of cooperative education, but only about 2 percent of the student population is involved in co-op programs. It should be noted, however, that throughout the 1980s, programs have tended to become somewhat larger. While the median program size today is 105 students, in 1978 it was 70 students.

Diversity of participation in cooperative education is not limited to fields of study. There is a mix of demographics, as well. Fifty-five percent of all co-op students are male. This represents a considerable shift in the proportions of male and female co-op students over the past twenty years. Although we do not have direct evidence, it seems reasonable that the shift is due to the large increase of programs in the liberal arts and in business fields, as well as to an increasing number of females entering traditionally male-dominated career fields. Approximately one-fifth of all U.S. co-op students are members of minority groups—black, Hispanic, Native American, Asian. One percent are foreign nationals, fewer than 1 percent are handicapped, and 12 percent are adults (twenty-five years of age or older). The majority of the latter group are to be found in junior and community colleges.

Current Issues in Cooperative Education

The preceding sections have presented a largely statistical description of cooperative education as it exists in U.S. institutions of higher education in the mid-1980s. It is a fairly comprehensive picture, showing diversity in programming style and in students served. Additionally, there are concerns experienced by individual program personnel and issues challenging the cooperative education field as a whole that are a part of the current co-op picture. These will be discussed here.

Support and Viability. With but few exceptions, cooperative education programs have been initiated within an existing institution, generally an institution with a long tradition and well-established educational practices. Cooperative education impacts upon a good many other units of the institution, such as the registrar's office, admissions, housing, financial aid, and, most of all, curricula and course scheduling. Co-op, if it is to function successfully, disrupts accustomed practices throughout the institution. One key to program success, then, is for staff and faculty throughout the institution to support the co-operative education effort sufficiently to be willing to be disrupted. Winning this support is a matter of considerable concern for a good many programs, especially those initiated within the last three to five years and those with very few participating students. It is a concern that is expressed and discussed at virtually every national, regional, and state cooperative education conference and at every co-op workshop.

Two sources of support are of principal concern—faculty and top administration. Faculty support provides co-op with academic sanction and validity, important ingredients of the long-term development and institutionalization of the program. Moreover, faculty often hold the key to student participation and to developing course schedules necessary for the smooth rotation of students from school to work and back to school.

Administrative support provides the endorsement that helps to incorporate co-op into the character of the institution. With public statements, both within and outside the institution, supportive administrators give credence to co-op and an integral instructional strategy (Wilson and others, 1974). The single most vital and sought-after administrative support is financial. To survive and develop, programs require adequate financial backing, and this comes from the administration of the institution. The two most cited reasons for program failure are lack of faculty and/or administrative support. Hence, it is understandable that they are matters of considerable concern and that strategies for their achievement are eagerly sought.

Attracting Students. It has already been observed that U.S. co-op programs tend to be relatively small. In fact, whereas about one-third of the nation's colleges and universities offer co-op, only 2 percent of enrolled students participate. The staffs of practically all new and developing programs have found attracting students to be one of their greatest challenges. As in the case of institutional support, many discussions and workshops have addressed how best to recruit students to co-op. This concern is generally tied to that of faculty support because, with most programs being elective, faculty exert considerable influence on student decisions to participate or not.

This issue of attracting students is important to staff for two reasons. First, if the program is to impact upon educational policy and practice, it must be large enough to be visible within the institution, and it must be large enough that policy and practice considerations must take it into account. Second, there is a critical mass necessary for any co-op program to become financially viable. How large is sufficient and what constitutes critical mass cannot be stated as a generalized quantity because it differs for each institution, but it does exist and for many programs it is greater than their current number. Hence, striving to attract more student participation is a very real concern.

Attracting Employers. Finding cooperative work assignments is a continuous concern for program staff. It is perhaps more keenly felt by those working in fledgling and developing programs, but staff of all programs must actively work to nurture existing jobs and establish new ones. Interestingly, job development is almost always the single greatest source of concern and anxiety for those just initiating programs but, again, is almost always more successfully accomplished than is recruitment of students to the program. Concern regarding employer participation is, of course, a fluctuating one, the intensity matching economic conditions and employment levels.

Professional Identity of Coordinators. It is surely not the case with all coordination staff of cooperative programs, but the question of professional identity is raised with sufficient frequency to justify noting it. It has been observed frequently and accurately that the position of co-op coordinator entails many diverse responsibilities. The position requires a coordinator, for example, to find suitable jobs and establish working relationships with employers, to determine student needs and assist students to set achievable goals, to assist students in the selection of an appropriate work assignment, to monitor the work situation and, in concert with the employer, to assess the students' work and learning, and in many programs to help recruit co-op students, as well. The coordinator has been described variously as a job developer, placement officer, counselor, educator, and manager. Within the institution, the coordinator generally does not fit neatly into any existing position classifications. As noted, in one-third of all U.S. programs, coordinators have faculty status, but they are seldom like most faculty. They do not teach or undertake research and other traditional forms of scholarly endeavor, and promotion in rank necessitates either different or differently interpreted criteria. In most programs, however, coordinators are classified as administrators and have no clear promotional avenues within cooperative education per se. The consequence is that persons beginning their professional careers in cooperative education—and most coordinators in the country are relatively young—find no clear promotion opportunities or career paths. This is a source of real concern to them and poses a long-term problem for institutions, because the most able and energetic seek and find other opportunities outside cooperative education.

Cooperative Education in Graduate Programs

Thirty-five percent (197) of senior institutions with undergraduate programs of cooperative education also operate programs for graduate students. They serve approximately 4,300 graduate students. Although in absolute terms this is neither many programs nor many students, it is a proportional gain of considerable magnitude over the past twenty-five years. In 1971, there were only twenty graduate co-op programs serving 730 students (Borman, 1971).

Table 3-4 shows that, as with undergraduate co-op programs, there is a concentration of students in business administration. Law and the social and behavioral sciences each account for the next two most heavily populated curriculum areas, with over 500 students participating in each.

The vast majority of graduate-level co-op programs are, in contrast to the typical undergraduate program, loosely structured, informally administered, and only sporadically used (Brown and Whitten, 1977; Davies, 1979). Often, however, there appears to be a close and positive relationship between the degree of program structure and the number of participating students

Table 3-4. Co-op Students by Graduate Curriculum Areas.

Curriculum Area	Number of Students
Agriculture and Natural Resources	98
Applied Arts	83
Business	1,090
Computer Science	280
Education	348
Engineering	374
Health Professions	167
Home Economics	19
Humanities	334
Law	570
Natural Sciences	127
Social and Behavioral Sciences	517
Technologies	18

(Brown and Wilson, 1978). Most, but not all, are administered through the undergraduate co-op program. Unlike undergraduate co-op, graduate co-op most often involves students in a single period of work. This may be one academic term or it may be organized to cover a longer period of time, six months to a year.

There are several factors that impede both the adoption of graduate programs of cooperative education and student participation in them. First, as noted, they are frequently extensions of undergraduate programs and constitute an overload responsibility for coordinators. Hence, graduate students tend to be served as time and energy permit, and little is done to attract students (Brown and Wilson, 1978). Second, graduate schools have traditionally used fellowships and assistantships to provide financial assistance, introduce students to academic functions of teaching and research, and give direct assistance to faculty so they may more ably pursue their research. Quite simply, faculty are often reluctant to support efforts that take away their student assistants (Brown and Wilson, 1978; Davies, 1979). Third, there is some reluctance on the part of many employers to employ graduate co-ops. They would prefer to encourage an existing employee whom they know and expect to remain with them to attend graduate school part-time.

Despite these deterrents, interest in graduate co-op continues, and each year new efforts are expended to initiate programs at this level.

Summary

Cooperative education in the United States is varied and serves a varied student population. These two facts attest to the adaptability of cooperative education to a broad range of institutional settings and conditions and to its appropriateness to varieties of students with widely differing academic and career interests. This adaptability, in turn, is testimony to the strength of cooperative education as an instructional strategy.

Diversity of programming is indeed a principal characteristic of cooperative education in America. Beneath this diversity, however, one finds a conceptual core, which is shared by all who engage in this form of education. All are committed to the proposition that important learning can and does occur outside the classroom; they all believe that the workplace provides an environment for important learning and that students' performing productive work is an excellent means for achieving that learning; and they believe that work experience must be viewed as an integral element of the students' educational program. Hence, we find that cooperative education in the United States holds firmly to the concept of integrating work and study but implements that concept in diverse ways, appropriate to the nature of the institution and to its student body.

References

Borman, A. K. "Graduate Programs." In A. S. Knowles (ed.), *Handbook of Cooperative Education*. San Francisco: Jossey-Bass, 1971.

Brown, S. J., and Whitten, C. J. *Cooperative Education for Graduate Students*. Boston: Northeastern University, 1977.

Brown, S. J., and Wilson, J. W. "Cooperative Education for Graduate Students." In J. W. Wilson (ed.), *Developing and*

Expanding Cooperative Education. New Directions for Experiential Learning, no. 2. San Francisco: Jossey-Bass, 1978.

Davies, G. "Better Career Education for Chemists." *Journal of Chemical Engineering,* 1979, *56,* 504.

Wilson, J. W. "Cooperative Education and Degree Credit." *Journal of Cooperative Education,* 1973, *9* (2), 28-38.

Wilson, J. W., and others. *Implementation of Cooperative Education Programs.* Boston: Northeastern University, 1974.

Four

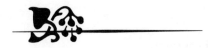

Comparing Programs Worldwide

Solveig M. Turner
Antoinette Frederick

Since the early 1970s, the number of higher education institutions adopting some form of cooperative education has been steadily increasing worldwide. Evidence of this growth can be found by comparing two studies made only seven years apart. The first, a survey done by Wanda Mosbacker (1977), indicates that in 1975 some form of cooperative education existed in fifty-five countries. In 1982, a study undertaken at Northeastern University identified seventy-six countries with some form of cooperative education—an increase of 38 percent (International Center for Education and Work, 1983). That survey also showed some 272 separate institutions, excluding U.S. institutions, offering some form of co-op. It was not, however, all-inclusive, since no responses were received either from the U.S.S.R. or from several Eastern bloc countries, which are known to stress a work component in educational programs.

The purpose of the following chapter is to explore some of the reasons for the evident growth of cooperative education and to examine the kinds of programs and support structures

Note: The authors are indebted to Gill Trevett, senior assistant registrar, Brunel University, for the discussion on "sandwich" program organizations contained in this chapter.

that have developed. Also included are seven "country studies," on grounds that a detailed examination of specific examples will serve to illuminate the more general observations made elsewhere.

Types of Programs

Most current studies indicate that, with the exception of the United States and Canada (where the cooperative education concept has been widely accepted by universities), the cooperative method has been most successful in nonuniversity institutions—British polytechnics, German *Fachhochschulen,* Dutch higher professional colleges, Australian colleges of advanced education, and technical institutions at the secondary and post-secondary levels. In general, universities have resisted the adoption of co-op, on the grounds that they are elite institutions whose function is to provide a highly theoretical education to a chosen few, and that the inclusion of a practical work component in the curricula is seen as antithetical to that mission.

Countries with the elitist view of higher education usually think of institutions that provide practical work as "different." Indeed the UNESCO *World-Wide Inventory of Non-Traditional Post-Secondary Educational Institutions* (1984) still labels cooperative education "nontraditional education."

It is true, however, that cooperative education schedules frequently do differ from those of more traditional programs. In some instances, the cooperative programs are briefer and more tightly structured than the purely academic programs. Such is the case with those offered in the German *Fachhochschulen* and Dutch higher professional colleges. In other instances, for example in some of the sandwich (U.K. terminology for cooperative programs) programs in India and the United Kingdom, the co-op component lengthens the time required to earn a standard degree or diploma.

Unfortunately, this difference in time connotes to many a lower or inferior educational level that has little to do with course content. Even more important in shaping attitudes toward the cooperative method is the necessarily close relationship that exists between a cooperative education institution and industry, an alliance regarded by some as contradictory to the very essence of "true" education.

So entrenched have these attitudes been that in some countries, notably France, the Scandinavian countries, and Germany, technological and business subjects have not been offered in traditional universities but have been relegated to technical universities or colleges, such as the French *grandes écoles,* the German *technische Hochschulen,* and the Swedish *handelshögskolor.* Lately, however, many of the barriers against practical education have been breaking down, and, as a consequence, co-op has become more acceptable. France now offers cooperative education in its new Technological University of Compiègne; Scandinavian universities are introducing co-op programs in almost all fields of study; and German universities are beginning to use the method in certain fields.

Undoubtedly contributing to this change of heart is the publication of employment statistics for many European countries (United Kingdom, France, Germany) which reveal that university graduates are under-represented in industry and commerce (Commission of the European Communities, 1985). A further factor is the growing number of proposals by organizations, such as the Commission of the European Communities, that advocate the implementation of training partnerships as a way to foster closer relationships between universities and industry (Commission of the European Communities, 1985). The proliferation of such proposals suggests that university programs —especially in Europe—may move toward adopting some form of cooperative education in the next decade.

Despite the growing acceptance of co-op programs by the traditional institutions, co-op still seems to be most successful when it is part of the educational plan of a new institution. As a corollary, it can be noted that, because most recent educational growth has occurred in short-term, technical institutions—junior colleges in the United States, *instituts universitaires de technologie* (IUTs) in France, technical colleges in Singapore and Hong Kong, and two- and three-year technical schools throughout the Commonwealth countries—new co-op programs have also grown most rapidly in these places.

As cooperative programs have expanded, so too have the

fields of study where the method is used. In 1986, these fields ranged from traditional engineering programs to more experimental programs, such as the one in catering and hotel management introduced at Footscray Technical College in Australia. In general, and not surprisingly, developing countries tend to be more conservative in their offerings, with co-op clustered in engineering and related fields, while European institutions show greater diversity.

Thus, until recently, co-op programs in Africa, for example, were characteristically in engineering and related technical areas, but efforts to introduce the method into business and some public administration and health curricula have begun. Institutions in Latin America show a similar pattern, with co-op programs clustered in engineering and technological areas, although, again, a small number of programs are beginning in health areas and in education. A comparable distribution is found in Asian institutions.

Cooperative Education Administration

There is no worldwide pattern for the administration of cooperative programs, nor is there a national pattern, since differences are common within every country. The administration of cooperative education seems to be a case of each individual institution's attempting to find its own solution relative to its philosophy, its own strengths and weaknesses, and the demands of its government or the cooperating employers and students. The section below will examine some of the variations that exist in length of programs, sponsorship, salary, and supervision. The major source for this examination is the 1982 Northeastern University study (International Center for Education and Work, 1983).

Length of Co-Op Period. As the *1982 International Directory of Work Experience Institutions* (International Center for Education and Work, 1983) and numerous individual case studies mentioned below clearly demonstrate, a bewildering number of combinations exists. We find endless variations of "thick or thin sandwiches" (see United Kingdom, Types of Sandwich Programs, later in this chapter). These range from the classic five-year program, which alternates three-month periods in school and at work; to one-month and six-month periods at the Université de Technologie Compiègne in France, which has three work periods—1-6-6—in a three-year program; to the "parallel sandwich" pattern of two days of work/three days in school in Cape Technikon in South Africa. In some cases the co-op requirement lengthens the program of study by six to twelve months. In a majority of cases, however, vacation periods are eliminated so that programs are not lengthened.

Many institutions find that at least two work periods are necessary—the first to introduce the student to the world of work and the second to give him or her a chance to actually perform useful work. On the other hand, many institutions using the one-year "thick sandwich" placement report that the length of the placement allows students to both learn and perform actual work even during the initial assignment.

Sponsorship of Programs. Here there is also considerable variation. In some countries and institutions the government mandates the structure of the program and also foots the bill. This is true, for example, in the German *Fachhochschulen.* In other instances an employer may approach an institution to set up what amounts to a company training program. This was the situation in the establishment of the Shell Expro Technician Scheme in the United Kingdom, which is a joint program funded by the Grampian Regional Education Council and Shell United Kingdom. The program enrolls fifty trainees annually and leads to a Higher National Certificate. All trainees are employed by the company, which supervises their study in cooperation with Aberdeen Technical College (Wilson, 1985).

Still another very typical approach is that used by Birla Institute of Science and Technology in India, which first set up its programs and then went in search of cooperating employers. A steady and often rapid development of programs is possible when the program is solidly entrenched within the educational system, as is the case with *Berufsakademien* (career academies) and the *Fachhochschulen* in Germany. Growth is slower but can be successful when the institution has to build its employer contacts over time, as did Swinburne Institute of Technology in Australia.

Salary of Sponsored Students. Whether or not to pay students for the cooperative work experience is a question that has been widely debated. A majority of programs indicate that students are usually paid by the employer, although some are paid by the government. The amount of salary varies not only from country to country but also in programs within each country. For instance, the salary fluctuations in the *Fachhochschule* programs are reported as a great source of irritation to the involved students (Schindler and others, 1981).

Generally, the programs that seem to work best are those in which the employer is closely involved in the program design and pays for the services rendered by the co-op students. In contrast, students who are employed by industry but are reimbursed by the government are not as readily accepted in the work situation. Examples of both these situations exist in India. Students at Birla Institute, who are paid directly by industry, are more readily accepted into the work team than students at other institutions who are reimbursed through the government's apprentice scheme.

Supervision. Available information seems to indicate that the basis for a successful program is the quality of student supervision. Supervision is provided not only by the employer on the shop floor or in the office but also by the institution. This latter supervision can be provided by co-op coordinators, as is common in a majority of U.S. institutions. Outside the United States, supervision by faculty members is more common. In either case, experience indicates that institutional supervision is most important for a successful co-op experience.

A recent study of German students shows that they felt a strong need to meet regularly with their professors to settle job questions and discuss work dynamics (Schindler and others, 1981). Many institutions, for example Birla Institute and the Université de Technologie Compiègne, recognizing this need for tight supervision, require written and oral reports from the students and extensive evaluations from employers. Such requirements necessitate close collaboration between the institution and industry, which must be seen as equal partners in the learning process, with equal privileges in setting learning goals. If faculty are to supervise students adequately, there must be suitable reimbursement, or at least the teaching burden must be lightened. A willing and interested faculty member can enhance the co-op program, while an overworked and poorly paid professor can seriously undermine it.

This observation is underscored by two recent studies. One from Brazil indicates that the slow growth in Brazilian co-op programs was affected by both the lack of involvement in planning and the low remuneration of faculty (de Souza, 1981). A second study from India indicates that the growth in Indian polytechnic co-op programs was also hampered by low salaries and a lack of arrangements for faculty to participate both in the planning and in the supervisory aspects of the co-op process (Chandrakant, 1982).

Specific Development Patterns

The development of cooperative education around the globe has been uneven. In general, the method has been a Western educational phenomenon and an anglophone one at that, with the greatest growth in the United States, Canada, and Australia. Not surprisingly, considering the character of the method, most growth in cooperative education has occurred in more industrialized nations, although recently there has been significant expansion outside this traditional sphere. To provide insight on some of the developmental variations, seven detailed studies of representative patterns are presented.

Australia

Cooperative education, referred to as "sandwich education," was introduced in Australia in 1962-63 with mechanical engineering courses at Footscray Institute of Technology and Swinburne Institute of Technology. The former program, which was conducted in parallel with a traditional full-time program, was not successful and was soon abandoned. The Swinburne program, however, flourished and led to the adoption of cooperative education in all engineering and applied degree courses at the institution (Davie, 1979).

Despite the success of the cooperative engineering courses at Swinburne, no new programs were introduced in the country until 1969, when New South Wales Institute of Technology (NSWIT) in Sydney established eight engineering and applied science courses (Davie, 1979). In 1971, the Royal Melbourne Institute of Technology pioneered cooperative courses in business studies (Cooper and Siemensama, 1985). Other programs in other disciplines soon followed. These included a geoscience program at New South Wales in 1973 (Sappal, 1985) and a graphic design program at Swinburne in 1974 (Francis and Martin, 1983). The cooperative system has also been used at the graduate level. NSWIT introduced a master's-level program in engineering in 1973 and a legal program in 1981 (Matthews and others, 1985; Handler and Winsor, 1985). An advanced occupational safety and health diploma program began at Ballarat College of Advanced Education in 1979 (Woolley, 1985). There are also cooperative graduate courses in accounting at both Royal Melbourne Institute of Technology and Bendigo College of Advanced Education, to mention only a few (Field, 1983).

The reasons for the introduction of all these programs and the philosophies directing them have varied. At some institutions, such as Swinburne, co-op engineering programs were introduced as a replacement for traditional full-time programs that had not been successful (Davie, 1979). At New South Wales Institute of Technology, on the other hand, co-op engineering programs were used to replace part-time programs because co-op programs allowed more latitude to students who could only find jobs at great distance (Buchner, 1983).

Distance was also a factor in the introduction of a co-op legal program at NSWIT. Since the nineteenth century, the Articles of Clerkship in New South Wales have demanded that law graduates have a certain amount of practical training. In the late twentieth century, however, since the legal profession has become increasingly centralized in the business district of Sydney, it has become more and more difficult for students enrolled in widely separated universities to secure part-time placement. Cooperative legal programs, which allow for concentrated and extended periods of work and study, directly and satisfactorily address this problem (Doyle and others, 1983).

In other disciplines, for example geophysics at NSWIT, the justification for introducing the co-op system was the nature of the discipline itself. The contention here was that most activity in the field was based on visual observation and that co-op was most appropriate for giving the student hands-on experience (Sappal, 1985). In still another discipline, graphic design as offered at Swinburne, the cooperative method was initiated largely to give students exposure to the very specialized equipment and professional skills that were only available in a truly professional environment (Francis and Martin, 1983).

Types of Programs: Length, Patterns, Placement. The length and patterns of the cooperative education programs vary from institution to institution and from discipline to discipline. In general, most require the same academic time as conventional courses or slightly less. Thus, most traditional engineering courses require eight semesters of academic work. The co-op engineering program at Swinburne, however, requires only seven academic semesters and two work semesters, while NSWIT requires six academic and six work semesters on an alternating basis. In both instances the reduced class time is justified on grounds that work experience has improved class performance. As indicated in the above examples, some programs are "thin sandwiches" while others are "thick sandwiches" (Davie, 1979).

The methods by which jobs are secured also vary. Most institutions use academic staff to find placements for the students, but at some institutions students must find their own jobs. This is the case at the colleges of engineering and of law at NSWIT, where students are generally employed before enrolling in programs (Handler and Winsor, 1985). At Royal Melbourne Institute of Technology, a structured placement program, which includes a series of interview preparation sessions and "Open Days" at which potential employers speak to students on the positions they are offering, is an apparently effective employment device (Cooper and Siemensama, 1985).

Control of cooperative education programs may be in the

hands of faculty or industry, and students may be college- or
industry-based. In the first instance, students are allowed time
off from university study to work in business or industry. In the
second instance, it is the employees of a given industry or business who are released from their work commitment to become
students for a specified amount of time. At the Royal Melbourne Institute of Technology, co-op is controlled by academic staff, and students are university-based. The reasoning
here is that the faculty should be involved if the development of
co-op as an integral part of the academic program is to be ensured. In contrast, students working for the graduate-level diploma in occupational safety and health at Ballarat College in Victoria are industry-based, with the employer releasing them for
six weeks' study and with industry exerting major influence on
the programs through participation on an advisory panel (Woolley, 1985).

Co-op Organizations. In 1974, a Cooperative Education
Centre with members drawn from employers, college staff, and
students, was established at Swinburne College of Technology
and subsequently grew to include other institutions in Victoria,
such as the Royal Melbourne Institute of Technology and Footscray Institute of Technology. The objective of the center is to
develop cooperative education through the use of the combined
resources of education, business, and industry; to promote an
awareness of cooperative education as a beneficial strategy; to
encourage discussion between the involved groups; to act as a
center for information; and to influence government and government policies (Davie, 1979). The center has been instrumental in promoting the co-op concept and recently hosted the
Third World Conference on Cooperative Education.

Canada

Cooperative education began in Canada at the University
of Waterloo with the introduction in 1957 of a single engineering program in the faculty of engineering. For the next eight
years, this was the only cooperative education program offered
in the country. Then, in 1965, the university instituted addi-

tional engineering cooperative programs. These were followed by still other co-op programs at other universities—namely, at Sherbrooke in Quebec in 1966, Memorial in Newfoundland in 1969, and Regina in Saskatchewan in 1970 (Tausig, 1980).

In the mid-1960s, a number of Canadian provinces began to establish community colleges. These colleges were designed both to serve an expanding college-age population that could not be accommodated by traditional universities and to answer the growing need of business and industry for persons with specialized skills, particularly in the area of rapidly changing technology. To help accomplish these purposes, many of the new colleges adopted the cooperative system. Since that time, the number of colleges and universities offering some form of co-op has accelerated, until by 1985, the Canadian Association for Cooperative Education listed forty institutions offering cooperative programs. Of these, twenty-three were at the senior or university level, while seventeen were at the junior level.

Types of Programs. By 1985 there were some 20,000 students enrolled in cooperative education programs throughout Canada (Poole, 1983). Of these, by far the largest numbers were in engineering, which attracted approximately one-third of the total. Other disciplines with relatively large enrollments were business administration, natural sciences (biology, mathematics, physical sciences), and computer science. Each of these listed between 2,200 and 2,300 students. Technology programs attracted some 1,100 students. Enrollments in other disciplines ranged from almost 1,000 in applied arts (architecture, commercial art, communications, crafts, fine/performing arts) to a mere seventy-two listed in education. Other disciplines offering cooperative programs in 1985 were health professions and vocational arts, each with approximately 700 students, and humanities, agriculture, and social sciences, with between 200 and 350 students apiece (The Cooperative Education Research Center, 1985).

Because most colleges and universities in Canada have sixteen-week terms, with two or three such terms a year, there is considerable uniformity in cooperative patterns across the country. Most are integrated thin sandwich courses, with students alternating a semester of classroom study with a semester of full-time paid work. A few institutions—five in 1985—reported using a field work pattern. Four of these are Okanagan College, Kelowara; Confederation College, Thunder Bay; Dawson College, Montreal; and Fanshawe College of Applied Arts and Technology, London. The fifth, University College Cape Breton, varies its pattern from one department to another, while the University of Lethbridge offers both an alternating pattern and a parallel pattern whereby students attend classes and work during the same day (The Cooperative Education Research Center, 1985).

Typically, cooperative education programs in Canada take longer for the student to complete than traditional programs. As the 1985 *Undergraduate Program of Cooperative Education in the United States and Canada* (The Cooperative Education Research Center, 1985) made clear, only ten of forty institutions reported that cooperative programs required no more time. Almost all programs are mandatory. The work situation is generally developed by the institution, which also monitors student performance. There are exceptions. At the University of Lethbridge, for example, students who already have jobs are encouraged to apply in the applied studies program, which is conducted on the cooperative system. This is the reverse of the usual pattern, wherein students first enroll in the academic course and then seek employment. The Lethbridge pattern, however, is particularly suitable to the liberal arts courses that dominate the program and in which finding suitable jobs has traditionally been a problem (Atkinson and Collis, 1985).

Women and Cooperative Education. Cooperative education has proved to be a way of providing new opportunities for women in Canada. In 1977, for example, the dean of women at the University of British Columbia (UBC) used a start-up grant for cooperative programs to encourage women students to enter the traditionally nonfemale faculties of applied science (engineering) and of forestry. As a result of opportunities provided through the cooperative program, the number of women in this field at UBC increased from 58 in 1977-78 to 203 in 1984-85, or from 4.7 percent to 11 percent of the total UBC enrollment in applied science (Gilmore, 1985).

Still other co-op programs that have been particularly significant for women are those offered at Mount Saint Vincent, a
women's university in Halifax, which introduced co-op in 1979
in the department of business administration "to better equip
women to assume decision-making and leadership roles" (Shore,
1980, p. 2). The program rapidly expanded to include courses
in French, Spanish, home economics, and public relations, with
enrollments increasing from 65 in 1980 to 115 in 1984–85 (The
Cooperative Education Research Center, 1985).

Problems. The geography of Canada, which involves great
distances between cities, has necessitated some long-distance
placement and consequent difficulties in placing and supervising
students. This has been somewhat alleviated by asking other
cooperative education colleges to assist in these tasks. More can
be done in this area.

A more difficult problem to resolve concerns funding. In
Canada the provincial governments have responsibility for education, while the federal government is concerned with employment issues. This means that cooperative programs can count
on receiving federal funds only to the extent that the programs
are explicitly related to resolving manpower issues. In 1977
Canadian Employment, a federal agency, did make available
start-up grants for cooperative education programs (Gilmore,
1985). As noted above, such money was used by UBC for co-op
engineering and forestry programs. In 1983 a second federal
funding program, the Canadian Employment Career Access Program, included a school/work component that reimbursed companies for employing students. As a result, ten new employers
became available to UBC co-op programs (Gilmore, 1985). As
these examples suggest, the federal government can be an important catalyst in developing cooperative programs and in the
general funding of postsecondary education. Unfortunately,
however, as the government receives little political benefit from
these actions, there is limited incentive to do much. Nevertheless, in 1986 a National Office for Cooperative Education was
established that was at least partially funded by the federal government. In the meantime, provincial governments have been
less than enthusiastic in diverting education funds from traditional methods of education to co-op.

Adding to the economic problems of co-op is the fact that when the program is not mandatory, it is more expensive than traditional programs. At the University of Mount Saint Vincent, for example, it is estimated that co-op costs the university about 10 percent more than regular programs (Shore, 1980).

Still a third problem confronting those interested in developing more co-op programs is the entrenched attitude of many who tend to view education in traditional terms and are still suspicious of a method that considers work an integral element of education. With only 14 percent of the 275 degree and diploma-granting institutions in the country providing cooperative programs, it is clear that the majority still have limited first-hand understanding of the programs.

Although the problems are substantial, they are not without possibilities of solution. The introduction of a new Cooperative Education Program in Exploration Geophysics, which cuts across provincial lines and involves three universities—Regina, Saskatchewan, and Calgary—and two major Canadian industries—mining in Saskatchewan and oil in Alberta, indicates that problems can be resolved when politics are ignored and institutions and industries are willing to be innovative (Robertson, 1983).

Germany

Although the term "cooperative education" is not used per se to designate practical work experience, programs in German institutions such as the *Fachhochschulen* and the *Berufsakademien* are sufficiently similar to justify their inclusion in any discussion of co-op.

The Fachhochschulen. The *Fachhochschulen* were established in 1970-71 to help train students to meet the manpower needs of German industry and commerce. An important element in founding the new institutions, which replaced two-year engineering schools (*Ingenieurschulen*) and many vocational schools, was the chance to forge a closer link between institutions and industry—between theory and practice.

Cooperating in the development of the *Fachhochschule* programs were faculty of the institutions, potential employers, and professional associations, such as the Association of German Engineers.

By 1984 there were 118 of these schools in all parts of Germany, enrolling 292,000 students (*Grund- und Strukturdaten 1985–86,* 1985). The demand for admission in the *Fachhochschulen* has also rapidly outstripped available places. In 1984, in Bavaria, for example, there were 48,000 applicants for 25,000 places.

Types of Fachhochschule *Programs.* The majority of the students enrolled in the *Fachhochschulen* participate in the practical work component. Fields of study include engineering, business, and social pedagogy, with specializations provided in agriculture, food and health technology, textile technology, computer science, and translating and interpreting.

Programs vary in length and structure according to state, institution, and department. Most range from four-year programs, which include two semesters of practical work, such as those in Baden-Württemberg, Bavaria, and Saarland, to three- or three-and-one-half-year programs, with varied periods of work in other states.

The placement of practice periods also varies. In Baden-Württemberg and Bavaria, they fall in the third and sixth semesters, but other states offer a variety of combinations, with some work periods following after the second or third semester or even coming much later.

Most *Fachhochschulen* require practical work in all departments, although some have optional participation. Students generally find their own positions (Schindler and others, 1981). Students retain their student status during the work period and thus also their government financing. While there may be no salary or a very low salary during the practical work period, the one-year practicum completed by social work graduates is invariably fully salaried.

Benefits and Problems. Schindler and others (1981) found ready acceptance of the practical work semesters by all those involved: students, institutions, and employers. The survey indicated no problems in finding work placements. Students were satisfied to find their own jobs, most of which are located within eighty kilometers of either their institution or home. Other satisfactions included close contact with counselors at the workplace and the institution. Problems centered on the timing of visits and the unevenness of salaries.

Berufsakademie *Programs.* Another manifestation of the cooperative education method is found in the Berufsakademie Baden-Württemberg. In 1974 two institutions were established to provide an education that would integrate theory and practice even more closely than did the *Fachhochschulen.* By 1982 there were eight such programs.

The *Berufsakademie* offers three years of education to secondary school graduates in alternating, complementary periods of classroom theoretical study and practical work in business or industry. The total program requires three years, with a less prestigious diploma available after two years. Students are employed throughout their full period of study. Programs are offered in three major specializations—business, technology, and social work—with a number of different majors, although not all specializations are available at all *Berufsakademien.* Curricula are drawn up by committees consisting of equal numbers of representatives from the universities, the *Berufsakademien,* and the training companies. There is also a student member.

While the German universities and the *Fachhochschulen* generally employ full-time faculty, the *Berufsakademien* have an 86 percent commitment of part-time faculty. Of these, 38 percent are from industry, 13 percent are from universities, 16 percent are from *Fachhochschulen,* and 19 percent from secondary schools. The *Berufsakademie* has received strong support from the state of Baden-Württemberg and from employers and in its first ten years has grown from 163 students in two institutions to 4,400 in eight institutions. A similar type of education is now being offered in other states, including Schleswig-Holstein and Hamburg.

Practical Work in the Universities. Although most of the growth of the co-op method in Germany has occurred outside the universities, there are some, especially the *Gesamthochschu-*

len, that have begun to incorporate practical work as part of the academic program. The *Kasseler-Reformmodell* at the Gesamt-hoschschule Kassel, for example, integrates two semesters of practical work within the university-level study program. The university also organizes month-long seminars of job evaluation to assess the value of the completed practical semester and an orientation period which is designed to give students a view of their projected careers. Furthermore, since government plans indicate an interest in increasing cooperative education, the method may soon occupy an even greater role in the universities ("Das Kasseler Reformmodell der Gesamthochschule," 1979).

Women in German Cooperative Programs. In 1984 women constituted 44 percent of enrollment in the *Berufsakademien.* In the *Fachhochschulen,* women constitute 29 percent of total enrollments. A majority were enrolled in business, where they made up almost 50 percent of total enrollments. Only some 10 percent enrolled in engineering subjects (*Grund- und Strukturdaten 1985-86,* 1985).

India

The first sandwich course in India was instituted in 1900 by the Eastern India Railways in its Central Training School in Jamalpur. Its objective was to train engineers and technicians for the railway's workshops. Students received an equal mix of practical work and theory, spending half their time in actual work situations with the company (Shahani, 1979). Although the program had a good reputation, it did not attract many imitators, possibly because it was not in the interest of the colonial government to develop an extensive industrial base or an independent, professionally trained, native, middle-class work force.

Following independence in 1947, India did experience vast industrial expansion and a simultaneous expansion of engineering education. The number of engineering institutions providing engineering education—including polytechnics—increased from 53 to 500 between 1947 and 1977.

Despite the proliferation of these institutions, there has been a continuing problem correlating industry and education.

Constant attempts have been made to bridge the gap, but most have met with only marginal success. Included among these efforts were those made by India's Scientific Manpower Committee, which in the late 1940s recommended a "Practical Training Stipend Scheme." The scheme gave a monthly stipend to undergraduates and diploma students who undertook practical work during their educational careers. By 1966, over 3,000 graduates had been served by the program. In that year the Education Commission reaffirmed the government's commitment to practical training as a part of engineering education when it urged the establishment of sandwich programs at the undergraduate level (Mandke, 1980).

In the early 1970s, in response to continued government recommendations as well as to the inclusion of sandwich education in the Apprenticeship Act (1973) Amended, several regional engineering colleges and a number of polytechnics introduced sandwich programs. By 1975, 44 of the existing 284 polytechnics had such programs, but the real pioneering effort to link industry and the university came in 1973–74, when Birla Institute of Technology and Science (BITS), Pilani, launched the BITS Practice School Programme. This is a system of education that places teams of BITS students in industrial work situations throughout India.

Types and Length of Programs. Practical work as a component of education exists in polytechnics and regional colleges as sandwich programs. It is also provided as part of the Practice School Programme of Birla. A third combination occurs in the conventional engineering curriculum when students undertake practical work during summer vacations. Variations also exist in the length of programs, the level of integration between work and study, and the level at which programs are offered.

In general, programs vary from three and one-half years for co-op programs in the polytechnics to five or more years for programs at the university level. The work component also varies from six months for certain polytechnic programs to several years for doctoral programs. Finally, and as indicated above, the levels show great variation. The most sophisticated programs are those offered at Birla Institute of Technology and Science. These are conducted at three levels—the Practice School

Programme at the first-degree level; a related M.E. (collaborative) program, which is a two-year master's degree program; and a further related off-campus Ph.D. All of these are implemented from Practice School stations, which are established in selected industry and government agencies. The stations are staffed by off-campus faculty who supervise the students. The major difference between Practice School and other cooperative education programs is that faculty are residents at the Practice Station and that the program is offered in all disciplines within the institution, from humanities to engineering.

The Birla program has now been in operation for over a dozen years. Evidence of its success is clear in the growing enrollments and in the growing number of involved industries, which has gone from 2 in 1973 to 130 in 1985. Furthermore, industry now pays 50 percent of the cost of the program. Another indication of success is the increased popularity, as evident in the fact that initially the program was optional and today the entire student body participates.

In summary, through the Practice School a new model of the Indian university has evolved, with a modular degree structure, a semester system, multi-entry admissions, and summer semesters. Thus, Birla is able to provide a degree in almost the same period of time as traditional programs.

Problems. Despite continuing pressure for education and industry to form closer links, the development of cooperative and sandwich programs in India has been slow. Partially, this is the result of weak educational leadership. A further contributing factor is the lack of national or state policies relative to sandwich education, while the administrative structures that do exist lack the coordination to bring together industry and educational representatives.

A 1984 study of 142 representative polytechnics from a total of almost 400 indicates that 15 percent of polytechnics have active sandwich programs, that private as opposed to government-run institutions were more likely to have closer ties with industry (possibly because they were run by industrialists), and that large polytechnics had better collaboration with industry (Inderisan, 1984).

Using Birla as the example of a successful program, other

points become clear. The more structured and organized the program is and the more involved industry is with the program, the better the chance for success. Other factors influencing success include the selectivity of the program and the totality of the commitment of all those involved—students, faculty, and industry representatives.

Nigeria

Like many Third World countries, Nigeria had no formal educational system prior to colonization. One generation learned from another through the informal apprenticeship system (Allen, 1982). Because this indigenous system, by its very nature, involves work/study, some are tempted to identify it as cooperative education. To the degree, however, that the cooperative method suggests a formally structured yoking of theory and practice, the apprenticeship method cannot be truly called cooperative. It can be seen as an alternative educational and vocational training method, one that is particularly well suited to the transmission of skills that can be attained through imitation. In general, the apprenticeship system does not lend itself to educating students in sophisticated disciplines because it lacks the formal classroom component found in the cooperative method.

The roots of cooperative education, then, as it is understood in this book, can be traced to a period shortly after independence. At this time, the Nigerian Post and Telecommunication introduced a day-release workers' training program. The program, which, as M. A. Iroegbu, President of Industrial Practice Officers of Nigeria, remarks, "married work and education," was designed to produce skilled professionals (Iroegbu, 1985, p. 694). Such a program had been urged by the Nigerian Labour Organization before independence but was rejected during colonization. Shortly after this program was instituted others followed. In the 1960s, Nigerian railroads, the armed forces, and the police established training schools capable of producing administrative, maintenance, and engineering crews.

In the late 1960s, the federal military government began to charter management development and training organizations and gave support to work/study programs. This support was formalized in 1971 with the passage of the Industrial Training Fund (ITF). The purpose of the ITF was to develop an indigenous work force to meet national, industrial, and commercial needs. As part of fulfilling this objective, ITF funded and supervised the Student Industrial Work Experience Scheme (SIWES), which began to coordinate cooperative education programs (Olawuni, 1985).

In 1977, another step occurred in the development of cooperative education in Nigeria. National educational policy changed, highlighting technological education and making it mandatory for a student at a technological institution to work for a specific time in an industry related to the student's field of study in order to graduate. The report further stated that these students should receive a stipend for their work from the federal government (Iroegbu, 1985).

In 1978 the Nigerian University Commission (NUC) assumed responsibility for funding SIWES at university institutions, and the following year the National Board for Technical Education assumed similar responsibilities for polytechnics and colleges of technology. These organizations supervise the development of cooperative education programs in the mid-1980s (Olawuni, 1985).

Types of Programs. In 1986 cooperative, or sandwich, programs are available at both Nigerian universities and colleges of technology. At Ahmadu Bello University, Center for Educational Technology, Zaria, a cooperative program in applied arts was begun in 1978. Work experience takes place in the year after class studies are completed. Students are paid by the government and the institution and share the responsibility of evaluating the program. At the College of Technology, Owerri, cooperative programs are provided in technological courses leading to a diploma. Work periods are three to four months and students are reimbursed by the government. Rivers State University of Science and Technology at Port Harcourt also provides a diploma course in a variety of fields, ranging from business administration to town and country planning. Each requires three semesters of class study plus two semesters of supervised industrial work experience. These examples do not exhaust the list of institutions providing some form of postsecondary sandwich plan education (Iroegbu, 1985).

Problems. As implied above, government has played a central role in fostering cooperative education programs in Nigeria, and a tripartite approach to education involving government, industries, and higher education institutions is national policy. Despite such support, however, the system has encountered several problems. These include organizational problems, inadequate industrial facilities, inadequate student boarding and transportation facilities, and inadequate funding.

Although the organization of cooperative programs varies from institution to institution, very few have clear policies governing coordinators, particularly at the university level. As a result, a great deal of the administration of programs is done on an ad hoc basis, with students left to find their own jobs. They are also poorly supervised, if supervised at all (Olawuni, 1985).

While the number of co-op students has grown considerably, the number of jobs available in industry has not kept pace. In fact, as a result of the global recession in 1983-84, the number of jobs has dropped. As a result, many students cannot find suitable employment. For others who do find jobs, the position may be far from home and, in these cases, affordable travel and accommodations may prove an insurmountable barrier. Finally, funding cooperative programs has proved difficult, particularly because many employers have been reluctant to pay students, claiming that they are the ones who benefit most from the experience (Olawuni, 1985).

Venezuela

The first cooperative education, or sandwich, programs in Venezuela were established in higher education institutions in the early 1970s. The impetus for the development of these programs was a growing sense of national identity that occurred when the rise in oil prices in the early 1970s caused a boom in the economy of this oil-rich country. The suddenly available funds prompted the Venezuelan government to take a careful look at its future. One of the consequences of this assessment was the determination on the part of the government planners to diversify the country's industry and develop a skilled, native work force that would be independent of foreign assistance. To achieve these aims, the government encouraged much closer cooperation between education and industry than had been usual in Latin American countries. It is no coincidence that cooperative education programs were begun at this time (Ardagh, 1974).

Two institutions in particular are identified with the introduction of cooperative education. The first is Simón Bolívar University (SBU), which was founded in 1969 and which in July 1972 opened two cooperative programs, one in chemical engineering and one in mechanical engineering. Together these enrolled fourteen students and involved eight companies (Bescanza, 1983). The second was a UNESCO-aided polytechnic in the steel town of Ciudad Guayana (Ardagh, 1974). This institute, which was designed to graduate technicians and engineers at the ordinary degree level, had an elaborate program of sandwich courses. It also had problems determining at what level training should be aimed.

Since that time, the cooperative education programs at Simón Bolívar University have expanded, as have those in the polytechnics. In addition, Venezuela provides related programs that are designed to encourage the development of a well trained work force.

Types of Cooperative Education Programs at Simón Bolívar University. Of the thirteen Venezuelan national universities, Simón Bolívar University has the most extensive co-op program. SBU is a technological university enrolling 9,000 students. It provides six engineering degrees and four basic science *licenciado* degrees, and town planning and architecture degrees. In general, these programs last five years, each year being divided into three terms. The exceptions are the materials engineering and biology programs, which take thirteen terms, and architecture, which requires eighteen. The first two years focus on a basic cycle of studies—mathematics, science, general studies. During the final three years, the curriculum is designed to lead to a career, and it is during this period that co-op programs are undertaken (Bescanza, 1983).

SBU's co-op program requires every engineering, town

planning, biology, and chemistry student to have two periods of industrial training. The first period, called the "short *pasantía*," lasts a minimum of six weeks and carries three academic credits. During this period, the student works in a setting relevant to his or her anticipated career. The object is to learn aspects of the profession not easily available in the classroom—labor relationships, decision-making procedures, and organizational structures. The second period, called the "long *pasantía*," lasts twenty weeks and requires a university defense of the work done. It carries nine credits and requires completion of a report, which is considered equivalent to a graduation project or thesis (Bescanza, 1983).

The work program for cooperative students must be approved by academic and industrial tutors. The student must contact his academic tutor every two weeks, while the tutor must visit the industry every six weeks.

Other Work/Study-Related Programs. In addition to the co-op programs offered by Simón Bolívar University, there are those provided through polytechnics, the *institutos universitarios politécnicos.* Originally conceived as short-cycle (three to four years) programs of study leading to the title *tecnólogo* in four years or the *técnico superior* in three years, the programs now emphasize five-year engineering degrees. It is considered, however, that the engineering degrees from the *politécnicos* that incorporate a required amount of practical training are far more practically oriented than those at the universities. For instance, the Instituto Politécnico Barquisimeto includes two major co-op periods.

Problems. By 1973 educating students to assume a meaningful place in industry had become a top priority in Venezuela. But, although cooperative programs offered through polytechnical schools were seen as one solution to this problem, it was nevertheless difficult to overcome entrenched feelings of skepticism about practical education. Traditionally, higher education in Venezuela had been linked to prestigious diplomas and titles and to training in the classical manner. The need, however, was for practically oriented graduates who could exercise entrepreneurial skills and participate in development activities. The major problem, then, was to assure that this was recognized and the desire for prestige put aside in the interest of useful education.

Between 1974 and 1985, inroads were made in meeting this problem, as the very number of students enrolled in cooperative education programs indicates. These numbers make it clear that cooperative education is no longer quite the stepchild it once was. A more acute problem in the mid-1980s is the state of the Venezuelan economy as a whole. The sudden plunge in oil prices will undoubtedly have its effect on education. What this effect will be and how it will shape the future of the cooperative method of education in that country remains to be seen.

United Kingdom

In the United Kingdom, courses which combine academic study with periods of practical work experience are known generally as "sandwich courses." The first documented sandwich course in England was offered in 1903 at Sunderland Technical College in engineering and naval architecture programs. No further significant expansion of the method occurred until the late 1950s, when the Colleges of Advanced Technology started the expansion of sandwich courses.

The 1960s saw a general growth in all higher education in the United Kingdom. During this period, many of the institutions that were providing advanced-level programs became designated as polytechnics, and in 1966-67, the Colleges of Advanced Technology became technological universities (Davie, 1977). It is these nine technological universities and the thirty polytechnics that offer the majority of sandwich courses in the United Kingdom. Recent developments in the approach to engineering education, however, indicate that older, more traditional universities may also be offering sandwich courses in engineering in the near future.

During the last decade, there has also developed a new program designed to raise the level of industrial performance by effective use of academic resources. This program, called the "Teaching Company Scheme," is not identical with the sandwich method of education. It is similar to the extent that it functions to bring universities and polytechnics together with industrial companies and works to train able graduates for careers in industry. For these reasons, it should be considered in a discourse on cooperative education in the United Kingdom.

Types of Sandwich Programs. The sandwich plan of education in the United Kingdom is most often employed in engineering and technology programs. Other fields of study in which the method is frequently used include vocational programs, such as business studies or hotel and catering, and nonvocational programs, such as mathematics and physics.

In most instances, sandwich programs in the United Kingdom require an additional year over the conventional, three-year program and fall into one of two patterns. The "thick sandwich" pattern requires that the student have one full year of work experience in addition to three academic years. By custom, the work period begins after the second academic year but may be taken earlier. The "thin sandwich" pattern consists of two to five work periods, varying in length, and interspersed throughout the total program.

In Britain, students following the sandwich plan of education may be either college- or university-based or industry-based. Until the mid-1970s industry-based students—particularly in engineering—were most common, reflecting sponsorship of sandwich programs by local industries. In recent years, the proportion of university- or college-based students has begun to exceed the numbers that are industry-based (Gordon and others, 1985), reflecting the move in sandwich programs into areas other than engineering, where sponsorship has traditionally been the most common. Some 25 percent of engineering students are currently sponsored by companies (Gordon and others, 1985).

Responsibility for coordinating academic and work experience is generally the task of the institution's teaching staff, who in the case of college-based students also assist in finding appropriate positions. The staff provides guidance and evaluates and assesses the student's work experience. This differs from the North American and Canadian systems, where such roles are often assumed by a nonacademic coordinator. The student is generally reimbursed by the employer for his work at regular salary scale. Unless industry is sponsoring his attendance at the college or university, the student is not reimbursed by the employer for the academic portion of the program.

Sandwich Program Organizations. In the 1970s, two groups with a prime concern for sandwich education emerged. The Universities Committee on Integrated Sandwich Courses was established in 1972. It promoted the integrated sandwich course system in the university sector by providing a forum for collaboration and sharing information among the universities. The committee also worked with government departments to promote the expansion of sandwich education. In 1976 a Polytechnics' Committee on Sandwich Courses was formed with the object of promoting the sandwich course system in the polytechnic field. The committee encourages an exchange of views and experience in the design and operation of sandwich courses and provides a national voice on matters of common concern to those involved with placing sandwich students into suitable training in industry and commerce.

Although the existence of these two organizations had assisted in discussion and coordination of issues concerning sandwich education, in 1979 it was considered that an association that could bring together the employing organizations and the academic institutions would be of mutual benefit. Thus the Association for Sandwich Education and Training (ASET) was set up to bring together, and to some extent represent, all those interested in sandwich education and training, namely employers, educators, and students. The association produces an annual journal that provides the main source of statistical information about sandwich education in the United Kingdom discussed in this chapter and offers a perspective on the provision of placements (Daniels, 1981).

The Teaching Company Scheme. Closely related to, but by no means identical with, the cooperative or sandwich method of education is the "Teaching Company Scheme." The scheme was devised in 1974 by the Science and Research Engineering Council (SREC) and the Department of Trade and Industry (DTI) to facilitate the flow of scientific and technological expertise, which exists in the universities and polytechnics, into the right place in industry. To implement this process and to ensure that relevant academics were kept up to date on industrial practice, SREC and DTI developed a program whereby companies were paired with academic institutions. Each partnership was called a "Teaching Company Programme." Within this program, academics became involved with company managers in the joint supervision and direction of a group of high-caliber young graduates who are called "associates." These associates are appointed by the university or polytechnic academic department and are paid full industrial salaries to work on specific projects. The associates are working in industry and for industry, but are doing so with the support, expertise, and facilities of the partner academic institution (*Information Sheet: The Teaching Company Scheme,* 1985).

The similarities between cooperative, or sandwich, education and the Teaching Company Scheme are clear. Both depend on a close working relationship between industry and academe; both help train graduates for careers in industry; and both assume that a period of paid work in industry working with senior company and academic staff is a major step toward achieving that career.

There are also significant differences. Associates in the Teaching Company are not undergraduates enrolled in an institution. Rather they are graduates recruited through the placement of advertisements in the media. Applicants who are accepted are considered employees of the academic institution, although they work primarily in the partner industry. Finally, expenses are met by SREC and DTI, operating through a "directorate" that, in its turn, is advised by a "Central Management Committee." From this source, grants are made to individual programs to cover basic salaries and to support costs.

Since their inception, Teaching Company Programmes have grown rapidly until, in 1984, over 200 companies of all sizes have been matched with a variety of academic teams from over fifty institutions. Furthermore, the budget for these programs now stands at 5 million pounds a year, and it is hoped that this will rise to at least 11 million pounds by 1988.

Problems and Conclusions. In 1983-85, 88,668 students were enrolled in sandwich programs in British universities, polytechnics, and further and higher education colleges. Of these, 65,480 were degree students and 23,188 were diploma students. Total placement numbers, however, were only 35,686 (Association for Sandwich Education and Training, 1985).

As these figures indicate, the number of suitable placements for students on the sandwich program is a source of concern. Anxieties about the provision of suitable placements for the growing number of students on sandwich courses at a time of recession in the United Kingdom resulted in reviews by the Department of Education and Science and the former Council for Tertiary Education in Scotland in 1981. They were concerned in particular to assess the extent and implications of a reported decrease in sandwich placements offered by employers. In 1982, following these reviews, the Committee on Research into Sandwich Education (RISE) was set up to coordinate a program of research on this issue. The overall conclusion of the RISE report found in favor of sandwich education but recorded a need for greater critical evaluation of student placements to assure suitability, greater effort to ensure a practicable relationship between work and academic pursuits, greater flexibility in institutional organization of sandwich programs, and greater employer awareness of the benefits of the program (Department of Education and Science, 1985).

The problems with sandwich education are, of course, very closely tied with those of the economy as a whole. In the mid-1980s, the United Kingdom is experiencing very high unemployment—roughly 11 percent. Under such circumstances, it is not surprising that the placement of students in industry would be difficult. Somewhat less vulnerable to these conditions is the Teaching Company Scheme. Because the associate is supported by a grant, because he or she is older, and because the function of the associate in the industry is to actively contribute to the solution of an industrial problem in addition to learning about the industry, the associate's presence is less likely to be perceived as a drain on the resources of the industry and is more likely to be perceived as a positive asset than is the sandwich student.

What all these conditions portend for the future of cooperative education in the United Kingdom is hard to say. What is clear is that the partnership between industry and education has a long history in the United Kingdom and that this partnership has become increasingly well regarded.

References

Allen, R. "Capitalist Development and the Educational Role of Nigerian Apprenticeship." *Comparative Education,* 1982, *18* (2), 123–137.

Ardagh, J. "Training Rides High on Crest of Oil Wave." *London Times–Higher Education Supplement,* no. 52, September 13, 1974, p. 11.

Association for Sandwich Education and Training. *1985 Journal.* Uxbridge, England: Brunel University, 1985.

Atkinson, D. W., and Collis, K. "A Model for Experiential Education." In *The Fourth World Conference on Cooperative Education.* Edinburgh, Scotland: Napier College, 1985.

Bescanza, C. H. "Simón Bolívar University Co-op Programme: Ten Years." *The Third World Conference on Cooperative Education.* Vol. 2. Melbourne, Australia: Swinburne College of Technology, 1983.

Buchner, T. E. "The Development of a Program of Co-operative Education in the School of Civil Engineering at the New South Wales Institute of Technology." In *The Third World Conference on Cooperative Education.* Melbourne, Australia: Swinburne College of Technology, 1983.

Chandrakant, L. S. *Sandwich Course Revisited—A Study on Technical-Industry Co-Operation in Indian Setting.* Bangalore, India: Indian Institute of Management, 1982.

Commission of the European Communities. *Proposal for a Council Decision.* Brussels, Belgium: Commission of the European Communities, 1985.

Cooper, B. J., and Siemensama, F. "Facilitating Productive Relationships for Co-operative Education in Business." In *The Fourth World Conference on Cooperative Education.* Edinburgh, Scotland: Napier College, 1985.

The Cooperative Education Research Center. *Undergraduate Programs of Cooperative Education in the United States and Canada.* Boston: The Cooperative Education Research Center, Northeastern University, 1985.

Daniels, A. "Foreword." In Association for Sandwich Education and Training. *1981 Journal.* Uxbridge, England: Brunel University, 1981.

"Das Kasseler Reformmodell der Gesamthochschule." *Informationen Bildung Wissenschaft,* 1979, *9,* 177.

Davie, R. S. "Sandwich Plan in the Commonwealth Nations." In A. S. Knowles (ed.), *The International Encyclopedia of Higher Education.* San Francisco: Jossey-Bass, 1977.

Davie, R. S. "Cooperative Education in Australia." In *The First World Conference on Cooperative Education.* Windsor, England: NFER Publishers, 1979.

Department of Education and Science. *An Assessment of the Costs and Benefits of Sandwich Education: RISE Report.* London: Department of Education and Science, 1985.

de Souza, H. G. "Cooperative Education in Brazil." *CIHED Newsletter,* 1981, *4,* (2), 13–14.

Doyle, K. J., and others. "Co-operative Practical Legal Training: A Survey of Employer Attitudes." *The Third World Conference on Cooperative Education.* Melbourne, Australia: Swinburne College of Technology, 1983.

Field, D. D. "Co-operative Course Students and Graduates in the Accounting Profession." In *The Third World Conference on Cooperative Education.* Melbourne, Australia: Swinburne College of Technology, 1983.

Francis, R. A., and Martin, B. D. "Cooperative Education in Graphic Design." In *The Third World Conference on Cooperative Education.* Melbourne, Australia: Swinburne College of Technology, 1983.

Gilmore, M. "The Government as Catalyst in Co-operative Education: A Canadian Perspective." In *The Fourth World Conference on Cooperative Education.* Edinburgh, Scotland: Napier College, 1985.

Gordon, A., and others. "Industrial Sponsorship of Engineering Undergraduates." *Studies in Higher Education,* 1985, *10,* (1), 33–42.

Grund- und Strukturdaten 1985-86. Bonn, West Germany: Bundesminister für Bildung und Wissenschaft, 1985.

Handler, L. G., and Winsor, K. "A Model for Co-operative Professional Legal Education." In *The Fourth World Conference on Cooperative Education.* Edinburgh, Scotland: Napier College, 1985.

Inderisan, J. "Profile and Index of the Polytechnic: Industry Collaboration—An Empirical Study." *Journal of Higher Education,* 1984, *10,* (1-2), 29-44.

Information Sheet: The Teaching Company Scheme. Swindon, England: Science and Engineering Research Council, 1985.

International Center for Education and Work. *1982 International Directory of Work Experience Institutions.* Boston: International Center for Education and Work (Center for Cooperative Education), Northeastern University, 1983.

Iroegbu, M. A. "Student Industrial Attachment—The Nigerian Experience." In *The Fourth World Conference on Cooperative Education.* Edinburgh, Scotland: Napier College, 1985.

Mandke, V. V. "BITS Practice School: A Case Study in Industry-University Collaboration." *The Birla Vidya Vihar Bulletin,* 1980, *23,* (3), 3-103.

Matthews, C. T., and others. "Insights from a Unique Cooperative Education Program." In *The Fourth World Conference on Cooperative Education.* Edinburgh, Scotland: Napier College, 1985.

Mosbacker, W. "Cooperative Education Worldwide." In A. S. Knowles (ed.), *The International Encyclopedia of Higher Education.* San Francisco: Jossey-Bass, 1977.

Olawuni, O. R. "University of Ibadan." *The Fourth World Conference on Cooperative Education.* Edinburgh, Scotland: Napier College, 1985.

Poole, W. J. H. "The Canadian Government and Cooperative Education: The Employment-Education Connection." *The Third World Conference on Cooperative Education.* Melbourne, Australia: Swinburne College of Technology, 1983.

Robertson, B. E. "The Political Context of a Cooperative Education Program Involving the Cooperation of Three Universities." In *The Third World Conference on Cooperative Educa-*

tion. Melbourne, Australia: Swinburne College of Technology, 1983.

Sappal, K. K. "The Australian Experience in Cooperative Education for Geosciences." In *The Fourth World Conference on Cooperative Education.* Edinburgh, Scotland: Napier College, 1985.

Schindler, G., and others. "Praktische Studiensemester in Fachhochschulen in Bayern." *Beitrage zur Hochschulforschung,* 1981, *2,* 153-165.

Shahani, H. S. "Development of Sandwich Courses in India." In *The First World Conference on Cooperative Education.* Windsor, England: NFER Publishers, 1979.

Shore, V. "A Miracle on the Mount." *University Affairs,* 1980, *21* (8), 2-3.

Tausig, C. "Cooperative Graduates Get a Head Start." *University Affairs,* 1980, *21* (8), 2-3.

UNESCO. *World-Wide Inventory of Non-Traditional Post-Secondary Educational Institutions.* 2nd updated and revised ed. Paris: UNESCO, 1984.

Wilson, D. J. "A Partnership in Training for the Offshore Oil Industry." *The Fourth World Conference on Cooperative Education.* Edinburgh, Scotland: Napier College, 1985.

Woolley, D. "The Development of Teaching Programs for Occupational Safety and Health in Australia Using the Cooperative Method." In *The Fourth World Conference on Cooperative Education.* Edinburgh, Scotland: Napier College, 1985.

Five

Planning, Implementing, and Assessing Programs

Harry N. Heinemann

Successfully establishing or expanding a quality cooperative education program is a complex process. It requires no less attention than bringing about any major change within the institution, perhaps even more. This appears to be true regardless of program size. In order to accommodate both students and employers, which is necessary for a program to expand, many changes must be made within the administrative and academic areas of the college. It does not take many students entering the cooperative education program before the institution feels the pressure for change.

Cooperative education affects virtually all areas of the college, but none more than the academic area. As a nontraditional, experiential approach to learning, cooperative education raises philosophical and curriculum issues that lie at the heart of the academy. It calls into question the educational mission of the institution and the objectives of the curriculum.

When the academic programs of the institution satisfy its constituents, faculty, students, administration, parents, and the public at large, little rationale exists for introducing major changes. Few colleges and universities today can consider themselves in this enviable position. Quite the contrary, serious questions concerning the quality of higher education in this country, especially when considering the costs involved, are being raised.

Incorporating out-of-classroom learning opportunities into the curriculum, such as those offered by cooperative education, is one possible change that can strengthen the learning process by bringing the college experience closer to the world beyond the classroom. Further, cooperative education offers the possibility of getting the students more actively involved in their own learning.

In order to meet the needs of most employers, the college may have to adopt a year-round calendar, with students either attending classes or on their cooperative education assignment. Having a pool of appropriate positions, as determined by the college, is the foundation upon which any successful cooperative education program must be built. Once a placement that meets these criteria has been developed, it is important that it be filled with qualified students on an ongoing basis. Many cooperative education programs lose employers because positions that need to be covered year-round go unfilled. Quite understandably, employers turn elsewhere for personnel. In such situations, the cooperative education program staff will find themselves on a treadmill, constantly having to develop new positions to replace those lost. Accommodating the current level of student enrollments under these circumstances becomes difficult, while any considered program expansion is next to impossible.

The schedule of courses may also need to be revised so that students will have necessary courses available to them upon their return to campus. This is a commitment that the college must make lest the participation in cooperative education result in an unanticipated delay in graduation. In many programs cooperative education does delay graduation beyond the normal two or four years, but this is known to students prior to their enrolling in the program. Any further delay quickly results in a loss of student interest, keeping the program small.

Probably, the curriculum itself will need to be examined in order to ease the alternation of classes and work for students. Prerequisite relationships among courses and the sequencing of courses will need to be examined and most likely modified. When the curriculum does not accommodate the program, the class schedule for each student may have to be developed on an individual basis. This is costly and time consuming. Where such a situation exists, it is very unlikely that the program will be able to serve many students.

Offering academic credit for cooperative education is another issue that must be resolved. This is not merely a question of whether to award academic credit and, if so, how much. It must be recognized that the credits generated by cooperative education must substitute for existing courses, either in the required or elective distribution. Otherwise, these credits become merely an add-on, increasing the number of credits required for graduation. It would not be unusual for some faculty to challenge cooperative education for fear that it will substitute for a course they teach. In effect, providing cooperative education is likely to trigger a thorough curriculum review, which, as difficult and time consuming as it may be, offers the faculty the opportunity to carefully examine the current curriculum for changes that could go far beyond meeting the needs of cooperative education. It is in the faculty's best interest to become actively involved in the decision-making process and to help shape the program rather than to view cooperative education with hostility, indifference, or benign neglect, which is all too often the case.

Having a large number of students away from the campus affects other areas of the college as well: the registration system may have to be modified to accommodate students on their co-op assignments; the financial aid package may need to be changed to include student co-op earnings; the impact on housing for institutions with dormitories will need to be assessed.

While establishing a comprehensive cooperative education program is not a simple matter, a well-designed planning process involving close cooperation among faculty, other members of the professional staff, and administration can result in establishing a quality program that serves both students and employers.

Cooperative Education Program Process

Four stages can be identified in the program development process: institutional readiness, planning and development, implementation, and evaluation.

Institutional Readiness—The First Stage. The top administration of an educational institution can be seen as having two basic functions. First is helping the institution achieve its goals, which presumes that the administration will institute a process whereby the organization will periodically review and, when appropriate, recast its goals. The second function, survival, depends upon an institution receiving a mix of public and private financial support, political support, community support, and, most of all, student enrollments. Today, this support must be sustained at a time of increasing competition from both public and private institutions of higher education for their share of shrinking resources, political and public unhappiness with the educational system, and keen competition for a smaller pool of students. The process of instituting a cooperative education program begins when top administration determines that cooperative education can assist the institution in better achieving its goals and enabling it to survive.

All too often, cooperative education is introduced to an institution as a result of receiving grant funds, but without the institution being either fully prepared or fully cognizant of the impact that the program will have. An administrative assessment of cooperative education should reveal whether the institution has the potential for developing and sustaining a program of sufficient size to meet anticipated student interest. The institution should be relatively free of faculty and administration conflicts. There should be a core of faculty and administrators who are open to considering cooperative education and are willing to carefully examine the possibility of a significant cooperative education program on the campus.

Further, the administration must have some sense of how the developing cooperative education program will be financed both now and in the future. Although outside funding support is currently available from sources such as Title VIII of the Higher Education Act, the institution will quickly have to assume financial responsibility for the program. While there is evidence that cooperative education does attract students, it is highly unlikely that cooperative education can be supported entirely from increased tuition revenues stemming from increased student enrollments. In fact, cooperative education may not result in any increased tuition revenues but may be a key strategy in stemming enrollment declines.

In the near future, colleges are going to be competing more intensely than ever for a smaller pool of high school graduates. A number of strategies, such as attracting new populations, is one approach toward moving the institution into a more competitive position. Offering new programs such as cooperative education is another. In its assessment, the administration must identify possible ways to reallocate internal resources, both dollars and staff. Without the support of top administration and faculty leaders, there seems to be little point in continuing the planning and implementation process.

The nature of the decision-making process in academic institutions necessitates input from areas across the college. In general, if an institution has successfully developed a mechanism for introducing change in the past, for example a major new program, then it should consider using the same process to introduce cooperative education. The mechanism used at most colleges is likely to be the establishment of a task force to conduct a study of institutional readiness. Selection of the individuals to serve on this committee takes careful consideration. Its membership ought to include the best and most creative minds within the institution. It should include individuals who are seen as leaders. Moreover, as this committee may well become the support base for the evolving cooperative education program, representatives from key constituencies within the college, as well as representatives from those areas that will be particularly impacted by the program, should be appointed to the committee. These would include the office of the academic dean; the office of student affairs; administrators from various schools or departments involved; offices such as financial aid, counseling, and placement; students, if they are normally included in the decision-making process; and representatives of the instructional faculty. If the college already offers a cooperative education program, then the director is the key person in the process and must obviously be involved. Should the college offer separate off-campus field experience programs, then thought should be given to include representatives from these areas.

It is important that the committee not develop a narrow, restricted view of cooperative education. Rather, the group should be encouraged to carry out its assignment in a creative manner. To accomplish this, assistance from outside consultants may prove very helpful. Also, to give the committee a sense of the importance of this undertaking, it should be appointed by either the chief executive officer or the chief academic officer of the institution. Finally, the group should be chaired by a recognized leader from either the faculty or the administration.

Need and Rationale for Cooperative Education. A careful and detailed study of existing cooperative education programs, both within the institution and at other colleges, could prove helpful to the committee in its determination of whether cooperative education has a place within the institution. The committee should first examine the need and rationale for cooperative education within the institution. All institutions have concerns they wish to address and goals they wish to achieve. The institutional needs that cooperative education has the potential to address can be drawn from a number of sources, including the institution's mission statement, the master plan, self-studies conducted for regional accreditation, existing institutional concerns, departmental concerns, and faculty member interests.

Identifying Program Objectives. Specific objectives for the cooperative education program can be grouped into two categories: administrative and student learning. Administrative objectives are directed towards meeting the needs and/or achieving outcomes that are of concern to either the institution, the department, or both. To the extent that cooperative education is seen as helping to attain important administrative goals, it is likely to receive administrative and financial support. Colleges differ in their expectations of cooperative education, but some objectives to which cooperative education can contribute include: increasing student recruitment, reducing student attrition, reducing pressure on facilities utilization, enhancing fundraising efforts, increasing community support, providing financial assistance, strengthening the education program, keeping curriculum courses current, and identifying new program areas.

It should be recognized that cooperative education by itself cannot achieve these administrative objectives. For instance, the experiences of colleges with cooperative education programs support the idea that cooperative education can be a strong recruitment attraction for students. Yet, cooperative education cannot compensate for insufficient resource allocation to the recruitment effort, a less than adequate staff, poor recruitment materials, or a poor public image. As with any other promising idea, thinking of it as a "quick fix" and "easy solution" to administrative problems is self-defeating.

Student learning outcomes are the heart of the academy. Each institution and/or department should have or will need to develop its own set of those learning objectives it deems important and appropriate. The range of possibilities includes: strengthening the learning process by applying and reinforcing classroom-taught skills and concepts; gaining new knowledge outside of the classroom; developing and strengthening learning skills, such as problem solving and synthesizing concepts across disciplines; enhancing personal growth and development; reality-testing career choices; facilitating career exploration; and broadening horizons through exposure to other people and cultures.

Establishing a Program Philosophy. Every institution of higher education holds at least one philosophy of education that is the underpinning of its educational programs. Different colleges within a university and different departments within a college may have their own educational philosophies, so that a single institution can have several philosophies existing side by side. For a cooperative education program to be successful, it must relate to and be compatible with the existing educational philosophies of the institution and of the departments involved.

A useful classification has been proposed (Jabs, Jabs, and Jabs, 1977): intellectual, subject matter, functional, humanistic, and systems education. Intellectual education derives from the philosophies of idealism and rationalism, holding the view that education is primarily an intellectual activity having the function of transmitting internal truths, absolute principles, and cultural heritage. Mastery of subject matter, the second approach, sees education as a process of learning abstract content and theoretical knowledge. The third approach proposed, functional education, holds the chief purpose of education to be reconstructing society in order to address existing problems within the culture. Existence is seen as a series of transactions with one's environment, whereas truth is what is successful, and knowledge is assessed in terms of results. Humanistic education is seen as an action-oriented approach which maintains that learning should be individualized, moving people toward self-realization and self-actualization. The fifth philosophy, systems education, refers to individualized or competency-based education, which maintains that students can master any subject if allowed to proceed at their own rate. Understanding the existing philosophies within the institution will assist the committee in developing a compatible philosophy for cooperative education.

The view that cooperative education is an educational strategy enhancing the learning process is premised on the belief that significant learning directly related to departmental and college goals can occur outside of the classroom and at an employer site. In effect, the cooperative education placement becomes the means to open learning possibilities for the student. Many departments may already have internships or field experience components that fit comfortably within the philosophies of those departments. In those instances, cooperative education is not a departure from what already exists and is accepted.

Maintaining Academic Integrity. The academic integrity of the institution as affected by cooperative education is an appropriate concern of the committee. When academic credit is being awarded, the work experience must be seen as more than placing a student in a job, even when it is closely related to his or her major. Faculty must assume the responsibility of developing a means to guide student learning that will also allow for the evaluation of that learning. One such approach is the use of measurable learning objectives developed by the student with the approval of faculty and possibly of the employer. These learning objectives can be written so as to incorporate into each objective what is to be learned, how it is to be learned, over what time frame, and how the learning is to be measured. The fulfillment of these objectives forms a learning contract with the student and becomes the basis of assessing learning and giving a grade. Different programs have different policies on the number of objectives that the student needs to accomplish in order to earn a single unit of credit. A second approach views the work experience as a "field laboratory" where students can either apply or observe the concepts that have been previously taught in the classroom. Learning emanates from two sources: student mastery of the job tasks and, even more important, from the interaction between the students and the environment in which the work takes place. Students, while working on their job, function as "part..ipant observers" (Bruyn, 1966). Through personal observations, interviews, and review of written materials, students collect information relating to what has been taught in the classroom. This is done without interfering with the work routine. For instance, students who have studied cultural anthropology can be directed to examine such aspects of organization culture as rituals in the workplace, language, dress, sexual roles, and so on. At LaGuardia Community College, which pioneered this approach, faculty have developed field manuals for students that structure and guide learning on the co-op job (Heinemann, 1983). Students attend seminars held during nonworking hours, the syllabus for which consists of the assignments in the field manual. Students are evaluated based on the quality of the work handed in and their participation in classroom instruction. The LaGuardia approach also includes individual objectives developed by faculty and students that are germane to student needs and interests and are over and above the seminar requirements.

This is but one example of many that have developed in recent years which structure the cooperative education assignment from a learning perspective. The committee, in its assessment, must ascertain that the faculty are willing and able to undertake the challenge of developing those educational components of the cooperative education program that meet administrative interests and student learning needs while maintaining the academic integrity of the institution.

With the assessment of the factors discussed, the committee should be able to formulate a recommendation on the future of cooperative education. This recommendation would most likely be in the form of a report that could then move through the various components of the institution's decision-making process—for example, the faculty senate, administrative council, board of trustees. With a decision to develop and/or expand an existing cooperative education program, the process moves to the second stage, developing an implementation plan.

Planning and Development—The Second Stage. In some institutions, the decision-making process that resulted in the development of cooperative education moving forward may have included a determination of how the goals and objectives were to be achieved. However, in most instances, the plan to implement cooperative education rests within the various areas of the organization. For example, the decision to have cooperative education in the curriculum is, in all likelihood, the responsibility of the faculty of a particular school or of a certain department. The extent to which cooperative education will be available to students depends upon the support received from faculty across the institution. It is possible that faculty of specific schools or departments could decide on different characteristics for the cooperative education program within each department. These differences could include whether to award academic credit and the number of credits for each experience, the number of placements, whether cooperative education will be optional or mandatory, and the placement configuration of alternating or parallel plans. Other aspects of cooperative education that could vary among departments include job development responsibilities, student placement responsibilities, methods of integrating the classroom learning with the work experience, and the grading structure.

In order to avoid the proliferation of cooperative education programs with differing characteristics, it would be helpful to establish a planning committee whose responsibility would be to coordinate the development of the implementation plans across the institution. The makeup of this committee could well include the members of the original assessment committee but should also have representation from those areas very much concerned with implementation, such as the registrar's office, counseling department, and admissions. An agreed-upon set of parameters to which all programs must adhere is essential and should include: the overall mission and goals of cooperative education programs across the institution, a common educational philosophy for the broad-based policies governing cooperative education throughout the institution, similar credit structures and grading procedures, and a single tuition structure for cooperative education. Within these parameters, individual academic units could then have the flexibility of designing methodologies best suited to their individual areas. Programs with excessive flexibility often have a large variance in program quality. An important criterion that should be established and to which all areas must adhere is that the cooperative education program within each school or department must be financially viable. Those units of the institution offering cooperative education would then be free to plan and develop programs suitable for their areas. The planning committee could serve as a central clearinghouse for the various implementation plans, assuring that needs and objectives would be addressed and academic integrity would be maintained.

A useful by-product of a decentralized approach is the necessity of the faculty from each area to review their curriculum to determine how cooperative education can best fit into their program. This should include a review of the courses being offered to ascertain whether courses need to be added or deleted, individual course syllabi changed, or the prerequisites restructured, and what the sequencing of courses should be. Each area should also determine when cooperative education will begin, whether it will be optional or mandatory, and what will be the number of students expected to participate.

Organizational Structure. The planning committee will have to determine whether cooperative education will be centralized or decentralized. Virtually all comprehensive programs, such as those at Northeastern University, the University of Cincinnati, Drexel University, and LaGuardia Community College, have a central department or division that is responsible for job development and student placement. The reason is a matter of program efficiency and cost-effectiveness. The experience of institutions with a long-standing history of cooperative education strongly suggests that a full-time staff whose only responsibility is delivering the cooperative education program ultimately develops the skills and expertise necessary to sustain a quality program. From a job development perspective, a centralized effort is more effective. Few, if any, employers would welcome working with a number of individuals from different areas of the institution, each representing the cooperative education program.

Responsibility for awarding academic credit is another matter. Usually, faculty from the instructional area assume the responsibility of structuring, guiding, evaluating, and grading students for the learning that has occurred. In a few cases, such as at LaGuardia Community College, full-time cooperative education coordinators have faculty status and therefore assume this responsibility.

In terms of reporting relationships, the cooperative education director usually reports to a top administrator in either the student or academic area. As more and more colleges offer academic credit for the cooperative education program, the department is placed within the academic area.

With a centralized cooperative education office, strong lines of communication need to be established with the academic departments involved. The co-op office needs to know on a timely basis the number of students that are expected to go out and the types of placements that would be appropriate. The placement format must be such that students qualified for existing positions are available on a year-round basis. Once a position with an employer has been developed, it should not be lost because the institution is not able to fill the position with a qualified student.

The instructional faculty can be helpful to the placement process by providing cooperative education coordinators with information on technical capabilities of students. The faculty can be a rich resource for employer contacts. Also, the faculty can be very helpful in advising the cooperative education staff on the type of positions that would be most appropriate.

Class scheduling is another activity that will create serious difficulties for the cooperative education program if there is not close coordination between the academic department and the cooperative education area. If class schedules do not accommodate students participating in co-op, their inability to take necessary classes can delay graduation. On the other hand, the cooperative education staff can provide important feedback to the faculty on the curriculum. Faculty could obtain virtually instantaneous feedback on changes occurring in the marketplace that require course or curriculum change. Furthermore, the cooperative education staff may be the first to know of the changing needs of employers that might suggest new program options. Close cooperation and collaboration need to be established in order to develop and maintain an effective cooperative education program.

Strong communication links also need to be developed with other areas of the institution, such as the following.

1. The Registrar's Office. Oftentimes, separate registration procedures need to be developed in order to allow students on a cooperative education assignment to register for classes.

2. Financial Aid Office. Where it is anticipated that the student will have cooperative education earnings, it is the institution's obligation to make these a part of the student's financial aid package. Information on students scheduled to go out on cooperative education placements should be transmitted to the financial aid staff so that students are neither over- nor underpackaged. Further, many colleges make use of college work-study students to reach agreements with nonprofit employers to compensate students working in those organizations on their cooperative education assignment.

3. Admissions Office. Virtually all colleges adopting cooperative education expect it to strengthen their recruitment efforts. In order to accomplish this, admissions counselors need to be knowledgeable about the cooperative education programs and effective recruitment materials must be developed. In addition, the cooperative education staff, together with students in the program, could be very useful in presentations to high school students, parents, and counselors.

4. Placement Office. If the placement and career development office is separate from cooperative education, then close cooperation needs to be established between these two

areas. Many cooperative education employers join the program in order to obtain full-time employees after the students graduate. Companies that hire graduates are therefore likely employers of cooperative education students. To avoid confusion and competition, placement and cooperative education need to work together. It is for this reason that in a number of colleges cooperative education and the placement operation have been combined.

5. Counseling Office. Counselors can play an important role in support of the cooperative education program. The anticipation of leaving the college campus for a work assignment could place some students under undue stress. At times, certain students may find personal problems interfere with their ability to obtain the most appropriate position or may even prevent them from participating. Other students may develop problems in functioning effectively in the work environment. In these and other situations, the cooperative education coordinator is not likely to be well equipped to respond as effectively as the professional counselor.

Developing Program Components. Students need to be adequately prepared for the cooperative education experience if they are to gain as much from it as possible. First, students should fully understand the cooperative education program and its philosophy. For most students, this will be their first exposure to experiential education. It would be difficult for them to adjust to a different learning strategy without fully understanding the rationale and philosophy of the program. If the college chooses to use behavioral objectives as its principal learning technique, then students must develop skills to write appropriate objectives. If students are to function as participant-observers, they must be taught techniques for gathering information in the field.

Few students can prepare an acceptable resume or possess interviewing skills. These must be taught if they are to be successful in obtaining the cooperative education positions of their choice. If exploring career possibilities is one objective of the cooperative education program, then the question of whether students should be exposed to such career education concepts as values clarification, career opportunities, and understanding the work environment prior to placement must be asked. A number of colleges address this and similar questions by holding a pre-cooperative education course or workshops prior to the first placement.

LaGuardia Community College has developed a unique approach to teaching students career and life-planning skills as an integral part of its cooperative education program. The seminar that students take in conjunction with their second co-op placement directs them to prepare resumes that would qualify them for specific positions they might wish to apply for ten years in the future. In developing the resume, students must decide on each element of the resume and explain their decisions in writing. These elements include such personal life-style questions as where one wants to live and the level of income one wishes to have. The students need to make decisions on what degrees are necessary to qualify them for the positions they have in mind and which colleges would be most appropriate. Students also need to develop an acceptable career path of former positions qualifying them for the jobs they seek.

After having completed the "future resume," students are then directed to identify the problems they anticipate would block them from achieving their goals. They then develop strategies and solutions that address these problems. The purpose of the seminar is not to have students develop blueprints for their careers; rather, it is designed to develop a perspective towards the future as well as the thought processes that incorporate future goals into the current decision-making process.

Developing a Program Budget. The final activity in the second stage is developing a program budget. The budget should not only include anticipated costs to be incurred during the three- to five-year development period but also the benefits that the college anticipates over the same period of time. The most immediate benefit to the college would be tuition revenues coming from increased student enrollments. These increases would come from two sources: recruitment of new students attracted to the institution because of cooperative education, and increased retention of students as a result of their participation in the program. The experience of other institutions makes increased student enrollments a reasonable expectation. As pointed out earlier, this expectation is predicated on the college's undertaking an effective and thorough marketing effort in order to inform high school students, their parents, and their high school counselors of the program.

For cooperative education to be cost-effective, it does not necessarily mean that student enrollments must increase in absolute numbers. For an institution experiencing enrollment declines, if cooperative education were able to sustain current enrollments, this should be viewed as a major benefit—one that can be measured by comparing the tuition revenue differential from the current level to what that differential would have been if the decreasing trend line were to continue. Data from other institutions suggest that, once enrolled in the college, student retention increases as a result of several factors: income earned from cooperative education providing much-needed financial aid; the attractiveness to students of obtaining actual work experiences in their field of study; and the overall increase in motivation that results from the fact that the cooperative education experience often leads to stronger academic performance.

In calculating the income that can be expected from cooperative education, the analysis should take into account the fact that an entering student will provide tuition income over the several years required to obtain a degree. Therefore, for each year of the cooperative education program, the tuition revenues that can be attributed to that program will be the sum of revenues derived by all students, both new and returning, attracted to the institution as a result of cooperative education, modified to take into account projected attrition.

Major cooperative education colleges and universities also find that cooperative education greatly helps their fund-raising activities. The linkages forged with the private sector can result in increased financial support to the institution. There is some indication that having had a successful cooperative education experience can increase alumni contributions. Having cooperative education in place and using it as an implementation strategy can strengthen grant applications.

Cooperative education will incur costs through the establishment or expansion of the cooperative education office as well as participating academic departments. These include program staffing and "other than personal" expenses, such as staff training, travel, equipment, supplies, telephone, and printing. In addition, cooperative education may cause revenue losses from having unfilled dormitory beds as a result of students' being away from the college during their full-time cooperative education assignment. Academic departments with either a full-time alternating model or a parallel model might be faced with having to offer additional sections of courses in order to accommodate students in cooperative education.

The college can also expect a series of start-up costs in the period prior to the launching of the program, plus the development costs incurred during the earlier years. Start-up costs would include such activities as recruiting employers, designing program components, developing educational materials, recruitment expenses, and, if needed, consultants. Another set of costs that should be budgeted relates to summative evaluations, which should be conducted annually to ensure that the program is on the right track.

A program budget helps to determine the financial viability of a cooperative education program by identifying the extent of resources needed, whether they come from new sources or are reallocated within the institution. Reallocation of existing resources deserves close and careful consideration because it may be the only viable way to develop the support necessary for a strong, quality cooperative education program. Few institutions are likely to be in a position to obtain the amount of new funds necessary for an expanding program, regardless of size. Reassignment of existing staff, particularly those who are being underutilized, could greatly reduce the amount of resources required for the program.

Program Implementation—The Third Stage. At this point, the major policy decisions concerning the cooperative education program have been made, and plans for developing the program have been formulated. Questions about the number of departments that will offer cooperative education, the schedule of introducing the program, the location of cooperative education within the organizational structure, reporting relationships, the philosophy and objectives of the program, academic credit, and placement formats have been resolved. Program implementation is ready to begin.

Program Staffing. The staff of the cooperative education program wear many hats. They are the bridge between the institution and the employer community; they are educators as well as counselors to students. They must work effectively with all of these groups. In staffing the cooperative education area, whether the institution recruits from outside or reassigns current staff members, staff selected should possess these skills or have the flexibility to develop them quickly.

Policy and Procedures. Appropriate policies and procedures must be developed for cooperative education. These include policies on the cooperative education coordinator's student load, criteria qualifying students for exemption in mandatory programs, grading, the number of hours students must work in either full-time or parallel programs, criteria for accepting a student's current work situation as a cooperative education assignment, nonpaid positions, and so on.

When developed, the various policies and procedures should be incorporated into a manual for the professional staff involved with the program. Furthermore, a handbook for students explaining the policies and procedures pertaining to them would be very useful.

Program Control and Evaluation Systems—The Fourth Stage. Developing internal evaluation and control systems and procedures is the final step in building and sustaining an effective cooperative education program (Gordon and Heinemann, 1980). The system should provide information that guides the growth of the program, points out existing weaknesses that need to be strengthened and potential problem areas, enables administrators to assess the extent to which the cooperative education program is meeting its objectives, and indicates changes that should be made with regard to objectives.

It should answer such questions as, Are the students sufficiently prepared for the assignment and are they performing well on the job? Are employers satisfied? Is there a shift in a given employer's assessment of a student's performance and, if so, why? Is a changing technology indicating that changes need to be made in the curricula? Are policies and procedures effective? Are the educational expectations being met? And, most important, are the institution's goals for the program being achieved?

The evaluation system should link back to the second stage. Planning and program development are never-ending functions in a quality program, even when student enrollments have stabilized. Changing internal, as well as external, conditions are likely to impact the program, requiring that modifications be made. Furthermore, even when an effective program enjoys institutional support, that very support may push cooperative education to broaden its role by expanding its goals and objectives, involving new program areas and serving new groups of students, such as adult learners. A "management information system" providing data for effective program evaluation and control needs to be developed. Current information on students and employers in the program, records of employer participation, faculty and coordinator student loads, and employer evaluation of students are among the important elements necessary to maintain effective quality controls on the cooperative education program. For the system to work, it needs to be timely, efficient, and cost-effective. Questions concerning the determination of data needs and the responsibility for collection and analysis must be resolved. Program administrators and cooperative education coordinators must support the concept of internal evaluation. Finally, the information from the evaluation system must be used to strengthen the program while assisting staff to better carry out other responsibilities.

References

Bruyn, S. T. *The Human Perspective in Sociology: The Methodology of Participant Observation.* Englewood Cliffs, N.J.: Prentice-Hall, 1966.

Gordon, S. C., and Heinemann, H. N. "Structuring an Internal

Evaluation Process." *Journal of Cooperative Education,* 1980, *16* (3), 47-54.

Heinemann, H. N. "Towards a Pedagogy for Cooperative Education." *Journal of Cooperative Education,* 1983, *19* (2), 14-26.

Jabs, B., Jabs, M., and Jabs, A. "Cooperative Education Must Relate to Different Educational Philosophies." *Journal of Cooperative Education,* 1977, *14* (1), 74-88.

Six

Documenting Benefits
and Developing Campus
and Community Support

Paul E. Dubé
Alice F. Korngold

Significant academic and economic benefits will accrue to an institution whose cooperative education program serves the educational and career interests of its students and contributes to the human resource development of the community's employers. As the first step toward achieving an effective cooperative education program, an institution must design that program to meet the particular needs of its students and prospective employers, while also carrying out the institution's philosophy and mission. A program so designed is assured of support, involvement, and success on the campus and in the community.

Once the program is implemented, it is then necessary to establish an ongoing process to evaluate the benefits that are derived from a cooperative education program and the extent to which the program is achieving its objectives. This is important for at least two reasons. First, program policies and procedures may require modification as the program seeks to expand and improve its services, and program evaluation is a critical first step to making changes. Second, information derived from the program assessment can be used to document program benefits and to inform faculty, students, administration, and employers of these benefits. Constituents will increase their support and involvement in cooperative education when they see its value to them. Experience has shown that long-term success of a cooperative education program is virtually assured if it is conceived with an understanding of the interests of all its constituencies, is evaluated and modified on an ongoing basis, and convincingly demonstrates the benefits derived by those who participate in the program.

Benefits of Cooperative Education to Colleges and Universities

The most obvious and direct beneficiaries of cooperative education are the students and employers who participate. There are, however, potential spin-offs of these benefits to the colleges and universities providing the program, which, with proper effort, can be fostered.

Academic Benefits. There are several ways in which an effective cooperative education program can contribute to the academic programs of an institution and thereby to the esteem in which they are held.

1. Selective Admissions. Effective and well-publicized cooperative education programs have been found to increase the applications for admission (Korngold and Dubé, 1982). When the numbers of applications increase significantly, an institution may either increase enrollment or become more selective in its admissions. By raising the level of quality of students enrolled, the institution raises its standing in the higher education community. This increased stature is reinforced, since students seek out the most prestigious institutions. Any factor that helps an institution to be as selective as possible strengthens its academic and economic position.

2. Curriculum Assessment. Cooperative relationships between employers and the school can foster academic benefits to the institution. Employer contacts can assist the faculty in identifying the need for curriculum changes (Sparrow, 1981).

Through contact with co-op employers, faculty have the opportunity to test the effectiveness of their teaching and of their courses in preparing students to be productive members of society. This benefit is more often realized by institutions whose faculty have a direct role in the cooperative education program. For example, many community colleges and some senior colleges use faculty to monitor student learning and job performance. If in their monitoring efforts it is found that one or two students are weak in a subject, it is usually assumed that the fault is that of the students, but if all students are weak in a particular subject matter, then the courses or curriculum can be quickly modified to correct the difficulty. To illustrate, an effective communication course was added to the engineering curriculum of a university as the result of employer feedback. The need for improved communication skills among engineering and business graduates was determined during the conducting of one of the university's labor market studies (Center for Cooperative Education, 1985). This information was used by the chairperson of the university's English department to persuade the engineering college to add a course in effective communication skills.

It is not uncommon that students are the vehicle of feedback to faculty on curriculum matters. On their cooperative assignments they are often introduced to new procedures and state-of-the-art knowledge and bring it to the campus long before it might otherwise be communicated. Cooperative education offers yet another curriculum advantage to institutions. Students are frequently introduced to and learn to use the most advanced equipment, which the institutions could not possibly afford. Hence, the cooperative program can, and often does, extend and enhance the curriculum.

3. Employer Relations and Institutional Involvement. Institutions can also expand upon the cooperative education links created between the school and the co-op employers by sponsoring other mutually beneficial projects. For example, Pace University and Chemical Bank cosponsored a project to provide technical assistance to nonprofit organizations in the process of computerization. Through this joint endeavor, Chemical Bank hired Pace faculty to teach computer courses to administrators

of nonprofit organizations. For its part, the cooperative education program is recommending qualified co-op students to assist these organizations in systems analysis, programming, and staff training. LaGuardia Community College is also involved in this project, referring students for data entry jobs. In this way, Pace and LaGuardia students benefit from the work experiences, Pace faculty have opportunities to work in the community, and Pace and LaGuardia are serving Chemical Bank's interests in providing a public service. Thus, although the educational benefits of cooperative education are derived most directly by the students themselves, new opportunities for institutional development and faculty development are also created by the links developed between a co-op program and its employers.

4. Increased Academic Achievement. Comparisons of cooperative and traditional students in the same class show that proportionally more co-op students persist to graduation and obtain better grades (see Chapter Thirteen). Increases in grades and persistence are even more significant for cooperative students in the lower half of the class, suggesting that the clearer purpose for education and the greater motivation and financial support provided by the work experience affect achievement. Whatever the reason, if cooperative education programs attract students who complete more courses and degrees and achieve more, the academic and enrollment objectives of the institution are being met more completely.

Economic Benefits. While academicians are primarily concerned with the quality of the education that is delivered, the economic benefits of the cooperative plan are a significant consideration in the decision to implement a cooperative program (Knowles, 1971). In managing limited institutional resources, college and university administrators increasingly need to assess the financial benefits realized from all programs, including cooperative education. There are several potential economic benefits to be realized by institutions through the operation of effective cooperative education programs.

1. Increasing Enrollments. Using the student outcome information of a successful cooperative education program, the institution's admissions department and public information staff

can attract students by promoting the student benefits with high school guidance counselors, students, and their parents. College students use a number of criteria when choosing a college or university, but the most important one today is the access graduation will provide to jobs and professional schools (Krukowski, 1985). Institutions with co-op are attractive to potential students because it does provide this access. Because so many of the nation's leading firms and federal agencies utilize cooperative education as a means of recruiting long-term professionals, a majority of co-op seniors are invited to remain with these employers after graduation. In addition, many students have found that the credentials and references they acquired through their work experiences have been of substantial help in getting accepted into professional schools, such as respected medical, law, and business schools.

The increased likelihood of cooperative students graduating from college is especially important to parents and constitutes a persuasive force in recruiting potential students. To some degree, most parents are anxious about their sons and daughters succeeding in college. This is especially so among families with no tradition of college attendance. Similarly, parents whose children wish to pursue the liberal arts, particularly the humanities and social sciences, have a concern about the career direction and employability of their sons and daughters after graduation. Again, the concern will be greater among families sending children to college for the first time. Knowing that the cooperative program helps students acquire marketable skills and work experience that helps them get appropriate employment is reassuring to parents.

The ability to finance a portion (sometimes substantial) of their education is of significant concern to both students and parents. The costs of education have risen to a level that is becoming increasingly difficult for parents to meet. This, combined with increasing uncertainty of financial aid, could cause many potential students to forego college attendance. Cooperative work earnings give students and their parents an important, additional option for easing the cost burden.

Another group with which institutions can make good use

of the cooperative education outcomes are the guidance counselors. The guidance counselors know their students and most
will help them choose a college that is best for them. Through
their ongoing contacts with high school students, the guidance
counselors are keenly aware of the concerns of students for careers and their need for financial assistance. With a clear knowledge and documented benefits of cooperative education, the
high school guidance counselors are in a good position to advise
their juniors and seniors on the value of attending an institution
that operates a viable cooperative plan of education. As in so
many other situations, guidance counselors (and teachers) often
have more influence with young people than do their parents.

It is clear that information on student outcomes can be
used effectively by institutions to recruit students. Studies conducted in each of the past four years at Pace University provide
a good illustration. They show that more than half of the incoming students were aware of the co-op program when they
decided to enroll and that for more than half of those co-op was
a significant influence in their decision to attend. Moreover, a
substantial number of students asserted that they would definitely have attended some other institution had Pace not had a
cooperative education program. In the fall of 1985, forty-six incoming students said they would definitely not have enrolled
had they not had the opportunity to co-op. Those students represented a one-year tuition income of nearly $240,000 and,
given a high retention rate among the co-op students, an estimated income of almost $650,000 over four years. Using similar
analyses for the 1984 and 1983 entering classes, it was estimated that the co-op program was largely responsible for almost
$1,000,000 of tuition income, more than enough to offset the
operating costs of the program.

2. Increasing Enrollments Through Retention. Attrition
is costly to colleges and universities. It is particularly costly during a time when institutions are striving to keep their enrollments from falling, because of demographic changes. Lowering
their attrition of students is one means of achieving this. Studies
have clearly demonstrated that students participating in cooperative programs complete more courses and more degrees than

their non-co-op counterparts on the same campus (Lindenmeyer, 1967; Smith, 1965). Hence, institutions can use cooperative education not only as a means of attracting students but of retaining them.

3. Extending Financial Aid. Co-op student earnings constitute another economic benefit to the institution. They enable the institution to extend its financial aid resources to assist a greater number of students and thereby further help to reduce attrition. Co-op income helps in two ways. First, it is an additional source of funds in constructing a total financial aid package for students. Second, it can reduce the endowment necessary for scholarships and grants-in-aid. To illustrate, if 500 co-op students earned an average of $6,500 each in a given year, the total of their earnings would be $3,250,000. The endowment necessary to yield this amount would approximate $50,000,000.

4. Employer Contributions. Yet another potential economic benefit to institutions sponsoring cooperative education is to be found in employer contributions. Benefits of cooperative education to employers for both immediate and long-term human resources are well documented (see Chapter Fourteen). When these benefits are referenced for specific participating employers in college and university development programs, they become a persuasive argument for those participating employers to make substantial gifts.

Strategies for Maximizing Benefits to the Institution

A cooperative education program will achieve its greatest potential in benefiting students, employers, and the institution when the program is evaluated on an ongoing basis and program modifications are made as necessary (Korngold and Dubé, 1982). As stated by Wilson, ". . . an essential element of cooperative education and any work/education collaborative venture is periodic assessment to determine to what extent the mutual objectives are being met. The evaluation must be such that it points the way to any needed changes in the relationship and provides a sound base for making those changes" (1984, p. 37).

Further, the value of the cooperative education program

is maximized when program results are documented and publicized in order to reinforce and enhance support from all constituencies. This is a cyclical process: an initial group of faculty, administrators, students, and employers become involved in co-op and derive its advantages; the co-op staff evaluates the impact and results of the program and provides this information to the community; support for the program grows when its value is documented; and the capacity for co-op to serve all groups is further strengthened when program resources are increased; the expanded program is now planned, implemented, evaluated, and promoted on an ongoing basis to ensure long-term success.

A number of surveys and studies can be used to evaluate the extent to which a cooperative education program is achieving its goals, assess the effectiveness of the program's design and procedures, identify program strengths and weaknesses, and document program benefits (Korngold and Dubé, 1982). Surveys of students, employers, and faculty are key. Additional studies relating to admissions, retention, permanent placements, student income, and employer contributions complete the profile.

Student Surveys. A student survey can provide information about student goals and needs, student awareness of the cooperative program, and student perception of its value and the extent to which it meets student needs. With information gathered from surveys, the cooperative education department can make significant strategic decisions regarding: (1) the nature of the promotional and recruiting material needed to interest students; (2) the channels and media to be used to contact students (such as classroom visits and student newspapers); (3) the type and location of jobs to be developed; (4) the level of student interest in either alternating or parallel employment arrangements; (5) the emphasis that must be placed on salary as opposed to other job elements, such as career development; (6) the extent to which the staff is meeting student needs; and (7) operating procedures that require adjustments to accommodate students. With the information provided by surveys, directors and staff can make the programmatic changes necessary to improve the service to students. Additionally, student surveys that demonstrate program effectiveness can be used to reinforce in-

stitutional commitment, increase faculty support, and attract
new students.

   Employer Surveys. Findings from employer surveys can
also be used for management decision making, long-term planning, and gaining institutional and employer commitment. Employer satisfaction with the cooperative education program is
particularly important, since the level of employer support and
participation affects the size and direction of the cooperative
education program. Receptive employers will provide jobs in
the quantity and quality needed to make good experiences possible for all students. Additionally, high-quality work experiences engender increased program acceptance and support by
students, faculty, and administrators.

   Employer surveys provide the cooperative education staff
with clear insights about the employers' purposes for hiring students, the extent to which the institution's cooperative education program is meeting the employers' goals, and program
strengths and weaknesses. Long-term planning is facilitated
when the cooperative education staff can measure the degree of
employer satisfaction and their projections of new jobs in which
students can be employed. If the program staff can anticipate
future employment opportunities, then student recruitment and
job development efforts can be organized accordingly. Further,
insight into the potential growth of the program will enable the
director to provide the administration with realistic budget and
space needs. Finally, the survey may also provide information
useful in assessing potential policy changes such as co-op schedule (alternating or parallel patterns), job development, shifts in
occupational and career trends, and other policy or operational
changes that might strengthen the program over time.

   In addition to facilitating program planning, the results of
employer surveys will help to improve faculty awareness and support for cooperative education. Faculty who are aware of the
overall employer satisfaction with the cooperative education program will recognize the contribution their institution is making
to the human resource needs of the community. The greatest
impact of positive employer outcomes, however, will be with the
president, first-line administrators, and those concerned with

development and public relations. Demonstrating the employers' satisfaction to the president, trustees, and administrators will enable the program to gain in many ways. Presidents who know that the cooperative education program is helping to meet the human resource needs of the employer community will feel much more confident in publicly supporting the program on the campus to students and faculty and off campus to business and civic groups and alumni. Presidents will also be more inclined to commit the institution's resources to the expansion and strengthening of those programs that demonstrate their effectiveness.

Employer survey results can also be used to identify satisfied employers who are likely to make financial contributions to the educational institutions that help meet their hiring needs. Additionally, the admissions office and those in public relations can use positive employer support information to promote the institution's image and attract new students. On the campus, the co-op staff can publicize the information among the student body to recruit new co-op students.

Faculty Surveys. Faculty surveys are important in order to determine faculty knowledge and perception of their institution's cooperative plan and in terms of program goals, program operation, benefits to students, difficulties cooperative education may create for students, weaknesses in the program, benefits to the institution, and direct or indirect benefits to the faculty. The survey will identify the positive and negative views of faculty and the basis for their views. With this information, the program staff can determine steps to be taken either to reinforce faculty support or to correct the causes of concern.

Positive results from a faculty survey will be of interest to presidents and can lead to greater institutional commitment. The presidents, trustees, and first-line administrators will be more confident in their decisions to allocate resources to the program if co-op is not a political liability. Documented faculty support will also strengthen proposals for external funding, enabling the program to further expand, serve more students even more effectively, and gain still greater support on the campus.

The extent to which faculty support cooperative education also affects other long-term issues that vary among institutions. These include the extent to which faculty will be willing to serve as faculty coordinators, the expansion of the cooperative plan into new disciplines, changes in the program's policies and operating procedures, and the awarding of credit for work learning. Negative responses and expressed concerns will alert the cooperative education staff to the need to address the faculty's reservations and to inform them of measures taken to correct difficulties.

Admissions Surveys. Institutions will want to measure the impact of cooperative education on institutional enrollments. Admissions survey results will show the number of freshman and transfer students whose decision to attend the institution was influenced by the cooperative education program. Further, an admissions survey can identify the number of students who selected the institution solely because of its cooperative program. An admissions survey that demonstrates that cooperative education was the cause or a significant influence in the decision of a substantial number of students to enroll in an institution will attract the support of both the faculty and the administration.

A simple hypothetical example illustrates this point. Assume 100 students enroll solely because of the program in an institution whose tuition is $4,000 per semester. Income for semester one for those 100 students would be $400,000. If 80 percent were to continue into semester two, the second semester income from students who enrolled solely because of co-op would be $320,000 (80 X $4,000). The total one-year income attributable to these students and to the cooperative education program would be $720,000. While this income cannot be considered as surplus, the income contribution of the program is clear. It should be noted that this amount does not reflect the tuition income of those students whose decision to attend was significantly influenced by cooperative education.

Retention Studies. Studies of student retention, as previously noted, have found that students participating in cooperative education earned higher grades and had a higher persistency rate than non-co-op students in the same institution.

Cooperative education programs that can show significantly greater retention among co-op students than non-co-ops demonstrate their economic worth to the institution. When a student leaves college, there is an insignificant decrease in costs, but there is a significant decrease in income. For every semester completed by a student who might have dropped out but for the motivation and income benefits of cooperative education, there is incremental income of that semester's tuition attributable to the cooperative education program. Retention is demonstrated by tracking the co-op and the non-co-op students, starting with the year the students can participate in the cooperative education program.

A hypothetical example can illustrate the economic benefits of retention. In this example, tuition is assumed to be $8,000 annually and fixed for four years. It is also assumed that 80 percent of all sophomores who become part of the cooperative plan will complete their degree requirements in the following three years, as opposed to 60 percent of non-co-ops. Thus, in this assumed sample of 100 sophomores participating in cooperative education, 80 will complete their degree requirements, while only 60 of the 100 non-co-op students will finish. If it is further assumed that, by the end of the sophomore, junior, and senior years, the co-op and non-co-op samples have 90, 85, and 80 students versus 80, 70, and 60 students, respectively, then the annual student enrollment gains due to co-op over the three-year span would be 10, 15, and 20 students. These student gains translate into $80,000 (10 × $8,000) for the sophomore year, $120,000 for the junior year, and $160,000 for the senior year.

The total incremental increase for this hypothetical co-op sample is $360,000 dollars over three years. Assuming further that these same comparative retention rates were to continue over time and the same number of co-op students were to enter the program in the sophomore year, this would become an annual incremental income of $360,000. High co-op student retention can produce a significant return to an institution. It is much less expensive to keep a student than to go out and recruit a replacement.

Postgraduate Outcomes. Studies of graduates, particularly in relation to their career experiences and their perceptions of the values of their college and cooperative education experiences, are another source of information for gaining student and institutional support of the co-op program. The feedback from graduates of an effective cooperative program is generally very positive and points clearly to the impact of the program on their careers and how they feel about their careers. When this information is circulated widely within the institution, it will generate broad-based support for the program. Graduate studies can also provide valuable information for assessing the effectiveness of the program and establish a base for any needed program changes.

Student Salary Information. Information about co-op student salaries is important in documenting the financial benefits of the program. Students, parents, faculty, and the school administrators will be interested in the average annual earning of each co-op student. Data regarding average salaries by field are particularly useful to employers in determining the salaries they should pay students and to students in setting realistic expectations. Finally, total earnings for all co-op students in one year can be impressive in showing the economic value of cooperative education in helping students to pay their tuition and in assuring institutions of being able to count on students able to afford college.

Summary

The faculty, employer, student, admissions, retention, post-graduate, and salary surveys discussed in this chapter can all produce information for decision making, long-term planning, and gaining increased commitment and support on the campus. It is important to describe the studies, interpret the outcomes, illustrate the information, and disseminate the results in order to obtain their maximum value.

Any reservations held by presidents, trustees, and first-line administrators about cooperative education are often due to an insufficient awareness of the program's value to their institutions. An effective cooperative education program should be able to strengthen the curriculum, help maintain or increase enrollments, improve the employment opportunities for its graduates, and strengthen the institution's financial position as a result of greater enrollments and employer contributions. Where these benefits exist to a significant degree and when they can be solidly documented, a broader awareness and respect for cooperative education will prevail over the entire campus. Then, and only then, will a program gradually earn the support that is essential to long-term program development.

A Case Study: Pace University

The strategies described above are not simply academic reflections. They have been applied and the potential outcomes for institutions have been achieved. The following case study of one co-op program in one institution illustrates the value of self-evaluation and communication.

Since 1979, Pace University's cooperative education program has grown into the nation's tenth largest cooperative education program among senior colleges and universities. This dramatic success is the result of the program's ability to serve student, employer, and institutional needs and to gain broad-based support by documenting and publicizing the benefits of co-op to these key constituencies. Pace offers a good example of an institution that has maximized the rewards of establishing a major cooperative education program.

Pace University. A brief description of Pace will show that the concept and purposes of cooperative education are compatible with the mission and environment of the university. From its beginnings as a school for accountants in 1906, Pace University has grown to become a major, multi-campus institution enrolling 27,000 students in eight undergraduate and graduate schools for arts and sciences, business, computer science and information systems, education, nursing, and law. One of Pace's three campuses is located in lower Manhattan in the heart of the business district, with the two other campuses in Westchester County, New York, near the headquarters of some of the nation's and the world's largest corporations. Pace's mission is to provide a quality education, preparing its students to be productive members of the community. Pace students are ambitious and career-oriented, often earning their tuition by working while attending school. In order to provide the most relevant education to its students, Pace has established strong ties to the surrounding community. The leaders of hundreds of major national and multinational organizations are actively involved with Pace, and Pace cosponsors many educational programs with the world's largest corporations. Pace is also distinguished by the strong leadership of its chancellor, Dr. Edward J. Mortola. For thirty years, Dr. Mortola has created the vision and provided the inspiration and direction in the building of this major university.

Clearly, this is an environment in which cooperative education has the potential to succeed. Co-op serves the institutional mission and students' educational and financial needs, and co-op draws upon established links within a vast employer community.

Obstacles to Cooperative Education. Despite the positive factors inherent in the concept of co-op and its natural compatibility with Pace, there were significant, and perhaps fairly universal, obstacles to the growth of cooperative education at Pace.

1. Birth Pains. In order for co-op to build a strong identity and a more important position in the institution, it was established as a separate department, independent of Pace's Office of Career Planning and Placement. However, the establishment of the new cooperative education department initially drew resistance from career planning and placement, thereby hampering the co-op program's implementation at the earlier and crucial stages.

2. Faculty Resistance. Although most faculty members had a laissez-faire attitude toward the program, a few questioned the academic integrity of co-op; others expressed concern about the conflicts that students would face in their attempt to manage studies and co-op jobs simultaneously; still others were quite disturbed about the possibility that the co-

operative education staff would press the unpopular issue of credit for co-op. Adding to tension was the fact that a few academic departments were already offering nonpaid, study-related internships for credit. The faculty members involved with these internships were concerned that a nonacademic program would lure away their student interns.

3. Disruption of Operational Procedures. Key administrative departments were hesitant to consider the interests of this new program in their own department planning and responsibilities, since co-op appeared to be a burden rather than a benefit. For instance, admissions was not eager to promote cooperative education, being dubious that cooperative education would positively affect admissions; after all, before 1979, cooperative education at Pace had an erratic record, not fulfilling its promises to students.

In addition, cooperative education placed additional burdens on housing, alumni affairs, financial aid, and the registrar. For example, co-op requested that students in full-time, alternating co-op be allowed to remain in the dormitories during their co-op placement; co-op sought access to Pace alumni to develop jobs; co-op students needed special advising from the financial aid staff regarding the effect of co-op salaries on their loan and aid eligibility; and the registrar would have to keep new records of students in alternating co-op positions so they could maintain their full-time student status while working. Therefore, until co-op proved some degree of success, it intruded on the daily operation of the institution.

4. Competition for Institutional Resources. Co-op required a share of limited institutional resources, such as funding and space. Other departments viewed co-op as one more competitor for resources.

Change Strategies. Since there were formidable obstacles to the development of cooperative education at Pace, the key question was, How were these inhibiting forces to be overcome so that cooperative education could achieve its potential to serve the institution and community?

First, it was important to choose a program mission that would meet a vital need. Support for a new program is more likely to be developed if the program's purpose meets the interests of key constituencies, in this case students, faculty, administration, and employers. At Pace, the need was identified to place high-achieving students in paid, study-related positions that would serve as stepping-stones to successful postgraduation careers. By developing advanced preprofessional positions and assisting and preparing students to be hired in these positions, co-op would serve the students. At the same time, co-op would serve employer interests by providing access to Pace's top students, who could be trained and evaluated for long-term employment.

Second, it was important that the co-op staff demonstrate a commitment to excellence in serving and advising students, aggressively developing jobs and recruiting students, screening students for referral to employers, placing students in appropriate positions, and monitoring the quality and success of each placement.

Although it was fundamental to design a program that would meet a need and show a commitment to excellence, these factors alone were not sufficient to bring about significant program growth. In fact, a vital strategy that led to the expanded development of Pace's program was to document and publicize the impact of cooperative education on the institution and the community. This documentation was provided by the kinds of studies and surveys described in this chapter.

By providing information regarding the actual achievements of co-op and benefits derived by co-op, the program reinforced support from the top administration, and this endorsement proved to be an additional and vital factor in accomplishing program success. Support from Pace's chancellor, president, and provost included direct and significant involvement in program planning, such as creating the Cooperative Education Advisory Board, chaired ex officio by the chancellor, and including Pace administrators, deans, faculty, students, and employers; highlighting the co-op program in many talks to faculty, trustees, administrators, students, and employers; assisting in the preparation of federal grant applications; allocating financial resources and space to co-op; promoting cooperative education's place in the organizational structure of the institution; and personally and publicly recognizing the efforts and accomplishments of co-op staff members.

Finally, it was important to be flexible in program planning in order to accommodate various interests and alleviate the concerns of faculty and others. With flexibility and an effort to avoid conflict, co-op minimized friction and allowed the benefits of co-op to draw support.

Documenting the Cooperative Education Program's Impact at Pace. To build support for cooperative education and to reinforce interest in the program, the Pace co-op office began documenting program achievements in 1979. (Although co-op existed at Pace on an occasional basis for a few years before 1979, a real effort was made only in 1979.) Statistics and other information were gathered and reported to show the number and range of co-op placements, the number and range of participating employers, the quality of the co-op jobs, co-op student salaries, and the number of permanent postgraduation placements resulting from co-op. This material was provided in memos and newsletters to faculty, students, administrators, and the admissions staff. As a result, people began to recognize the accomplishments and value of co-op.

To expand on this information in 1981–82, the third year of co-op's growth at Pace, the co-op office conducted faculty, student, and employer surveys and studied the impact of co-op admissions, student income, and postgraduation placements. The faculty, student, and employer surveys indicated the major objectives sought by these groups through their involvement in co-op. The surveys also demonstrated that Pace's cooperative education program was indeed serving their interests most effectively in providing educational, career, and financial benefits to students and a good recruitment tool for employers.

These surveys also helped in planning program improvements. An example of an unexpected but important revelation in the first faculty co-op survey in 1981–82 was the indication that (based on a 44 percent response rate), only 64 percent of the faculty were "aware of the co-op program." Although this was disappointing, it was useful to the co-op staff in recognizing co-op's weakness in providing adequate information about the program to the faculty. This weakness could be addressed in an aggressive publicity campaign to faculty. In fact, in 1982-83 (based on a 35 percent response rate), 81 percent of the faculty said they were "familiar with" Pace's cooperative education program.

As surveys of employers, students, and faculty were conducted in 1981-82, 1982-83, and 1984-85, patterns began to emerge in responses to key questions on the surveys. A few examples are shown in Tables 6-1 through 6-5.

Table 6-1. Organizational Objectives in Utilizing Cooperative Education.

Employers: What are your organization's objectives in utilizing cooperative education? Please rank. (Originally, seven items were listed.)

	1981–82 *60% (51 total)* *responded*	*1982–83* *46% (57 total)* *responded*	*1984–85* *28% (101 total)* *responded*
Obtain productive work	1	1	1
Attract top-quality candidates	2	2	2
Recruit potential long-term employees	3	3	3

Table 6-2. Elements of Cooperative Education Important to an Organization.

Employers: What elements of cooperative education are important to your organization? Please rank. (Originally, six items were listed.)

	1981–82 *60% (51 total)* *responded*	*1982–83* *46% (57 total)* *responded*	*1984–85* *28% (101 total)* *responded*
Availability of top-quality candidates	1	1	1
Choice of more than one candidate	4	2	2
Continuity of job coverage	5	3	3

Table 6-3. Student Benefits of Participation in Cooperative Education.

Students: What are the greatest benefits of participating in the Cooperative Education Program? Please rank.[a]

1981–82 (67%—90 total—responded)[b]
1—The experience helped me plan my career goals.
2—The experience helped me gain a better understanding of my academic coursework.
3—The experience helped me make professional contacts for jobs after graduation.

1982–83 (35%—106 total—responded)[b]
1—To gain career-related work experience.
2—To make contacts and gain experience leading to jobs after graduation.
3—To relate my coursework to a work experience.

1984–85 (50%—322 total—responded)[b]
1—To increase my chances of getting a good job after graduation.
2—To develop professional skills.
3—To apply my coursework in on-the-job experience.

[a]Since the items were phrased differently each year, each set of the top three responses is provided.

[b]Each year, the financial benefits of the Cooperative Education Program were ranked fifth.

Table 6-4. Faculty Opinion of Benefits of Cooperative Education to Students.

Faculty: What do you consider to be the primary benefits to students who participate in cooperative education? Please rank. (Originally, eight items were listed.)

	1981–82 44% (74 total) responded	1982–83 35% (106 total) responded	1984–85 26% (134 total) responded
Provides study-related (career-related) work experience	1	1	1
Provides career direction	2	2	2
Enhances personal growth	5	5	3
Reinforces learning	3	3	4
Provides financial assistance	4	4	5

Studies of the impact of co-op on admissions, retention, salaries, and permanent placements documented important benefits of cooperative education. The results of admissions studies conducted in 1983, 1984, and 1985 are provided earlier in this chapter. The retention study, also reported earlier in this chapter, showed that the retention rate of co-op students was 96 percent, compared to a university-wide retention rate of 52 percent. Salary survey results indicated that Pace co-op students would earn approximately $6,750,000 in 1985-86; earned $4,705,538 in 1984-85; $3,766,840 in 1983-84; $2,419,787 in 1982-83; and $1,648,884 in 1981-82.

A study of permanent placements that occurred as a result of co-op placements is reported in Table 6-5.

Table 6-5. Permanent Employment Resulting from Co-op Placements.

	1981–82	1982–83	1983–84	1984–85
Number of co-op graduates surveyed	138	98	195	245
Response to survey	119 (86%)	79 (81%)	121 (62%)	175 (71%)
Number of graduates who received permanent offer from co-op employer	69 (59%)	39 (49%)	46 (36%)	81 (47%)
Number of graduates who accepted permanent offer from co-op employer	42 (35%)	21 (27%)	28 (61%)	52 (64%)

The reader will notice some inconsistencies in response rates and even in the results from one year to the next. One reason for the erratic response rate was the variation in methods for distributing various survey forms. Depending on the staff's time and availability in a particular year, the co-op office did one or two mailings and occasionally followed up with a telephone reminder. It is important to note that all of these studies were done by a co-op staff whose primary job was to place students and yet who realized that some time had to be set aside to gather some data to measure the program's impact.

Clearly, the results of studies and surveys conducted at Pace did document program benefits and provided information that was useful in planning and implementing program goals and procedures that best served the interests of students, employers, and the institution.

Conclusion

The success of Pace's Cooperative Education Program is apparent from its current status as one of the nation's largest co-op programs. In 1985–86, 1,350 students are being placed from Pace's undergraduate and graduate schools of business, computer science and information systems, arts and sciences, education, and nursing. There are over 400 participating employers, including Fortune 500 companies, medium-size and small firms, and government and nonprofit organizations.

Throughout the establishment and growth of Pace's program, co-op studies and surveys were conducted to provide a clear guide in assessing program strengths and weaknesses and in planning program improvements and expansion. Furthermore, the documentation of program benefits built a momentum of growing support for the co-op program. Pace's program proved that it serves the institution's mission in providing a relevant career-oriented education to its students; that the program enhances Pace's ties with the community; that cooperative education provides an income to Pace students who are earning their college expenses; that cooperative education experiences increase the likelihood that Pace students will find good jobs when they graduate; and that cooperative education increases institutional enrollments through recruitment and retention. Finally, Pace's co-op program demonstrated its value to employers by meeting their hiring and recruitment needs.

This is a model that can be applied at other institutions planning program improvements or expansion. By documenting and publicizing program benefits, support is easily developed among each of the major constituencies, so that the program thrives and brings benefits and rewards to the institution.

The questionnaires used at Pace University to survey employers, students, and faculty follow as Exhibits 6-1, 6-2, 6-3, 6-4, and 6-5.

Exhibit 6-1. Pace University's Cooperative Education Admissions Survey—Fall 1985.

1. Were you aware of Pace University's Cooperative Education Program when you applied to Pace?
   ☐ Yes   ☐ No
2. Was the cooperative education program a significant influence in your decision to attend Pace?
   ☐ Yes   ☐ No
3. Were you accepted to any other colleges or universities?   ☐ Yes   ☐ No
   If yes, please list the schools at which you were accepted:
   _____

4. If Pace did NOT have a cooperative education program, which of the following decisions would you have made? (CHECK ONE RESPONSE)
   ☐ Would not have attended college in Fall 1985.
   ☐ Would have attended another school (please specify school: _____)
   ☐ Would have attended Pace anyhow.
   ☐ Not sure.
5. Which Pace campus are you attending?   ☐ NY   ☐ Pleasantville   ☐ White Plains

If you would like to receive information about the cooperative education program, please print your name, address, and phone number below.

Name:_____

Street Address: _____

City, State, Zip: _____

Area Code & Phone No: _____

Please return to the Cooperative Education Office.

**Exhibit 6-2. Pace University's Cooperative Education Program—
Senior Placement Survey, 1986.**

Name: _____ Social Security Number: _____

Current Address: _____ Telephone: (___)_____

Date of Graduation from Pace University: _____

1. Please indicate your co-op placement(s):

Position	Company	Salary

2. Did your co-op employer offer you a permanent job? Yes _____
   No _____
   If no, skip to 3. If yes, please indicate position, company, and salary.

Position	Company	Salary

   Did you accept this offer? Yes _____ No _____

3. Did you receive a permanent job offer(s) from an employer other than
   your co-op employer? Yes _____ No _____
   If yes, please indicate position(s), company(ies), and salary(ies).

Position	Company	Salary

   Which position did you accept?

Position	Company	Salary

Please Remember to Complete All Questions.

Exhibit 6-3. Pace University's Cooperative Education Program—
Student Survey.

1. Please indicate your campus (CHOOSE ONE):
   (a) ☐ New York
   (b) ☐ Pleasantville
   (c) ☐ White Plains

2. Sex:
   (a) ☐ Male
   (b) ☐ Female

3. College Status:
   (a) ☐ Freshman
   (b) ☐ Sophomore
   (c) ☐ Junior
   (d) ☐ Senior
   (e) ☐ Graduate

4. How did you learn about the Cooperative Education Program at Pace University?
   (CHECK ONE OR MORE RESPONSES)
   (a) ☐ Pace Student Handbook
   (b) ☐ Faculty member told me
   (c) ☐ Poster on campus
   (d) ☐ Article in campus paper
   (e) ☐ Co-op staff person spoke in my class
   (f) ☐ Co-op Orientation Program
   (g) ☐ Learned of program through friends
   (h) ☐ Other: (please specify) _____

5. For what reasons did you decide to apply for a co-op position?
   (PLEASE READ ALL THE ANSWERS, THEN RANK YOUR ANSWERS FROM 1-5, WITH 1
   BEING THE MOST IMPORTANT AND 5 BEING THE LEAST IMPORTANT REASON)
   (RANK 1-5):
   (a) __ Earn an income
   (b) __ Gain self confidence
   (c) __ Apply my coursework in on the job experience
   (d) __ Increase my chances of getting a good job after graduation
   (e) __ Develop professional skills

Exhibit 6-3. Pace University's Cooperative Education Program—
Student Survey, Cont'd.

6. What were (are) the greatest benefits of participating in the Cooperative Education Program? (PLEASE READ ALL THE ANSWERS; THEN RANK YOUR ANSWERS FROM 1-5, WITH 1 BEING THE GREATEST BENEFIT AND 5 BEING THE LEAST BENEFICIAL) (RANK 1-5):

(a) __ Earn a good salary

(b) __ Gain self confidence

(c) __ Apply my coursework in on the job experience

(d) __ Increase my chances of getting a good job after graduation

(e) __ Develop professional skills

7. Did you participate in any co-op workshops or seminars in resume writing, interviewing, or career planning?

(a) ☐ Yes

(b) ☐ No

If yes, was the workshop helpful? (CIRCLE ONE NUMBER)

1   2   3   4
(not at all)   (very much)

8. Please indicate the level of effectiveness of each of the following services of the co-op office (CIRCLE ONE NUMBER FOR EACH ITEM):

	Improvement Needed	Satisfactory	Effective	Very Effective
a) Provided me with a worthwhile study related work experience	1	2	3	4
b) Staff counseled and assisted me during the co-op job search	1	2	3	4
c) Staff assisted me in resume writing and interviewing	1	2	3	4
d) Co-op staff was helpful and available during my placement (LEAVE BLANK IF NOT APPLICABLE)	1	2	3	4
e) Other (PLEASE SPECIFY): _____ _____	1	2	3	4

PLEASE RETURN TO THE COOPERATIVE EDUCATION OFFICE

Exhibit 6-4. Pace University's Cooperative Education Program— Employer Survey.

1. What are your organization's objectives in utilizing cooperative education?

(PLEASE RANK THESE ITEMS FROM 1-7, WITH 1 BEING THE MOST IMPORTANT OBJECTIVE. THEN INDICATE IN THE COLUMNS TO THE RIGHT TO WHAT EXTENT THESE OBJECTIVES ARE MET BY PACE UNIVERSITY'S COOPERATIVE EDUCATION PROGRAM).

	(A) RANK OBJECTIVE ACCORDING TO IMPORTANCE TO ORGANIZATION (NUMBER 1-7)	(B) EXTENT TO WHICH OBJECTIVE IS MET BY PACE CO-OP PROGRAM (CHECK ONE)	
		Good (1)	Needs Improvement (2)
(a) -meet cyclical, project, or short term work needs			
(b) -recruit potential long term employees			
(c) -attract top quality candidates			
(d) -obtain productive work			
(e) -cost efficient labor force			
(f) -affirmative action			
(g) -other (please specify)			

Comments: _____

2. What elements of cooperative education are important to your organization?

(PLEASE RANK FROM 1-6, WITH 1 BEING THE MOST IMPORTANT. THEN INDICATE ON THE RIGHT TO WHAT EXTENT THESE NEEDS ARE MET BY PACE'S COOPERATIVE EDUCATION PROGRAM).

	(A) RANK ELEMENT ACCORDING TO IMPORTANCE (NUMBER 1-6)	(B) EXTENT ACHIEVED BY PACE CO-OP PROGRAM	
		Good (1)	Needs Improvement (2)
(a) -continuity of job coverage			
(b) -availability of top quality candidates			
(c) -choice of more than one candidate			
(d) -length of work periods			
(e) -screening of candidates by co-op staff			
(f) -other (please specify)			

Comments: _____

3. What criteria do you use in selecting cooperative education students?

(RANK THESE ITEMS FROM 1-7, WITH 1 BEING THE MOST IMPORTANT. THEN INDICATE ON THE RIGHT TO WHAT EXTENT THE QUALIFICATIONS ARE MET BY STUDENTS REFERRED BY PACE'S COOPERATIVE EDUCATION PROGRAM).

	(A) RANK CRITERIA IN ORDER OF IMPORTANCE (NUMBER 1-7)	(B) EXTENT ACHIEVED BY PACE'S CO-OP PROGRAM	
		Good (1)	Needs Improvement (2)
(a) -related work experience			
(b) -academic preparation/coursework			
(c) -grades			
(d) -maturity			
(e) -interpersonal skills			
(f) -interest/motivation			
(g) -other (please specify)			

Comments: _____

Exhibit 6-4. Pace University's Cooperative Education Program— Employer Survey, Cont'd.

4. Is it more cost-efficient to utilize cooperative education to recruit permanent employees than to use standard recruiting methods?

   (a) ☐ Yes, we have data to support this

   (b) ☐ I think so, but there is no study to support this

   (c) ☐ No, the data refutes this

   (d) ☐ I don't think so

   (e) ☐ Not sure

Comments: _____

5. Do co-op employees who remain with the company after graduation advance at a faster rate than non co-op employees?

   (a) ☐ Yes, we have data to support this

   (b) ☐ I think so, but there is no study to support this

   (c) ☐ No, the data refutes this

   (d) ☐ I don't think so

   (e) ☐ Not sure

Comments: _____

6. Do co-op employees who remain after graduation show a higher retention rate than non co-op employees?

   (a) ☐ Yes, we have data to support this

   (b) ☐ I think so, but there is no study to support this

   (c) ☐ No, the data refutes this

   (d) ☐ I don't think so

   (e) ☐ Not sure

Comments: _____

7. Does your organization work with cooperative education programs at other schools?

   (a) ☐ Yes

   (b) ☐ No

Comments: _____

8. Do you have human resource needs not now being met by the cooperative education program, but in areas in which cooperative education students might make a contribution?

                (a) ☐ Yes   (b) ☐ No

Comments: _____

9. Additional comments: _____

_____

_____

10. If you would like to discuss this assessment, please provide your name and a number and our staff will call you.

_____

(Please print)

Exhibit 6-5. Pace University's Cooperative Education Program—
Faculty Survey.

1. Please indicate your campus:
   (a) ☐ New York
   (b) ☐ Pleasantville
   (c) ☐ White Plains

2. Are you familiar with the Cooperative Education Program at Pace University?
   (a) ☐ Yes
   (b) ☐ No

   IF YOU ANSWERED "YES" TO QUESTION 1, CONTINUE TO THE NEXT QUESTION.
   IF YOU ANSWERED "NO" TO QUESTION 1, SKIP TO QUESTION 8.

3. Are the co-op students you know satisfied with their cooperative work experiences?
   (SELECT ONE RESPONSE)
   (a) ☐ Yes, in almost all cases
   (b) ☐ In some cases
   (c) ☐ No
   (d) ☐ Do not know any co-op students
   (e) ☐ Do not have enough information
   Comments: _____

4. Do you think co-op positions are appropriate for your students?
   (SELECT ONE RESPONSE)
   (a) ☐ Yes, in almost all cases
   (b) ☐ In some cases
   (c) ☐ No
   (d) ☐ Do not have enough information
   Comments: _____

5. Based on your knowledge of the current cooperative education program, are you comfortable in en-
   couraging students to participate in the cooperative plan?
   (SELECT ONE RESPONSE)
   (a) ☐ Yes
   (b) ☐ No
   (c) ☐ Do not have enough information
   Comments: _____

Exhibit 6-5. Pace University's Cooperative Education Program—
Faculty Survey, Cont'd.

6. What do you consider to be the primary benefits to students who participate in cooperative education?
(PLEASE RANK IN ORDER OF IMPORTANCE FROM 1-8, WITH 1 BEING THE MOST IMPOR-
TANT BENEFIT AND 8 BEING THE LEAST IMPORTANT BENEFIT):

(a) __ Reinforces learning

(b) __ Provides financial assistance

(c) __ Increases motivation to continue in college

(d) __ Enhances personal growth

(e) __ Provides career direction

(f) __ Provides study-related work experience

(g) __ Helps students secure post-graduation jobs

(h) __ Other (Please state): _____

Comments: _____

7. Do you have any concerns about Pace students participating in cooperative education?

(a) ☐ Yes

(b) ☐ No

If yes, please indicate your concern(s): _____

_____

8. Do you believe that students at Pace University can benefit from a cooperative education program
that provides study-related paid work experiences?
(SELECT ONE RESPONSE)

(a) ☐ Most students can benefit

(b) ☐ Some students can benefit

(c) ☐ No students can benefit

(d) ☐ Not sure

(e) ☐ Do not have enough information

9. Please indicate if you would like the co-op staff to provide any of the following: (CHECK AS MANY
RESPONSES AS YOU LIKE AND PROVIDE YOUR NAME AND DEPARTMENT)

(a) ☐ Would like to receive literature about the program

(b) ☐ Would like to meet with a co-op staff member to discuss the program

(c) ☐ Would like a co-op staff member to speak briefly to my class

NAME: (Please Print) _____

DEPARTMENT: _____

10. Additional Comments: _____

_____

PLEASE RETURN TO THE COOPERATIVE EDUCATION OFFICE

References

Center for Cooperative Education. *Engineering Labor Market Study*. Boston: Northeastern University, 1985.

Knowles, A. S., and Associates. *Handbook of Cooperative Education*. San Francisco: Jossey-Bass, 1971.

Korngold, A., and Dubé, P. "An Assessment Model for Cooperative Education Program Planning, Management, and Marketing." *The Journal of Cooperative Education*, 1982, *19*, (1), 70-83.

Krukowski, J. "What Do Students Want? Status." *Change Magazine*, May-June, 1985.

Lindenmeyer, R. S. "A Comparison Study of the Academic Progress of the Cooperative and the Four Year Student." *The Journal of Cooperative Education*, 1967, *3*, (2), 8-18.

Robak, R. *Analysis of Cooperative Student Wages*. Boston: Northeastern University, 1985.

Smith, S. H. "The Influence of Participation in the Cooperative Program on Academic Performance." *The Journal of Cooperative Education*, 1965, *2*, (1), 7-20.

Sparrow, W. K. "Syllabus Revision Through Cooperative Education: Adapting Courses to the 'Real World.' " *The Journal of Cooperative Education*, 1981, *18*, (1), 94-98.

Wilson, J. W. "Analysis of Cooperative Education as a Work/Education Joint Venture." *The Journal of Cooperative Education*, 1984, *21*, (1), 29-39.

Seven

Achieving Cost Efficiency
and Program Effectiveness

James W. Wilson

A necessary element of cooperative education program development is sound financial planning. Unfortunately, however, awareness of this has frequently come too late to save a program from extinction. Since 1970, approximately one-quarter of all institutions that received one or more federal grants for initiating or expanding cooperative education have discontinued their programs altogether, and many more have sharply curtailed their scope. There is good reason to believe that at least some of these programs might have been saved had cost analysis and cost-effectiveness planning been incorporated into the development process from the start. More important, there are many programs that would benefit substantially from a better understanding of the financial elements that impact upon them and from careful planning based upon those understandings. The intent of this chapter, therefore, is to provide a framework for analyzing and assessing the cost-effectiveness of cooperative education programs and to propose ways to plan for financial viability.

Characteristics of Financially Cost-Effective Programs

In the most generic sense, a cost-effective cooperative education program is one that has achieved some previously decided-upon balance between investment in the program and outcomes of the program. Two contrasting mandates flow from this general proposition: For some predetermined level of investment, achieve the most and best possible. Or, achieve specified objectives for the lowest investment cost possible. The goal of cost-effective planning is to find an operational compromise between these extremes so that the objectives to be achieved are agreed on and adequate funds are made available to meet the costs of their achievement.

The difficulty many program administrators have encountered is achieving this balance without relying on funds from outside the institution, principally federal Title VIII funds. What cooperative education administrators seek, of course, is a viable and financially institutionalized program. The characteristics of such a program are that it (1) is sustained by institution funds through line items in the institution budget; (2) operates independently of external monies, except for special projects; (3) is able to grow in size and scope with a reasonable expectation that budget allocations will grow appropriately; and (4) shares equitable priority with other institutional units in the budgeting process. The discussion and advice to follow is aimed at helping program administrators reach these financial goals.

Analyzing Program Costs

All educational programs, including cooperative education, use resources to attain outcomes. The estimated value of those resources is the cost incurred by the program to achieve the outcomes. It is customary to equate program costs with program budgets, but for several reasons the budget is an inadequate measure of the true cost of operating cooperative education (Levin, 1983). First, the budget is at best a plan for the expenditure of money, not a report of actual expenditures. Second, not every cost item is necessarily included in the budget, for example, donated equipment, work-study students who devote fifteen hours a week to the program, or other "unpaid" services. Third, in most budgets the cost of any new equipment or other capital expense is accounted for in its entirety in the year in which it was incurred, rather than depreciated over its projected lifetime. This means, of course, that that particular program cost is overestimated in the first year and underestimated in each succeeding year.

Hence, while the budget is useful as a planning document, it is not an accurate source of information for cost analysis. Cost analysis requires that every ingredient used to produce the program outcomes be accounted for and its value or cost estimated. The "ingredients method" is a useful means to identify and estimate program costs and to determine how and by whom the burden of cost is being shared (Levin, 1983).

Identifying Program Ingredients

The first step in analysis is to determine every resource that is used to attain the program outcomes. Since our concern here is with cooperative education, it is important that we include every ingredient used for it, but only for it. If, for example, a cooperative education program were part of some larger program, it is essential that only those ingredients or proportion of ingredients actually used for cooperative education be included. The typical ingredients to be found include personnel, facilities, equipment and supplies, communications, and other resources.

Personnel. The personnel ingredients include all the human resources used to achieve the outcomes of the program. Typically, these minimally include a program administrator, professional staff, and support staff. The administrator is most often a director but sometimes will include a portion of some other administrator, such as an academic vice-president or a director of career planning and placement. If the program is sufficiently large, it may also entail an assistant to the director. The professional staff used may vary considerably, depending upon program structure and policy. The traditional position is the cooperative education coordinator, a full-time professional who counsels students, develops and maintains work positions, helps to place students, and monitors student experiences. There are today, however, other positions within this category of ingredient. There is the position of job developer, whose responsibility it is to establish work assignments, leaving the counseling and placement process to others. Teaching faculty are very often involved as advisors, providing academic counsel, assessing learning, and awarding academic credit based upon the cooperative experience. Support staff will include secretarial, data processing, and data entry functions.

These, it must be remembered, are typical program personnel. Any given program may not have all of these, or they may use others. The point to be remembered is that all human resources used in the program to achieve the outcomes of the program are ingredients that must be identified.

Facilities. Cooperative education programs need physical facilities, offices, reception areas, work rooms. They are a category of ingredient seldom found in budgets. Yet, they are an essential resource of the program and hence a cost. Most colleges and universities maintain records of kind, amount, and value of campus facilities for purposes of estimating total assets. From this information it should be possible to estimate the cost of those facilities devoted to cooperative education. It should be noted that if teaching faculty, or any other institution personnel, spend some portion of their time contributing directly to cooperative education and use their own offices to do so, the facilities cost thus encumbered must be allocated to the costs of cooperative education.

Equipment and Supplies. Cooperative education is labor intensive and does not rely heavily on equipment. Nonetheless, most programs use typewriters and, increasingly, word processors and microcomputers. Since these are a resource used to attain the objectives of the program, they constitute a program cost. Their total value, however, should be depreciated over their estimated life. For these particular pieces of equipment, five years is customary. For accurate cost estimates even donated equipment must be included.

Of course, all supplies used in conducting the business of the program must be included as an ingredient of the program.

Communications. Every cooperative education program must be in communication with persons and groups external to itself in order to achieve its intended outcomes. Hence, all post-age, telephone service, advertising, and publications must be charged as a cost to the program.

Other Services. This is a category of ingredient used to achieve the outcomes of the program which do not fit into any other category. It would include such specific ingredients as program-related travel, membership in professional associations, personnel training, and overhead charges.

Program and Incremental Institution Costs

Most programs of cooperative education have sufficient administrative integrity and unique function that they may properly be thought of and examined as independent totalities. Thus, it is appropriate to analyze the costs of cooperative education per se. It is also obvious, however, that co-op programs do not evolve or function in isolation from the institution of which they are a part. It might be assumed that in a hydraulic-like relationship, any program cost would transmit directly into an institution cost. For the most part this is so, but not in every instance, and it is important, as we shall see later, to distinguish between program costs and incremental institution costs. An incremental cost in this context is a new or additional cost to the otherwise total institution costs and is due solely to the existence of the cooperative education program. For example, a director of cooperative education, added to the institution payroll to direct the program, is both a program cost and an incremental cost to the institution. We will examine shortly some co-op ingredients which represent program costs but which are not incremental to the institution.

Using a Cost Worksheet

A useful strategem for organizing cost information is to construct a cost worksheet. This has the superficial appearance of a budget, but it has two major differences. First, it is not a planning document but a statement of actual costs. Second, it makes clear who shares in those costs.

The first step in creating a cost worksheet is to identify all program ingredients and list them in the left-hand column. The next step is to estimate the cost of each ingredient and report it in the second column of the worksheet. Normally, the market value of goods and services purchased or rented is the figure used. In some instances, such as the cost of facilities, more complex estimating may be required. The sum of these ingredient costs is the estimated total cost of the program. The final step in completing the worksheet is to determine who is actually paying. For cooperative education, those who are likely to share in the costs are (1) the institution; (2) the federal government; (3) the state government; (4) private foundations or corporations; and (5) parents and students.

The cost worksheet is illustrated in Table 7-1 with data from a hypothetical cooperative education program. Depicted are cost data for a program in an institution of 5,000 students, serving 200 co-op students. The program is staffed by a director, two full-time coordinators, two full-time support persons (one assigned to the director, the other to the coordinators), and twenty teaching faculty who provide academic counsel and assessment to an average of 5 students each and at a cost of $100 per student. Immediately following personnel ingredients and costs are those for equipment and supplies. Microcomputer, software, and printer costs are based on a straight five-year depreciation schedule. Communications, travel, photocopying, memberships, and any other like costs are straightforward summations of expenditures.

Overhead, on the other hand, is likely to be more complex, and what goes into it is likely to vary considerably from institution to institution. Usually, but not necessarily, costs for services such as space, light, heat, janitorial services, and sometimes even furniture are subsumed under this category of expense. Often, overhead is estimated as a percentage of wages and salaries. When, however, specific information is available, such as the square-foot cost of space or actual heating costs for areas occupied, direct summing may be used. In any event, the services usually lumped into overhead constitute a part of the total program costs and are to be included. In this example,

Table 7-1. Cost Worksheet.

Ingredients	Total Costs	Costs to Institutions	Government Grants	Private Gifts and Grants	Student and Family Costs	Resource Reallocation
Personnel						
Director	$32,000	$32,000				
Director's Secretary	15,500	15,500				
Coordinators	46,000	20,000	$26,000			
Faculty Advisors	20,000	20,000				
Coordinators' Secretary	14,000		14,000			
Fringe Benefits	21,500	13,500	8,000			
Equipment and Supplies						
Microcomputer	1,100	1,100				
Printer	360	360				
Software	300	300				
Paper	150	150				
Stationery	300	300				
Other Supplies	100	100				
Communication						
Telephone	4,500	1,800	2,700			
Postage	900	450	450			
Printing	1,500		1,500			
Other Expenses						
Travel						
Director	3,500	1,500	2,000			
Coordinators	5,000	2,000	3,000			
Photocopying	1,000		1,000			
Overhead	48,375	43,683	4,692			$43,683
Totals						
Costs	216,085	152,743	63,342			
User Fees		(15,000)			$15,000	
Other Cash Subsidies		(65,000)		$30,000	35,000	
Net Costs	$216,085	$72,743	$63,342	$30,000	$50,000	$43,683
Reallocation		(43,683)				43,683
Incremental Costs		29,060				

Source: Adapted from Levin, 1983.

overhead was estimated as 45 percent of salaries and wages. The sum of all ingredient costs for this hypothetical program is $216,085.

The cost worksheet also illustrates the distribution of these costs across all constituents. We observe first, for example, that line item costs have been allocated to the institution ($152,743) and to a government grant ($63,342). The total line item cost to the institution, however, is not the net cost to the institution because others share in paying for the program. Specifically, in this hypothetical situation, an industry grant of $30,000 reduces the net cost to the institution, as does a specific tuition increase of $7 for co-op to all students and a user fee of $75 for each of the 200 co-op participants. This reduces the net cost assigned to the institution to $72,743.

Within the net costs, however, are overhead costs, and these bring us back to the distinction between program and institution costs and to the notion of incremental costs. Most, if not all, of the ingredients of overhead entail costs which the institution would have even if there were no cooperative education program. Hence, while they are real costs to co-op and must be included in any analysis, they are not incremental costs to the institution. What the institution has done is to reallocate the resources comprising overhead from whatever their previous use to cooperative education. Although it may not be totally realistic, it is assumed for this hypothetical example that all of the co-op overhead costs represent resources the institution has reallocated. Thus, the final column of the cost worksheet, *Resource Reallocation,* lists a reallocation of $43,683, which is the institutions's share of the total overhead costs. One may question the wisdom of including a program cost, assigning it to the institution, and then effectively "writing it off." However, it is included because it is a cost incurred by the cooperative education program and therefore is a part of the total cost of having co-op. It also puts into perspective the institution's commitment to cooperative education through its willingness to reallocate existing resources. In this example, when the contributions of all constituents to the total program costs are taken into account, we find that the institution's financial outlay, its incremental costs, amount to $29,060.

In summary, the sum of costs for all ingredients, or the net cost of this hypothetical cooperative education program, is $216,085. This total, however, is distributed among several constituents. The federal government has made a grant of $63,342, reducing the institution's line item share to $152,743. Costs are further shared by an employer through a gift to cooperative education and by students and their parents through a specific tuition increase for co-op and a user fee. Thus, the co-op costs borne by the institution total $72,743. These are the real costs of co-op to the institution, but because $43,683 are costs the institution would experience with or without cooperative education, the incremental costs to the institution for co-op are $29,060.

The cost worksheet is an aid to the cost analysis of cooperative education. It provides a format for identifying all program ingredients and for estimating their cost. It also provides a mechanism for identifying who shares in these costs and to what extent. The result is a focused picture of program costs and their distribution among constituents. The analysis paves the way for planning and decision making. The initial question, of course, is whether the outcomes of the program, from the institution's point of view, are worth their cost: total cost, net cost, and especially the incremental cost. Examination of the worksheet will raise additional questions regarding the financial condition and future of the program. For example, Can the current level of external support be relied upon in the future? Can other sources, such as students or reallocation of existing resources, be used in the absence of external funding? Are there costs that might be reduced or eliminated and, if so, what would be the impact upon the quality of the program? Further exploration of these and other planning questions will be undertaken in the next section.

Cost-Effectiveness Analysis

At the outset of this chapter a cost-effective program was described as one in which an acceptable balance between program costs and outcomes had been achieved. The preceding section examined the cost side of the relationship. We turn now to the issues of program outcomes and assessment of effectiveness.

The literature of cooperative education provides ample evidence that benefits accrue to students, graduates, employers, and institutions (see Chapters Six, Thirteen, and Fourteen). The difficulty, from the perspective of financial assessment and decision making, is placing value on these benefits. The ideal is to be able to express both costs and effects in dollars, permitting calculation of benefit-cost ratios (Thompson, 1980). Some efforts have been made to express outcomes in monetary units for students and graduates (Cohen and others, 1977) and for employers (Wright, 1980; Wilson and Brown, 1985), but to date this has not proved practicable for institutions.

For situations in which outcomes are difficult to value, a strategy called "Cost-Effectiveness Analysis" (C/E) has been recommended (Thompson, 1980). C/E leaves evaluation of program effects to decision makers. The argument underlying this strategy as applied to cooperative education might be as follows: One cannot assign value in dollars or any other useful unit of measurement to the effects of cooperative education. But it is known that they are positive, giving students a better education than they otherwise would have had. Hence, cooperative education is good for the institution and the objective is to provide a quality co-op experience to as many students as possible for the least cost possible.

Since it is obvious that C/E compares monetary effects (costs) with nonmonetary effects (outcomes), the question becomes what nonmonetary effects might be considered. There are three criteria for their selection: They must be relevant; they must be measurable; and the unit of measurement must have meaning. In light of the C/E argument posed above, an appropriate outcome for a cooperative education program might be participation. The C/E ratio is calculated by dividing program costs by a measure of participation. For example, the hypothetical program of the previous section had a total cost of $216,085 and placed 200 individual students on co-op assignments. The C/E ratio is $216,085/200 = $1,080 per individual student placed on a co-op assignment. An alternative measure of participation could be placements per year rather than students per year. Thus, it may be that on an average, each student has one and a half placements in a year, yielding a total of 300 placements. In this event, C/E = $216,085/300 or $720 per placement. Decision makers at the institution must ultimately determine whether a C/E of $1,080 per individual student placed or a C/E of $720 per placement is acceptable or not.

Other outcomes measures are possible. One, for example, might be the number of students who may not have remained in college until graduation had they not entered a co-op program but, because (assumed) they did, do graduate. Suppose that this particular co-op program begins in the second year and that a study has shown that 70 percent of all students entering the sophomore year who do not co-op actually graduate. Applying this institution "survival rate" to the 200 co-op students, we would expect 140 to graduate had they not joined co-op. In fact, however, suppose 176 graduated. This is an increase of 36 students over expectation. The cost-effectiveness ratio for "saving students" would be C/E = $216,085/36 or $6,000 per student "saved." Again, decision makers must decide if this is an acceptable cost-effectiveness ratio.

The cost-effectiveness ratio may be used for particular elements within the co-op program, as well as with the program as a whole. For example, a project may be undertaken to recruit additional students to a program or to recruit additional employers. The cost per student or employer recruited can be determined.

The obvious limitation of cost-effectiveness analysis is the very reason it is used: the outcomes are not valued. Consequently, the C/E is value free and, hence, to make decisions regarding the program, someone has to decide upon its acceptability. On the other hand, it does relate costs and outcomes and gives additional meaning to the overall program effects. Cost-effectiveness analysis is most useful when costs and outcomes of alternative strategies to achieve the same objectives can be compared. Then, it is relatively easy to make a judgment, following the dictum of "the biggest bang for the smallest buck."

Planning Cost-Effective Programs

Cost analysis and cost-effectiveness analysis of cooperative education programs, as described and illustrated in the two preceding sections, will provide valuable information about the financial condition of the program and will give clues for possible financial strengthening. Another analytical procedure, "breakeven analysis" (Buffa, 1973), will furnish additional information. Further, because it permits the examination of the financial effect of alternative policies and procedures, it is a powerful "what if" tool and hence a substantial aid to the planning process.

In business-for-profit settings, breakeven analysis finds the point of sales and cost where neither a profit is made nor a net cost incurred. Applying this concept to a cooperative education program, breakeven analysis finds the point at which program income (constituent assumption of program costs) exactly equals total program costs. In brief, the breakeven point in the present setting is that point at which program costs and income are such as to make the institution's incremental costs for the program zero.

Fundamental to breakeven analysis is the assumption of a cost dichotomy: fixed costs and variable costs. In business, a fixed cost is one that is independent of the level of sales, whereas a variable cost is directly proportional to sales. In this application of breakeven analysis, *sales* translates into total income generated, which in turn relates, at least in part, to the level of student participation. Thus, fixed costs are those that remain essentially constant, regardless of student participation, while variable costs are closely tied to participation. Typically, fixed costs for cooperative education would include most costs that pertain to the director and the director's secretary: salaries; fringe benefits; office operations, such as telephone, postage, travel, supplies and equipment; and overhead. These are costs that would likely exist no matter how many students participated. In contrast, costs associated with coordinators and faculty advisers would likely increase more or less directly with the increase of student participation and hence are variable costs.

There are instances in which one might be uncertain as to how to classify costs. For example, how should one classify the cost of an associate director? Obviously, the need for an associate director arises when the program becomes large enough that the director needs to delegate responsibilities. On the other hand, the relationship between this position and student participation is not direct or proportional, as is likely to be the case for coordinators or faculty advisers. Generally speaking, unless the cost is closely tied to the level of activity (student participation), it is a fixed cost. For the hypothetical program used above to illustrate cost analysis, total costs would be divided as follows into fixed and variable costs.

Fixed Costs

1.	Director	$32,000
2.	Secretary to Director	15,500
3.	Fringe Benefits	9,500
4.	Equipment and Supplies	2,310
5.	Travel	3,500
6.	Communications and Other	5,200
7.	Overhead	21,375
		$89,385

Variable Costs

1.	Coordinators	$ 46,000
2.	Secretary to Coordinators	14,000
3.	Fringe Benefits	12,000
4.	Travel	5,000
5.	Payment to Faculty	20,000
6.	Communications	2,700
7.	Overhead	27,000
		$126,700

Breakeven analysis entails a relationship among fixed costs, variable costs, and income. In our application to cooperative education, income is the same as what we called cost-sharing constituents in cost analysis, minus the institution's share. Thus, for our hypothetical program the following is income.

Income

1.	Government Grant	$ 63,342
2.	Industry Gift	30,000
3.	Co-op Fee ($75 × 200 Students)	15,000
4.	Extra Tuition ($7 × 5,000 Students)	35,000
5.	Reallocation of Resources	43,683
		$187,025

Before explaining how to determine the breakeven point, an additional concept, "gross margin," must be introduced. Gross margin is the percentage of income that goes to cover the fixed costs and is calculated by dividing the variable costs by total income and subtracting the resulting proportion from one. In our illustrative co-op program, the gross margin is 0.3226. It is obtained by dividing $126,700 (variable costs) by 187,025 (income) and subtracting the resulting quotient (0.6774) from 1.00. The breakeven point is then obtained by dividing the contribution (0.3226) into fixed costs ($89,385). The result, $277,119, is the breakeven point, the income necessary after variable costs to just equal the fixed costs. At first thought, this may seem strange because, it will be recalled, the incremental cost to our hypothetical institution was only $29,060. This breakeven income is $90,094 more than the actual income. The reason for this discrepancy is that breakeven analysis assumes additional income is not obtained without additional variable cost. It provides an answer to the question, What level of program activity is necessary to break even, given the existing relationship among fixed costs, variable costs, and income? In short, how large must the program be?

Translation of breakeven dollars into student participation is achieved by dividing the breakeven amount by the per-student income. Estimating the per-student income, however, is somewhat complicated. There would be no difficulty if all program income were the same, but, like costs, some of the income is fixed and some is variable. In the present illustration, the following items constitute fixed income (income essentially unaffected by the number of students participating in the program).

1. Government Grant $ 63,342
2. Employer Grant   30,000
3. Extra Tuition   35,000
4. Overhead Reallocation for Director and
   Secretary (minus overhead from grant)   16,683
                                                                 $145,025

The variable income for our hypothetical program is as follows:

1. Student Fee $15,000
2. Reallocation of Coordinator and Secretary
   Overhead   27,000
                                                                 $42,000

The fixed and variable incomes must be treated differently to estimate the breakeven number of student participants. First, the fixed income must be subtracted from the breakeven amount, yielding a value of $132,074, which must be obtained as a direct consequence of student participation (variable income). Second, a per-student income level must be estimated. This will equal the sum of the student fee and the per-student value of the reallocation of overhead for coordinators and secretaries. The student fee, in this example, is $75. The per-student value of the overhead reallocation cannot be determined with precision, because the total overhead amount is not linked to an individual student but rather to a group of students set by the coordinator and secretarial load policies. Seemingly the most reasonable and surely the simplest means of estimating it, however, is to divide the total amount to be reallocated by the current number of co-op students, in this instance 200. Since the reallocated amount is $27,000, the per-student amount is $135. The total per-student income, then, is $210. When this amount is divided into $132,074 (the breakeven amount minus the fixed income), the result is 629 students. This represents the number of students needed to participate to break even under the assumption that the relationship (gross margin) among fixed costs, variable costs, and income remains the same.

There are two problems with this estimate insofar as planning strategy is concerned. First, although a reasonable long-range plan, expanding the program from 200 students to over 600 is not ordinarily a feasible solution to an immediate fiscal problem. Second, were this particular program, with its current cost and income characteristics, to expand to 600 students, it would experience an annual deficit of over $170,000. The two graphs below illustrate the rapidly increasing financial difficulties that this program would experience were it to expand as currently constituted.

Figure 7-1 graphs the fixed costs, total costs, and total income of the program from 0 to 900 students. It shows the ever-

Figure 7-1. Breakeven Analysis: Fixed Costs, Variable Costs, and Income for Hypothetical Program.

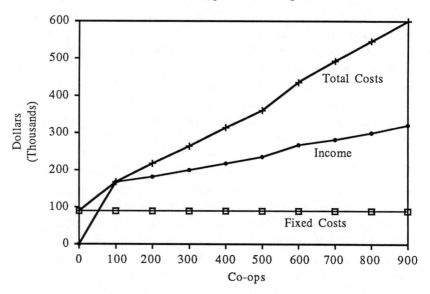

widening gap between total costs and income. It also shows the projected gap attributable to the program's variable costs (income rises substantially above fixed costs). This explains why the program appears to be financially sound at 100 students. It will be recalled that the program was assumed to have two coordinators. Hence, the analysis was conducted on the basis of a coordinator load of 100 students. Were the program at the level of 100 students, costs associated with one coordinator would be saved. Figure 7-2 provides another perspective on the same data.

Figure 7-2. Breakeven Analysis: Gross Margin for Hypothetical Program.

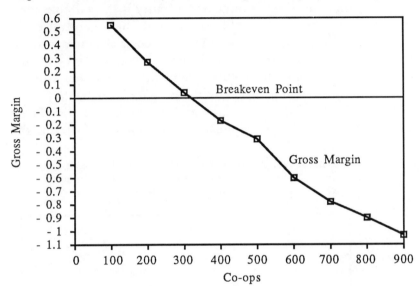

It plots the gross margin at each increment of student participation, showing that with each increment the gross margin decreases and hence, the income necessary to reach the breakeven point increases. It also shows, for this program, that the gross margin quickly becomes negative; that is, the variable costs are greater than the total income. When this occurs the idea of any breakeven point is illogical.

It appears that our hypothetical program is not only costing the institution $29,060 in incremental costs at its current level of 200 students, as shown in the cost worksheet (see Table 7-1), but is so constituted that it cannot expand without the certainty of ever-increasing incremental cost to the institution. It is not a viable program. To become one, it must modify its cost structure, or its income structure, or both. Every program ingredient, every cost, and every source of cost distribution (income) is a candidate for change in the planning process. It becomes quickly clear, however, that some are more likely candidates than others. For example, the travel cost of the director could be totally eliminated with essentially no impact on the future viability of the program. On the other hand, since it is apparent that the major source of difficulty is the variable costs in relation to income, variable costs would be a good place to start. The two major sources of variable costs are the coordinators and the faculty advisers. Although the load of 100 students per coordinator and the faculty payment of $100 per student may be desirable and justified by the program's goals, they must be examined carefully since they are very expensive ingredients of this program. Figure 7-3 illustrates the impact of altering the

Figure 7-3. Breakeven Analysis: Fixed Costs, Variable Costs, and Income for Hypothetical Program When Load Policy and Faculty Payment Are Altered.

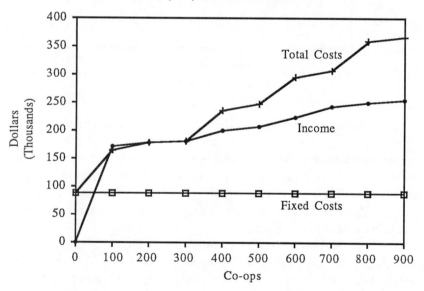

load policy from 100 students per coordinator to 200 and decreasing the faculty payment to $50 per student. While these changes will not yield an incremental cost-free program for all levels of student participation, they will for up to 300 students. Additional changes would be required for continued expansion.

All of the analyses reported here and the graphs based upon them were done with a microcomputer and spreadsheet. They are invaluable aids for this kind of analysis. Once a template or model incorporating all of the program ingredients and their costs, the elements of income, and the mathematical relationships among them has been created, it is possible to undertake "what if" analyses. These are little more (at least at the outset) than a series of trial and error changes in the cost and/or income assumptions. Since the spreadsheet program recalculates all mathematics in the model very rapidly, it is possible to posit many different "what if" assumptions and discover their effects in short order.

There are a number of values to be gained from playing "what if." First, of course, is the opportunity to experiment with a variety of financial arrangements without the necessity of actually implementing them to discover their impact upon the program. Second, there is the likelihood of finding, among the many arrangements tried, one or more that will achieve the financial goals of the program. The most important value, however, is the understanding that accrues regarding the relationship among the various cost and income variables. One begins to develop a sense about sound financial policy for a given program within a given institution. For example, the strategy for our hypothetical program began by recreating the exact conditions presented in the cost worksheet (see Table 7-1) and then asking a series of "what if" questions.

1. What if the coordinator load were increased from 100 to 200 students?
2. What if faculty were paid on the basis of $50 per student, rather than $100?
3. What if faculty were not used at all (presumably a no-credit-for-co-op policy)?
4. What if there were no external grants to support the program?

5. What if the co-op fee were increased from $75, decreased, or removed altogether?
6. What if tuition for the entire student body were increased by $10, $20, or $25?
7. What if, since our principal concern is with incremental costs to the institution, the institution reallocated the costs of unnecessary teaching faculty (because academic credit is awarded for co-op and replaces courses) to pay for coordinators?

All manner of potential policy changes and strategies can be explored. The result is a developing understanding of how the various program ingredients interrelate and lead to differing financial patterns. In turn, this understanding becomes the basis for developing a viable financial plan. Figure 7-4 illustrates the financial condition of our hypothetical program for various

Figure 7-4. Breakeven Analysis: Fixed Costs, Variable Costs, and Income for Hypothetical Program When Policies Affecting Costs and Income Are Altered Further.

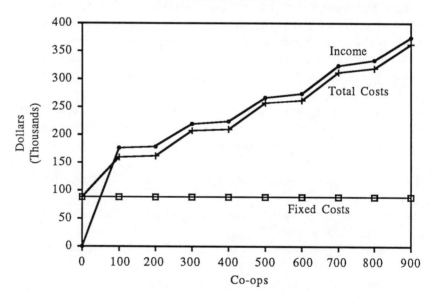

levels of student participation with a number of cost and income changes. The changes made are as follows.

- Coordinator student load is increased to 200 students
- Faculty compensation is decreased to $50 per student
- All coordinators after the first are faculty replacements and constitute reallocation of institution resources
- The "extra" tuition to support co-op is increased to $25 for all students in the institution
- There are no fixed-income external grants
- A College Work/Study Supplemental Grant (federal) of $12 per co-op student is added.

All other ingredients remained as originally presented.

The results of these changes present a financial picture dramatically different from that found in Figure 7-1. With this new configuration of costs and income, the program adds no incremental costs to the institution for any number of co-op students up to at least 900.

The great value of using an electronic spreadsheet for the planning process is that it permits unlimited experimentation. That experimentation will be more focused, if a few generalizations are borne in mind.

1. Variable costs tend to be insidious because they often are relatively inconsequential when the program is small, but growth is prevented because those costs can soon become prohibitive. Hence, financial planning should pay particular attention to keeping variable costs as low as possible without sacrificing the quality and objectives of the program. Since personnel costs constitute the largest portion of program costs, policies regarding coordinator loads, ratios of coordinators to support staff, and payments to faculty are crucial.

2. In contrast to variable costs, fixed costs assume a proportionately larger role in small programs and become less influential as the program grows.

3. Income, as used here, includes both incremental income and reallocation of existing resources to the program.

Incremental income is additional income due solely to the existence of the program and would include all external grants awarded to the institution for the co-op program, student fees for co-op, and any tuition increase levied specifically for the program. From the point of view of financial efficiency, the student fee for co-op is most effective because it is variable and grows in total income produced with the program. Its chief difficulty as a means of defraying costs is student resistance to a fee sufficient to acco nplish the task. On the other hand, an addition to tuition has the dual virtue of not having to be of the same magnitude as a co-op fee, because all students will share, and of not being a special fee. Tuition, however, is a fixed income and hence unless the institution itself is expanding will not increase as the program grows. It has been argued that increasing tuition to support co-op is unfair because it is taxing students who choose not to participate. This is true, but there is precedent for it—all students pay a student activity fee, but not all participate in the available activities. The opportunity is there, just as it is with co-op.

4. Reallocation of resources constitutes a special kind of income for a cooperative education program. It is an existing resource or ingredient of the institution, which would exist with or without the presence of co-op and which the institution has given to the program. It is not income to the institution; neither is it an incremental cost; it is, however, income to the program. Two examples of reallocation of resources were given. The first was all overhead costs. Overhead costs are ones that the institution would experience in any event and hence are not new or incremental costs. The other example was somewhat different. It was assumed because faculty advisers were used that the hypothetical program awarded academic credit to students based on their cooperative work experience. It is sometimes believed that awarding credit for co-op will in itself help meet the costs of the program, because tuition is charged for that credit. This is not the case, however, because that same tuition income would have been obtained without co-op—a course would have been taken instead. Nonetheless, when a program becomes of sufficient size (in the example here, 200), an additional coordinator

is needed, but one fewer teaching faculty is needed. Again, it is a reallocation of resources—from teaching faculty not needed, because students are earning credits outside the classroom, to coordinators.

Conclusions

Application of the financial concepts discussed in this chapter—program ingredients, incremental costs, fixed and variable costs, income, and reallocation of resources—and of the strategies suggested—cost worksheet, cost-effectiveness analysis, and breakeven analysis—can help significantly in understanding the financial condition of programs and in planning for their financial viability. But an ingredient without which no amount of planning would suffice is the commitment of the institution to a co-op program. That commitment may be based on any one or a combination of reasons: co-op is better education; it attracts new students; it reduces attrition; it attracts business and industry gifts. Whatever the reason or reasons, if the program is to survive, the leadership of the institution must be committed to its survival. The program can trim costs and operate with considerable efficiency; it can win external support through grants; it can probably assess a co-op fee. It cannot, however, raise tuition, establish a policy of resource reallocation, or, alternatively, approve a policy of some level of negative financing. These require action at the highest level of the institution and therefore commitment to the program.

References

Buffa, E. *Self Review in Production and Operation Management.* Homewood, Ill.: Irwin, 1973.

Cohen, A. J., and others. *Cooperative Education—A National Assessment: Final Report.* Silver Spring, Md.: Applied Management Sciences, 1977.

Levin, H. M. *Cost-Effectiveness: A Primer.* New Perspectives in Evaluation, vol. 4. Newbury Park, Calif.: Sage, 1983.

Thompson, M. S. *Benefit-Cost Analysis for Program Evaluation.* Newbury Park, Calif.: Sage, 1980.

Wilson, J. W., and Brown, S. J. *A Benefit-Cost Model for Employer Participation in Cooperative Education.* Boston: Northeastern University, 1985.

Wright, J. J. "Georgia's Cooperative Education Program." Unpublished report, Georgia Organization for Southern Bell, 1980.

Eight

Creating Information Systems
for Effective Management
and Evaluation

James W. Varty

Programs of cooperative education go through a series of "stages" in growth and development and are characterized by a variety of "organizational structures." In each of these stages and as a result of their particular organizational structure, special and different kinds of information/communication issues arise that need to be addressed. For the sake of simplicity we might conceptualize these stages as program implementation, initial program growth and consolidation, and continued expansion. The basic organizational structures can be characterized generally as centralized or decentralized. Of course, it is important to point out that both stages of growth and organizational approaches are on a continuum and intersect each other at myriad different points in different programs.

Given such program variety, this chapter will explore how individual programs can be managed systematically through an automated system for the collection, manipulation, analysis, interpretation, and the consequent use of program information.

A systematic approach to information management is important and is either a conscious or unconscious component of every cooperative education program; it is particularly critical to comprehensive cooperative education programs. For that reason, particular emphasis will be given to how such a management system can support and contribute to the administration and development of large established programs of cooperative education.

A Complex Educational Strategy

At first glance, cooperative education appears to be a relatively simple strategy. Students go to college, learn about cooperative education, are matched with interested employers, and rotate for the rest of their college experience between school and work. The pivotal person in this relationship is the co-op coordinator. Like a circus ringmaster, he or she ensures that the show goes on. More careful examination points out the complexity of the co-op strategy and its unique information and management needs.

As managers of individual students, co-op coordinators are responsible for placing students in appropriate work experiences related to their academic disciplines. At a minimum, appropriate placements require a good understanding of students' background, prior student orientations, resume development, the practice of interviewing skills, and an overview of employer expectations. Good placements do not develop spontaneously but are usually the result of careful cultivation of personnel officers and front-line supervisors and the subsequent development of position descriptions. The right placement for a particular student is the product of the coordinator's in-depth understanding of the work experience that a particular position provides and the referral of the student most likely to benefit from the same. Co-op programs are working with industries that are increasingly concerned with human engineering, or the appropriate fit between an employee, peers, and technology. Coordinators should expect that the demand for very careful placement will increase in the years to come. This will probably result in even more complex systems to achieve that goal.

Once into the co-op experience, learning is aided if a student sets specific learning objectives with his or her immediate supervisor, and the coordinator and/or faculty advisor needs to monitor and evaluate the growth that is occurring. Also, as a student grows through a series of work experiences, careful academic advisement needs to occur so that the mix of academic and work experience results in very carefully honed skills that lead to productive and satisfying employment following graduation. Co-op can be a tremendous learning experience, but it does require complex and careful orchestration of individuals.

On a broader programmatic level, the management of a co-op program is also complex. Coordinators have to monitor the pulse of the business community constantly. Within the institution, they need to garner support for this strategy, which continues to be a bit suspect among other educators. To be able to function, Ralph Tyler (1980) notes, cooperative education programs need to develop planned outcomes and that program activity needs to be reviewed to monitor whether and to what extent the planned and unplanned outcomes need to be evaluated. Only in this way will a program as a whole become more acceptable, be nourished, and develop.

A Cooperative Education Management
Information System

The complex elements of the co-op process described above require the effective collection and utilization of information and a well-developed management system for effective program operation. In many small programs this system is often implicit. The required information is stored in the memory of the coordinator. However, as a program expands or becomes more concerned with quality and efficiency, an explicit "Cooperative Management Information System" (CMIS) becomes very important, if not essential. For the purposes of this chapter, a CMIS is defined as a strategy of program management that depends heavily upon an information system (often automated) for data collection, storage, and processing. This system provides appropriate information in a timely and efficient manner to ensure effective program operation. It also provides accurate information to those served by co-op, including educators, students, employers, and the community at large.

A management system is not intended to merely collect

and report information but should integrate the collected information and available information-processing technology to manage the co-op program effectively and efficiently. What is being proposed is an integrated system for co-op management. Such a system considers the populations involved with co-op, the tasks involved, the available staff, and available technology and welds all of these elements into an effective, functioning management system.

Because each cooperative education program is unique, each CMIS will be unique and will develop as the program develops and grows. There are, however, a number of common problems with co-op management that need to be overcome and which will be addressed here. A more detailed approach to the development of the information collection and reporting component of the CMIS is found in *Developing a Management Information System for Cooperative Education* (Varty and Thompson, 1981).

Common Weaknesses in the Management of Co-op Information

To be able to manage effectively, coordinators or co-op directors need to have access to necessary information, at the proper time and place, on all facets of the co-op organization. They need to be able to view information comprehensively and, at the same time, be able to focus on individual issues within that comprehensive picture. This requires a systematic approach to information collection, storage, and retrieval.

Nearly all cooperative education programs do collect some information about co-op students and do evaluate student performance. Many even undertake occasional evaluation of the long-range effect of the cooperative education experience on student development, as well as the general effectiveness of the cooperative effort. Unfortunately, few coordinators or directors of cooperative education have ever spent time reviewing their information needs and developing that systematic approach to information management. As a result, certain weaknesses in information management are common. This section discusses these problems and indicates how an organized approach to information and program management, a CMIS, can avoid the same.

Irrelevant Data Collecting

Rather than collect too few data, some directors attempt to collect too many. Application forms, for example, may require coordinators to provide facts that are not utilized or to collect the same data items on various forms when they could be collected once. A functioning CMIS is organized to collect data once and to collect only the essential data necessary to conduct and manage the program and to evaluate program effectiveness.

Unorganized Data Collection

Often data collection occurs in such a manner that the ability to generate information is severely limited. For instance, coordinators might collect wage and salary data from students on one form and employer data on another. Consequently, a director finds it difficult to combine the data items to generate an information report that reflects salaries paid to students by specific employers. In the case of larger, decentralized programs with several coordinators, different units or individuals may be collecting different types of data or the same type of data in a different format—for example, wage information by monthly, hourly, and annual amounts. This severely limits the ability of a director to draw useful conclusions about co-op from an institutional framework. In a CMIS, all coordinators collect similar kinds of data in similar formats.

Untimely Collection and Processing of Data

Cooperative education directors may develop and distribute a particular form without establishing responsibility for who is to complete it or when it is to be returned. When timelines and responsibilities have not been established through a clear statement of procedures, facts are either not completely provided or are not provided by all coordinators in a timely manner. Under these conditions, the processing of data to provide information is either delayed or does not even occur. In both instances, information that could be very useful in program activity or planning is unavailable at the appropriate time. A CMIS establishes individual responsibilities and written timelines for all aspects of data collection and processing.

Inadequate Reporting of Information

Even though state and federal regulations often require co-op directors to collect data and prepare certain kinds of reports, directors seldom have the time to prepare accurate, timely, and clear reports on program accomplishments to justify the program's existence to top administration, to communicate with employers, and to attract additional students. Because of difficulties with timely and appropriate data collection and processing, as well as other program responsibilities, directors fail to present and interpret information about their program on a regular basis to those in the best position to use it. A CMIS lists key people who need to be routinely informed and details about when and in what format reports will be generated.

Program Management Independent
of Available Information

Often co-op directors make decisions based on hunches influenced by a few isolated facts instead of making decisions based on a broad, total program perspective. In effect, the program's information system and management process co-exist, but do little to influence one another. Instead of using information systematically, directors set program direction and then hunt for information to justify that direction. A CMIS includes clear guidelines for the presentation and utilization of information in program planning and management.

Person-Dependent Programs

Small co-op programs are often managed by a single coordinator. That same person often keeps records of employers, students, and active placement in his or her head or on a few pieces of paper in a system known only to that individual. Like the co-op program itself, such an information process poses few problems as long as this person is in charge and the program remains small. However, should the program grow or the person leave, chaos can result. Because a CMIS has established data collection instruments and information procedures, it is less person-dependent and provides for transition or growth more easily.

Stated positively, a cooperative management information system ideally:

1. Determines, collects, stores, and presents data important to routine program operations.
2. Aggregates the same data for routine information reports as required by the institution and external agencies.
3. Provides selected information for communication to various interested parties, including employers (a historical record of their co-ops), instructors (the worksite locations of students in their discipline), and institutional administration (cost-benefit analyses).
4. Manages communication linkages within the co-op staff and with interested and involved others. This is extremely important because co-op is a very interdependent strategy. Coordinators depend upon faculty for referrals, and several coordinators often work with the same employer.
5. Contains and manages pertinent program materials, including program objectives, procedures, advisory committee activity, program documents, grants, management calendar, program correspondence, co-op brochures and materials, and the co-op library.
6. Contains and manages program public relations and marketing activities, including listing employers, recording faculty

and staff contacts, and maintaining marketing materials and marketing strategy.

7. Provides basic data for program evaluation and forward planning, including demographics and reports on whether objectives were implemented, how they were implemented, and the impact of objectives on participants, thus establishing a base for future planning.

8. Manages the management system itself, including providing timelines and promoting re-evaluation of data collection methods and the types of data collected.

Principles for CMIS Development

Most co-op programs suffer from several or all of the information collection and management weaknesses mentioned, and many colleges are extremely interested in making progress toward these described ideals. The ability to picture and gain consensus about the ideal co-op program for a particular program and then to conceptualize how that program needs to be structured is essential to the development of a functioning CMIS. A description of how such a process might occur follows.

A Team Effort

CMIS development takes time and the full involvement of staff and interested others. It cannot be adequately covered as one topic among many routine staffing concerns and is probably best initiated through special meetings to brainstorm the issue, away from the office and day-to-day program operations. Ideally, a meeting needs to include others critical to co-op at the institution, for example, a representative of top administration, a knowledgeable representative of the institutional information or data processing services, key employers and students, and members of the co-op advisory committee. A neutral moderator or consultant knowledgeable about co-op might provide direction and keep the discussion on target.

Enlisting the effort of the entire staff makes good practical sense, since support and professional staff all play a part in maintaining the constant flow of co-op information. It also makes good psychological sense because the entire staff will feel ownership of the final product.

Moreover, the developed system must be supportive of staff and not counterproductive. Too often, data requests and procedures seem designed only to complicate the life of a staff person. If the developed system meets the needs of staff, requests for information will be much more acceptable.

Steps in the Development of the Management System

The process for developing an information system described in *Developing a Management Information System for Cooperative Education* (Varty and Thompson, 1981) can be a point of departure. As a first step, it is important to be able to picture in some detail the functioning cooperative education program at an institution, as well as the potential modifications that might make the program even more valuable to students, employers, and the community. With a picture clearly in view and some consensus about the direction the program should take, needs analysis can begin.

Needs analysis should be broad and encompass all aspects of the program. For example, it should not merely concentrate on data required for information reports but should be a comprehensive analysis of what is involved in program management. A staff needs to consider data collection for program operation, reporting, and evaluation; information retrieval and word processing for routine and special communication with students, staff, and employers; maintenance of a library of co-op materials, philosophy, and objectives; a developed schedule of annual and weekly program activities that would also capture and be used as a routine report of program accomplishment; and probably an electronic mail system.

It is not easy to extract all of these information needs and important processing procedures after picturing an ideal program. Still, when this is done well, the potential for building an effective integrated management information system dramatically increases. At times, a director is hesitant to think in such a global fashion, concerned that he or she will be overwhelmed by the effort involved in implementation. Realistically, many programs lack the resources to implement such an integrated system all at once. Still, if a director is guided by a well-conceived plan, the potential for a well-integrated and effective management system dramatically increases, and a director is able to identify resources and bring parts of the total system up as these resources become available. At the same time, it is less likely that the various parts of the developed system will prove incompatible or limited in their ability to interact.

A data management system needs to be carefully developed. To structure the collection, maintenance, and retrieval of data, as well as the communication of information, is time consuming and often seen as an unnecessary or impossible exercise by coordinators and support staff already burdened with many responsibilities. A properly conceived system will not eliminate collection, maintenance, and retrieval responsibilities. However, it can avoid duplicate collection of data and the collection of useless data, and it will result in the simplification of other time-consuming tasks that can be subsequently automated. For example, a management system that has integrated data collection and word processing can automatically generate routine correspondence to students and employers. Think of the time that can be saved when employer contracts and employer student evaluations are routinely word-processed from collected demographic data.

The examination of current forms and the development of a set of collection instruments that ensures pertinent information is collected only once is an essential step in the development of the data management process. Careful consideration of how the information will be stored for maximum utilization and analysis is also very important. The way the database is constructed can make a significant difference in how efficiently data can be used. For example, if data about a certain employer are stored in a central file or system, then all of these data can be used to provide an accurate picture of that employer's current level of cooperative education involvement or as material for a profile of employers in general. That central file might include the names of the various divisions in a company serviced by co-op, the contact person within each division, supervisors responsible for each co-op, the number of academic disciplines that an employer uses, the names of active and inactive students in co-op each term, and even the company's involvement with co-op advisory committees, career days, and the like.

If that employer file can be merged or connected with the student data file, then these employer data need only be collected once to be used in either the student or employer file. Data about a company collected from a student information report could be used to profile the company and the individual assigned. The University of Waterloo in Ontario, Canada, has a mandatory cooperative education program and has developed an extensive co-op database, described briefly in the proceedings of the Cooperative Education Association meeting held in Norfolk, Virginia (Beaupre and Ferdall, 1986). This very comprehensive system is worth careful review.

Many management information systems fail because they lack well-developed, written collection procedures and schedules. When an entire staff knows how information is to be collected, who is to provide and collect it, when it is due and how it is to be entered into a file, there is much more likelihood that accurate data will be collected in a timely manner. If collection instruments themselves provide details about the collection procedure and if an overall program management calendar identifies when data are due and monitors how collection is proceeding and when it is complete, data collection will probably occur on schedule.

Although collection occurs later in the chronological chain of events, data are used primarily in making decisions about what data should be collected, the collection schedule, and database construction. General issues, such as how information is to be used in program management, and specific issues, such as the type of reports to be generated, frequency of their generation, routine correspondence requested for program operation, the individuals to whom both reports and correspondence should to be directed, all need to be determined for an effective CMIS.

Thus far, this chapter has reviewed the complexities of the cooperative education strategy, pointed out common weaknesses that exist in most programs, and suggested principles to consider in developing a management system at a particular institution. Now it is important to suggest how a CMIS can be used to support and strengthen a functioning program. There are probably hundreds of applications that might be mentioned. The following are suggested to encourage creative application of the CMIS system at each institution.

Establishing Program Direction

A functioning management system measures what a program has accomplished and where it currently is and assists in setting a direction for further growth. When a director is able to measure, compare, and report the current level of co-op activity, he or she is in a much better position to develop a plan for the future that contains very specific and realistic goals and objectives. With a planned approach to program management, the data required for this type of analysis and forward planning are routinely collected, eliminating the very time-consuming need to go back and retrieve them at budget or annual planning time. When forward planning is a routine event in an annual program management cycle, it is much more likely to occur and to be well done.

A cooperative education program needs focused growth. Goals should only be established after careful consideration of various alternatives. These goals need to be both long- and short-range, and they need to be quite specific. For example, it is not sufficient to establish a general goal that growth will occur in co-op. It is better to determine that co-op in "materials handling" will be explored with the relevant associations of employers and that co-op will be increased 25 percent in public service because of employer demand. Students' academic preparation for co-op will be strengthened in design technology through a review of curriculum conducted by a study committee composed of staff, faculty, and employers. An established management system provides for this kind of precise planning.

It is important to emphasize that institutions, foundations, and federal and state agencies are much more likely to be supportive of efficient and productive programs that have a clear sense of their past and their present and have formulated a precise plan for growth.

Program Productivity

Without a well-developed CMIS, plans for future growth are less likely, will necessarily be less specific, and will probably be ineffective. Such programs are more prone to drift and tend to respond to external pressures as they occur, rather than following a planned approach to reasonable growth and development. In this situation staff tend to be less productive.

Conversely, if staff members understand where they are going and have an articulated set of procedures for reaching goals and the necessary resources available at hand, they will tend to be more efficiently employed. When a director is able to establish current levels of staff productivity, it is also possible to measure the impact of both new procedures that are initiated and new technology introduced. Worthwhile programmatic and technological innovations can be retained and enhanced, while less valuable ones can be discarded.

Clearly defined goals and procedures also enable a staff to make wise decisions about the kind of technology that will best support their operation. A small program with a few students and employers will probably not need to be connected with the college database for information about students, will at most need a microcomputer to manage information about students and employers, and will not need sophisticated word-processing capabilities to regularly communicate with constituents. However, a larger program would likely require college database access for student records, will probably need networked microcomputers with a college database or enhanced memory to manage program information, and will need to integrate word-processing equipment with that database to maintain efficient communication with students, employers, and faculty. The decisions that need to be made about the right technology to purchase and the kind of system to develop can occur only if goals and procedures are clearly understood. The increased productivity of the right system is clear in the following example.

Many programs require a written employer-student agreement and updated job descriptions each semester or at the beginning of an alternating placement. A word processor networked to the co-op database could automatically prepare the agreement and print prior job descriptions from data already on hand. It could personalize an accompanying cover letter, explaining the agreement procedure and requesting that the enclosed job description be updated, and, lastly, it would provide a mailing label. As the requested information is completed and returned, a coordinator might review it and note in the student data file that the agreement has been completed and the revised job description is on file. At an appropriate time, a secretary would review the file, and reminder letters would be automatically generated to nonrespondents. When time permitted, the revised job description would be entered into the system. An experienced director could easily point out numerous examples where such a configured information system could considerably simplify program operation and increase overall program productivity.

Improving Quality

As the mechanical aspects of cooperative education become routinized through the management system, staff will have more time to interact effectively with employers, students, and faculty to implement those added touches that make the difference between "average" and "superior." Handbooks for students and employers can be developed and maintained. The advisory committee can be utilized more effectively in program design and implementation. Supervisory training can be developed to strengthen the co-op experience for students on assignment. Faculty can be better informed about business and industrial development. Co-op seminars can be reviewed and strengthened. Students can be better informed about the purpose of cooperative education, better prepared for interviewing, and better assisted in the development of learning objectives. The college administration can be better informed of co-op direction, activities, and accomplishments. Co-op staff can grow in their understanding of their role and of the college and business/industrial environment in which they work. This may well result in a more proactive role in committees within the institution and in community projects. It may well contribute to co-op's academic credibility. When co-op staff members have time to get beyond the mechanics of "keeping track" of employers and students, their job is likely to grow more interesting. They will be doing a better job with employers and students alike and will be recognized for their accomplishments. They will feel good and their enthusiasm will result in even greater accomplishments.

An effective management system does free the staff from mechanical tasks and sets a clearer direction, increasing productivity to indirectly improve the quality of the co-op program. At the same time, it is important to note that the system directly contributes to program quality. A systematic marketing plan for co-op will attract better employers and result in stronger placements. A well-developed introduction to co-op for students will help them decide if co-op is appropriate and will enable coordinators to get to know students better and place them more appropriately. A program that is consistently able to listen to and communicate with employers, students, faculty, and staff will grow in quality. A program that is able to routinely evaluate its direction and its procedures will become a better program. The accomplishment and integration of all these activities and countless others is only possible through a systematic management strategy for cooperative education. A program might be able to do one or another activity well, but only a well-organized program can bring together the complete co-op strategy and do all of it well.

This chapter has explored the complexity of the co-op strategy, presented some of the common problems experienced in the management of cooperative education, and suggested principles that need to be considered in the development of a cooperative management information system. Finally, it has touched on how a CMIS can contribute to program direction,

productivity, and quality. The author hopes that his colleagues
have found this helpful in their review of program direction and
in the strengthening of their program management.

References

Beaupre, D. J., and Ferdall, S. A. "An Integrated Co-operative
    Education Information System: A Live Demonstration." Pa-
    per presented at 23rd Annual Conference of the Cooperative
    Education Association, Norfolk, Virginia, Apr. 1986.
Tyler, R. "A Brief Overview of Program Evaluation." *The Jour-
    nal of Cooperative Education,* 1980, *16* (3), 7-15.
Varty, J., and Thompson, D. *Developing a Management Infor-
    mation System for Cooperative Education.* Warren, Mich.:
    Macomb Community College Press, 1981.

Nine

Legal Rights and Obligations of Students, Employers, and Institutions

Michael B. Goldstein
Peter C. Wolk

As cooperative education is the joining of the worlds of work and learning, so the law of cooperative education is a confluence of the laws of the workplace and those of higher education. The need to work within two very different legal arenas both complicates and illuminates the principles under which cooperative education programs must operate.

The law of the workplace is both venerable and, to a very large degree, enshrined in statute. Some of the key legal principles go back to British common law, but most of the statutory framework was developed during the first half of the twentieth century. The first child labor laws of the 1900s were followed in succeeding decades by a stream of legislation that regulated the workplace and sought to protect the interests of the workers. The governing law is now a mixture of federal and state statutes, the former providing the general framework and the latter filling in the detail. The rights and duties of workers and their employers, to a very great degree, can be determined by looking to the statute books.

The law of higher education, on the other hand, is still in its evolutionary stage. There is precious little statutory law that governs the relationship between the student and his or her institution, and the case law that exists, being substantially in the state courts, lacks consistency as well as depth. The rights and duties of students and their institutions continue to be defined by the nature of their relationship, which is characterized by a rather complex and sometimes amorphous contract of enrollment. Overlaying this is a relatively thin veneer of statutory law, primarily relating to civil rights and due process.

The cooperative education participant sits squarely between these two legal worlds. He or she is a student, enrolled at an institution of higher education, subject to its rules and requirements, and holding certain enforceable expectations of that institution's behavior. But he or she is also a worker, employed by an entity separate and apart from the college or university, and subject to the laws, rules, and expectations of the workplace. To further complicate this picture, the participant's school and his or her employer have a relationship between each other, either expressed or implied. Thus, what emerges is a tripartite relationship, with rights, duties, and obligations flowing between and among the student, the institution, and the employer.

As a worker, the co-op participant has a specific set of responsibilities to his or her employer. The participant must have the capacity to perform the work and in doing so must be able to both serve and protect the interests of the employer, as well as those of third parties, such as co-workers, clients, and the general public. Conversely, the employer has the obligation to provide the participant with suitable work, in a safe environment, with adequate supervision and proper tools and equipment, and to compensate the participant in accordance with both the understanding between employer and employee and the governing law.

As a student, the co-op participant has a set of responsibilities to his or her institution. These include, in addition to performing the work involved in the co-op placement, carrying out any assigned academic responsibilities and, in performing the work, protecting the interests of the institution. In return, the student's college or university may have the obligation to properly assess the student's skills, capabilities, and limitations; place the student in a suitable position where he or she will be reasonably protected from harm; and fulfill its part of the academic bargain in the form of the award of appropriate certification and other recognition.

Between the institution and the employer lies yet another set of relationships. To the extent that the school is involved in the placement process, it assumes the obligation to adequately screen and assess each participant, make placements based upon a reasonable matching of skills and requirements, and apprise the employer of any limitations that may affect the student's performance of the work or impact upon his or her health and welfare or that of others with whom the student may interact. In turn, the employer implicitly or explicitly commits to appropriately utilize the services of the student, to protect the institution from risk of loss or harm, and to comply with whatever academic reporting and supervisory requirements may be a part of the cooperative education program.

The law of cooperative education seeks to define the nature of those interlocking rights, duties, and obligations within the framework of the legal system.

The Co-op Student as Worker

The most critical question to be answered in looking at the legal relationship between a cooperative education participant and the entity at which he or she is working is whether the student is an employee. Determining whether a co-op participant is an employee entails examination of several areas of law, with varying definitions and standards for each. Simply put, a co-op participant may be an employee for some purposes, but not an employee for others, such as unemployment compensation. The status of the co-op participant carries with it certain legal rights and responsibilities and imposes upon the school and the employer corresponding legal duties.

Under common law, analysts looked to four elements

when they attempted to determine the existence of an employment relationship: selection and engagement of the purported employee, payment of wages, power of dismissal, and the power of control over the person's conduct. Of these, the last, the power to control an employee's conduct, was the most important.

During the Great Depression, Congress sought to ameliorate the lot of American workers by establishing a minimum wage. The Fair Labor Standards Act of 1938 (FLSA) did not look to the common law for a definition of "employment" (U.S.C., title 29, sec. 201 et seq., 1978). Rather, it established a new theory of the employment relationship, one that was much broader than that hammered out by judges under common-law definitions. The new act neatly cut away all the previous encrustation by simply defining the term "employ" as "to suffer or permit to work." "Employee" was then defined, rather circularly, as "any individual employee employed by an employer" (U.S.C., title 29, sec. 203(e)(1)(3)(g), 1978). In an attempt to remedy this ambiguity, Congress sought to make it clear that it did not intend to reorder all of the relationships between employers and employees simply by passing the Fair Labor Standards Act but that it did want to ensure broad, "commonsensical" application of the Act [*N.L.R.B.* v. *Hearst Publications, Inc.,* 322 U.S. 111 (1944)]. Yet, questions concerning that relationship were raised almost immediately. Of particular note to the cooperative education community, the Secretary of Labor began to pursue companies that maintained unpaid or subminimum wage trainee programs. Over time, this ambiguity has become significant as various types of relationships have been spawned by co-op programs, particularly where there is not regular compensation or the compensation level is below FLSA requirements.

In a leading case, the Secretary of Labor determined that the Fair Labor Standards Act applied to an uncompensated training program for prospective railroad personnel. In the case of *Portland Terminal* [*Wallery* v. *Portland Terminal Co.,* 330 U.S. 148 (1947)], the Supreme Court disagreed. The Court found that one of the purposes of the Fair Labor Standards Act was to determine who received the primary benefit of the training program: the employer or the employee.

This issue arises most clearly in the case of the co-op student who is not receiving any compensation. It would appear on its face that a volunteer is a kind of employee, rendering service to an employer, but without the expectation of being compensated. In this context, it is extremely important to note that an individual cannot contract away the right to compensation under the FLSA. Thus, were an individual to enter into an employment agreement with an employer which stated that the individual would render service to the employer and would receive no compensation for reasons of the individual's own, that individual would still have the right, despite the agreement, to payment in accordance with the FLSA. If the employer refused payment, the individual could ask the Department of Labor to intervene and potentially receive not only the compensation due him or her but statutory damages as well. In other words, the parties' intent to not create an employment relationship does not control, since application of the Act does not depend on subjective intent [*Brennan* v. *Partida,* 492 F.2d 707 (5th Cir. 1974)].

The volunteer who agrees not to be compensated raises an interesting question: May an individual provide useful services on a voluntary basis and contractually agree that the employer is not liable to pay compensation? The Wage-Hour Administrator of the Department of Labor, the official charged with administering the FLSA, has weighed in on the side of excluding volunteer services for nonprofit organizations such as schools, hospitals, and the like from the coverage of the FLSA (Opinion Letter, 1968). The cases interpreting this ruling suggest that an individual's status as an employee may depend upon the nature of the entity for whom he or she is rendering service. If the enterprise is organized for profit, then the individual rendering service is more likely to be considered an employee. Conversely, if the entity is nonprofit, the "volunteer" worker is less likely to be considered an employee.

The courts have attempted to formulate a set of rules to govern when certain educationally related work does or does not constitute employment. Generally, the cases point to a set of attributes that would indicate the existence of an employment relationship subject to the FLSA.

The Department of Labor has established a set of criteria to distinguish employees from trainees, the latter being excluded from coverage under the FLSA:

1. the training, even though it includes actual operation of the facilities of the employer, is similar to that which would be given in a vocational school;
2. the training is for the benefit of the trainees or students;
3. the trainees or students do not displace regular employees, but work under their close observation;
4. the employer-trainer derives no immediate advantage from the activities of the trainees or students, and occasionally work operations may actually be impeded;
5. the trainees or students are not necessarily entitled to a job at the conclusion of the training period; and
6. the employer and the trainees or students understand that the trainees or students are not entitled to wages for the time spent in training [U.S. Department of Labor, n.d.].

The FLSA was amended in 1985 to exclude from the definition of "employee," and thus from the act's coverage, any individual who volunteers to work for a nonfederal public agency, even if the person is paid expenses, reasonable benefits, or a nominal fee to perform the services, unless the person is also employed by that same public agency to render those services (U.S.C., title 29, sec. 203(e)(4), 1985).

A special situation arises in the case of co-op placements with agencies of the federal government. Until recently, federal agencies were categorically prohibited from accepting the services of an individual without paying regular compensation. This requirement derived from a Depression-era statute passed to prevent post office employees from being coerced into accepting unpaid days to avoid being laid off. Only in 1978 was this law amended to permit students to serve internships with federal agencies on an uncompensated basis. However, the definitions of individuals eligible to participate in such programs are rather narrowly set forth, including the requirements that the student be enrolled in a qualified institution at least half time or be on leave for not more than five months for the express purpose of participating in the work-experience program, the program was established by the federal agency, the student participates with the express consent of his or her institution, and no employees will be displaced. The regulations contain an interesting provision proscribing the use of students "to staff a position which is a normal part of the agency's work force" (C.F.R., title 5, sec. 310.101, 1986). How this differs from the prohibition against displacing existing workers is undefined.

An explanation of how the federal FLSA applies only to the employees of those employers who can reasonably be tied to "interstate commerce" is far beyond the scope of this chapter. Suffice it to say that many employers whose work is performed only in one state are nonetheless covered by the FLSA, as are schools, colleges, and universities. For those employers who are not covered, however, state minimum wage laws may apply, as they do for all employers within a state if they set higher wage bases than does the federal law.

Of considerable importance to co-op programs are the provisions of some state laws that set a time limit on the duration of work-experience activities, after which covered employment will be found to exist, even if the putative employee is a student intern. For example, the Attorney General of Michigan has construed that state's minimum wage law to impose a limit of thirteen weeks of exempted employment, after which the minimum wage statute becomes applicable. Similarly, the minimum wage law of Massachusetts, which provides for the payment of overtime for persons employed in an "occupation" (Annotated Laws of Massachusetts, title 151, sec. 1A(17), 1976), defines "occupation" as not including "work by persons being rehabilitated or trained under rehabilitation or training programs in charitable, educational or religious institutions." However, what constitutes "training programs" is not defined.

Collective Bargaining and Civil Service. If a co-op student may be, and indeed often is, an employee, the question frequently arises whether he or she is subject to civil service laws or collective bargaining agreements in place at the worksite. Many states facilitate cooperative education and internship programs through special provisions in their civil service system. In Massachusetts, for example, the State Personnel Administrator is empowered to exempt co-op students from many of the formalities of the Civil Service law, providing there is a formal certification of participation in such a program by the student's college or university.

Whether a co-op participant may (or must) be included in a collective bargaining unit is a more difficult question. The National Labor Relations Board has ruled that

> [W]here a student is employed by a commercial employer in a capacity which is related to the student's course of study the student will be excluded from a unit of full-time nonstudent employees . . . . This conclusion is based upon the fact that the commercial employer in these situations is acting as a surrogate for the educational institution, and thus, unlike the non-student employees, the students' interest in their employment is primarily educational in nature. Accordingly, the students' long-term interest in the employment relationship, including wages, hours, and conditions of employment, is necessarily minimized [N.L.R.B., Report, Vol. 229, p. 1000, 1977].

However, a co-op student may be included in a collective bargaining unit if there is a sufficient "community of interest" between the student and the workers. The tests for such inclusion are complex but merit careful scrutiny lest the co-op placement run afoul of delicate labor-management relations. Indeed, when students are to be placed with entities governed by collective bargaining agreements, program directors must pay careful attention to the terms of the existing agreement, for in some cases students are mentioned specifically. What constitutes an excluded student worker may be specifically defined, although all too often in a fashion that applies only to secondary school students. Often, however, collective bargaining agreements do not mention students directly but cover them implicitly, frequently under the rubric of "occasional employees."

It is interesting to note that at least one large labor organization, the American Federation of State, County, and Municipal Employees, has prepared suggested contract language specifically to address the use of uncompensated students at organized sites: "If volunteers are brought into any bargaining unit work area, their services shall not replace, in whole or part, nor substitute for, the services provided by regular employees. Volunteers shall not be assigned to activities which have historically been performed by regular employees within the bargaining unit" ("Beware of Volunteers," Nov.–Dec. 1981).

Application of OSHA Requirements. It is important to note that the application of the Fair Labor Standards Act is not the only attribute of employment. There are certain responsibilities of the worksite that exist independent of any agreement between student and worksite or between institution and worksite. The Occupational Safety and Health Act (OSHA) was enacted by Congress to establish minimum safety and health standards at most workplaces. Like the Fair Labor Standards Act, it is a remedial statute and thus, it is interpreted broadly and its provisions cannot be waived (U.S.C., title 29, sec. 651 et seq., 1985).

One example of "employee" status under OSHA involved some individuals who were referred to a job site by a temporary agency, but they were to remain at the site for a period of time. These individuals were considered employees of the job site for occupational safety and health purposes. The employer could not escape liability for unsafe conditions at the job site by claiming that he did not owe the duty of safe conditions to these individuals because they were not employees of his. The application of this reasoning to the co-op situation, particularly where the student is placed by his or her institution, is of considerable importance.

Another, more subtle duty that is imposed by OSHA is

the obligation to adequately train new employees. There is a line of cases that finds violations of OSHA by employers who have failed to instruct new employees adequately in the use of sophisticated equipment. A recent case, *H. C. Nutting* v. *OSHRC* (Vol. 1977–78, Par. 22016, 1980), held that "the regulation requires that an employer inform employees of safety hazards which would be known to a reasonably prudent employer or which are addressed by specific OSHA regulations."

Given that most co-op students are likely, at least at the outset of their program, to be untrained, the cases indicate that OSHA may impose additional obligations on job site supervisors to train them in proper safety procedures.

Co-op Students as Independent Contractors. All co-op students are not employees. There is a way for an individual to perform valuable services at any worksite without triggering the provisions of the FLSA or its state equivalents: establishment of independent contractor status (U.S.C., title 29, sec. 203(e)(1), 1986). The central issue when examining a relationship for possible independent contractor status is control. An independent contractor differs from an employee in that the services rendered to the employer represent the will of the employer only as to the result, not as to the means by which the results are accomplished. Thus, an employer may tell an independent contractor what it wants done, but the independent contractor decides how to do it. The courts have created an "economic realities" test to determine independent contractor status. In terms of the standards applied, an independent contractor will typically have

- Greater specialized skill than an employee
- More opportunity for profit and loss
- Greater investment in facilities of his or her own, often with employees of his or her own
- A less permanent relationship with the employer
- Less control by the employer as to the manner through which the work is performed

A highly trained or experienced student thus could qualify as an independent contractor if the specific circumstances of his or her activities meet the requirements of the five-point test. However, it should be pointed out that in setting up a work agreement, it is helpful, but not conclusive, to use the term "independent contractor"; the tax authorities, agencies, and courts uniformly look behind the label to the economic realities of the situation. If an individual is an independent contractor, not only is there no obligation on the part of an employer to pay minimum wage, withhold taxes, or pay unemployment compensation or social security taxes, but the status affects issues of liability and risk, discussed elsewhere in this chapter.

Tax Consequences of Co-op Employment. Not infrequently, students enrolled in cooperative education or other forms of experiential learning seek to avoid the withholding and even the payment of federal and state income taxes on the basis that they are not receiving compensation but rather a nontaxable "stipend." Others seek to classify their earnings under the category of "fellowships and scholarships," which under certain circumstances are exempt from taxation in accordance with the provisions of Section 117 of the Internal Revenue Code. In almost all cases, however, the earnings of students participating in compensated cooperative education programs are in fact fully taxable as ordinary income. The law is clear that where the work is being performed for the benefit of the entity that is paying the compensation, there is no avoidance under the Internal Revenue Code provision for scholarships and fellowships. Furthermore, the 1986 Tax Reform Act amends Section 117 to further limit the excludability of even a qualified scholarship or fellowship to that amount required to be used, and in fact used, for tuition, books, supplies, and equipment.

However, a co-op student may properly avoid withholding of federal and state income taxes in two fashions. If he or she is determined to be an independent contractor, there is no obligation on the part of the employer to withhold taxes. Alternatively, if the student files a certificate with the employer attesting to the expectation that he or she will not have any tax liability for the year, then the employer may avoid withholding income taxes. But neither of these approaches in any way alters the obligation of the student to report the co-op earnings as taxable income on his or her annual tax returns.

Firing Co-op Students: Rights and Consequences. A co-op student is generally subject to all of the ordinary attributes of employment, including termination. However, this power on the part of the employer may be modified under the terms of an agreement entered into between the employer and the student's institution, which may impose certain specific requirements or procedures in the event that it is determined that the student's participation should be terminated. Such agreements may provide for notice to the student or the institution, or both, and may also afford certain procedural rights. When entered into with the proper authority of the parties involved, such agreements are enforceable in the courts and can afford students a certain degree of protection that they may otherwise lack.

One ordinary consequence of being involuntarily discharged is eligibility to receive unemployment compensation. One may also be eligible for unemployment benefits if the position one is employed in ceases to exist. Illogical though it may appear at first, this theory has been advanced by a few co-op participants when they filed for unemployment compensation benefits at the end of their work period.

The Federal Unemployment Tax Act (U.S.C., title 26, sec. 3302 et seq., 1986) imposes on employers an excise tax equal to a percentage of the total wages paid to an employee, except, among other specified groups, to students enrolled in nonprofit or public educational institutions whose work is integral to the students' education program. What is important, it is not enough for the student to make such a declaration; the institution must formally certify the student's participation. Without such a certification, an employer could find itself faced with an unemployment compensation claim upon the completion of the work period. Since unemployment insurance premiums are based on claims made against the employer, such an outcome could seriously jeopardize future participation at a placement site. However, as in the case of FLSA, a student may not be required, nor indeed is he or she permitted, to waive the right to unemployment compensation if it is due.

Some states have resolved this issue by amending their

statutes, which effectuate the federal law, to exclude students engaged in work-experience programs or those who are concurrently enrolled in school. However, like the provisions of some federal regulations and collective bargaining agreements, it is not uncommon for such statutes to speak only of high school students.

The Co-op Participant as Student

The nature of the relationship between students and their institutions has undergone significant change over the years (Reidhaar, 1985). Institutions once were able to argue that since enrollment was a privilege, the rights of students were definable totally by the institutions they attended. By and large, the courts accepted this premise, so that colleges were afforded almost unmitigated discretion. "Conduct unbecoming a student" was thus deemed adequate grounds for summary dismissal. Even in the landmark case establishing that students have a constitutional due process right to a hearing prior to dismissal from a public institution, the appellate court had to reverse the trial court decision according the university unfettered authority [*Dixon* v. *Alabama State Board of Education,* 186 F. Supp. 945 (M.D. Ala. 1960) *rev'd* 294 F.2d 150 (5th Cir. 1960)].

Another popular theory was that institutions took over the role of parents when students entered institutions; whatever powers the parents had to discipline students were transferred to the institution upon the students' arrival on campus [*Stetson University* v. *Hunt,* 102 So. 637 (Fla. 1924); *Gott* v. *Berea,* 156 Ky. 376, 161 S.W. 204 (1914)]. However, this *in loco parentis* theory gave way in the late 1960s and early 1970s to what is currently the dominant explanation of the student-institution relationship, that there is a contractual relationship between the parties (Nordin, 1981-82; Ray, 1981; Jennings, 1980-81).

The relevance of this discussion to the rights of a co-op participant lies in the conception of the "contract of enrollment," an agreement that the courts have found to exist in part through the terms of formal understandings and in part through the totality of the circumstances that surround a student's enrollment, for to a very substantial degree it is the nature and content of that "contract" that defines the rights and obligations of students and institutions to each other. The definition of these rights and obligations are of particular importance in the case of activities, such as co-op participation, that may be outside the customary processes of the institution.

It is important to recognize that a binding contract may exist between an institution and its students on particular matters, such as whether a student is entitled to a co-op placement, without a "formal" contract. Thus, an institutional representation as to the nature of a cooperative education program or the rights of students who participate in it may create a contractual obligation upon the institution even though the institution never formally intended to be so bound. It is essential, therefore, that such a relationship be set forth with specificity and mutual assent. That this is often not done is the cause of much disagreement and, increasingly, costly litigation.

Indeed, some of this litigation has been spawned by the careless use of the term "learning contract" by academic officers and students alike. Yet, when properly utilized, the learning contract represents a major source of protection and guidance for the student and his or her institution. If the general "contract of enrollment" covers the traditional academic context, the cooperative education learning contract should be viewed as subsuming those elements that go beyond that traditional framework. For example, the right of the student to a co-op placement, his or her tuition and fee liability during a co-op period, the conditions under which academic credit will be awarded for the successful completion of a co-op period, and, indeed, the definition of "successful completion" all need to be incorporated within an appropriate understanding between the student and the institution. To the extent that this is embodied in a single cohesive document, the risk of confusion and misunderstanding is reduced. Conversely, to the extent the above elements must be gleaned from a variety of sources, some formal and some not, the risks are heightened.

Some of the elements that a cooperative education learning contract should contain are

- The specific responsibility of the student and the institution in identifying and consummating the co-op placement
- The nature of the relationship between the student and the institution arising out of the co-op placement
- The nature of the student's status vis-à-vis the placement site—for example, employee or independent contractor
- The duration of the co-op placement as well as the starting and ending dates
- The academic remuneration arising out of the student's participation in the co-op program—for example, the credits awarded and the terms of their award
- The method and frequency of evaluations and the manner through which such evaluations will affect the credits earned or grade received
- A description of the relative rights and responsibilities of the student, the institution, and the employer with regard to acceptance, job duties and supervision, and termination
- A description of how disputes between the student and his or her employer, or between the student and the institution, arising out of the placement will be resolved

While the cooperative education learning contract may be very effective in defining respective rights and obligations, there are certain caveats that must be observed in its use. First, if the institution is too specific concerning its own obligations, the student may well be able to enforce provisions that the institution intended to be merely exemplary. The opposite outcome is also possible. If the institution binds itself to nothing at all, a court may find that it is illusory, seeking to bind only one party (the student) while not obligating the institution to do anything. In such a case, it is likely that a court would find that no bargained-for exchange exists, relieving the student of any obligations.

Also significant is the risk that the learning contract may unwittingly establish duties from which unintended results could follow. For example, if the agreement provides that the co-op coordinator will visit the student on the job site during the first month of a semester-long program, an obligation is created not only that such a visit will take place but that it may have certain consequences, such as determining the appropriateness of the placement. If the promised visit does not take place, and the student suffers harm as a result, a breach-of-contract action may lie against the institution.

If there is no cooperative education learning contract, the terms and conditions of the program will be deduced from the entirety of the circumstances. Determining the nature of that agreement is not always a simple matter. Once there is deemed to be mutual assent to an agreed-upon set of conditions, a contract exists, even if all the terms are not specifically agreed upon; if the essential terms are set, the courts will infer those additional terms to effectuate the intent of the parties. And, where there is no meeting of the minds and yet one person has rendered service or has given up something for the benefit of another in the belief that a contract exists, the courts may order the benefitting party to appropriately compensate the party who provided the service. Also, the contracts need not be made only by a party or its principal officers; often a party's agent, remote from formal authority, will be held to have the power to bind a party by contract where another has reasonably relied on that person's conduct or representations. Thus, there have been examples of successful student suits based upon improper counseling by faculty members, even though the faculty member lacked the formal authority to bind the institution [*Blank* v. *Board of Higher Education,* 51 Misc. 2d 724, 273 N.Y.S. 2d 796 (1966)]. The "contract of enrollment" between the student and the institution was sufficiently modified by the faculty representations that the student's reliance became cognizable under law. Likewise, a program announcement that sets forth conditions or attributes of the co-op program, and upon which a student relied to his or her detriment, may effectively modify more formally adopted institutional policy if the student's reliance was not unreasonable under the circumstances.

The recourse available to students for violation of their rights has been considerably broadened in recent years. While in some respects any discussion of rights arising out of student-institutional contracts is premature because the law is not yet settled, there are enough cases to allow one to begin to discern a pattern. Certainly, students have been victorious in cases that once were shunned by the courts as involving academic judgments [*Steinberg* v. *Chicago Medical School,* 371 N.E.2d 634 (Ill. 1977)]. Indeed, the traditional distinction that once existed between "disciplinary" actions and "academic" concerns is fast eroding [*Brookins* v. *Bonnell,* 362 F. Supp. 379 (E.D. Pa. 1973)]. Both of these facts imply increased judicial intervention into institutional conditions. On a more subtle note, they change the institutional atmosphere: more is now negotiable and more is enforceable on both sides. More attention must therefore be given to agreements that predetermine respective rights and responsibilities. It is obvious, for example, that an institution must represent itself fairly to a prospective student. If an institution alleges that it offers a co-op program, students who enroll in or attend the institution may justifiably rely on the program's existence [*Peretti* v. *Montana,* 464 F. Supp. 784 (D. Mont. 1979) *rev'd on other grounds*—661 F.2d 756 (9th Cir. 1981)].

Co-op placements raise another set of institutional issues that transcend the academic. What are the rights of the institution to discipline a student for conduct arising out of his or her cooperative education activities? Until recently, the "academic-disciplinary" distinction was talismanic. If an institution could convince the court that the dispute was best characterized as an "academic" matter, then, subject to very limited exceptions, the court would uphold the determination of the institution. If, however, the student could persuade the court that the matter was "disciplinary" in character, then the results were quite different [*Sofair* v. *SUNY Upstate Medical Center College of Medicine,* 377 N.E.2d 730 (1970)]. Today, however, this distinction is in danger of evaporating. In the landmark *Horowitz* case [*Board of Curators of the University of Missouri* v. *Horowitz,* 435 U.S. 78 (1978)], the student achieved excellent grades in all of her classroom work. Yet she was dismissed from the University of Missouri Medical School because she failed to perform well in the clinical experience (practicum) component of her curriculum. The student sued for reinstatement, alleging an abridgement of her fundamental rights. The Supreme Court, in deciding for the institution, reaffirmed the traditional judicial uneasiness to become involved in academic decision making. However, in a strong dissent, Justice Marshall compared the *Horowitz* case to earlier high school disciplinary dismissal cases. He noted that in both cases, students were being dismissed from their institutions on account of their conduct, not their academic performance. (In the high school case, the Court had required some form of hearing before the student could be suspended, while in *Horowitz* the majority did not address squarely the question of whether a hearing should have been required.)

This case has triggered considerable interest on the part of those responsible for experiential education programs. Analysis of the case indicates that academic deference is likely to be less justified when conduct is at issue, rather than achievement in a traditional academic context. Following this line of reasoning, a court might well find that students in a co-op program have a right to a hearing if they are dismissed from their placement, or if they are dissatisfied with the nature of the work to which they have been assigned. A court is likely to be more willing to examine the evaluation of a student in an experiential context, although the same court might be loath to do the same in a traditional academic course.

The conclusion for those involved in developing and administering experiential learning programs is the need to ensure that the relationship among the student, the employer, and the school is, to the maximum extent feasible, regularized and committed to a set of consistent standards. The right of the employer to accept, supervise, and dismiss students should be clearly stated and, where limited by the institution, those limitations should be enshrined in the form of an enforceable agreement. It is no longer sufficient to claim that the conduct of the employer is separate and apart from that of the institution. If the co-op program is an integral part of the academic enterprise of the institution, then the conduct of the employer may well be ascribed to the school itself, with the result that due-process standards may apply to any action that adversely affects the interests of the student. Whether a court would find that a co-op placement constitutes a property interest is unsettled, but such a conclusion would not require the breaking of any new legal ground, given the comparable treatment of job tenure.

Cooperative Education and Student Financial Aid

A very substantial proportion of college students receive some form of assistance under one of the several federal and state student financial aid programs. The proper treatment of cooperative education employment earnings is essential to ensure that the student is treated fairly and that participation in the co-op program does not work to the student's disadvantage. The problems with co-op programs as they relate to student aid are twofold. First, the institution must be careful to properly treat co-op earnings so as not to effectively negate the economic value of the placement. Second, the institution must configure the placements so as to enable the student to obtain all of the financial assistance he or she requires and is eligible to receive.

Except where cooperative education placements are need-based and their earnings are packaged by the institution as part of a student's financial aid program, as would be the case where the co-op placement is funded under the Federal College Work/Study Program, co-op earnings are not supposed to be treated as financial assistance (U.S. Department of Education, 1981). Rather, to the extent they are known to the institution, they should be counted as part of a student's own financial resources. The difficulty comes in where the institution does not know, at the time it packages aid for the student, whether or not the student will be participating in a compensated cooperative education placement during the forthcoming academic period. Where the institution does not know that a student will be participating in a compensated co-op placement, it is not under any obligation to hypothesize earnings. Thus, where the financial aid office has no knowledge of a student's participation in compensated co-op placements or, even when knowing of the placements, has not received accurate information as to the level of compensation, then the earnings do not have to be taken into account. Conversely, of course, where the financial aid office is aware of the prospective earnings or obtains reliable information during the course of the award year that a student has a new source of income through a co-op placement, the student's resources must be credited with the prescribed proportion of the earnings and the student's aid award adjusted accordingly.

The second issue concerns the treatment of the period of cooperative education participation as continuing enrollment. Were the school not to treat the co-op period as a period of enrollment, the student would be deprived of access to student aid for that period. Where the student is receiving academic credit for the co-op period, particularly through the vehicle of enrollment in a catalogue-listed co-op course, the school should regard the student as maintaining his or her enrollment.

The institution must also determine the equivalent intensity of enrollment of the co-op period. Many colleges construe a co-op period as equivalent to full-time study, rendering the student eligible for the maximum financial assistance consistent with his or her demonstrated needs. However, in doing so, it is not necessary for the school to grant a student the credit equivalent of full-time enrollment. It is acceptable for the institution to afford the student the level and type of credit commensurate with its own academic standards for co-op participation, while still declaring the student to be on full-time status.

Finally, it has always been the case, and in recent years it has become explicit, that College Work/Study (CWS) funds may be used to support credit-bearing co-op placements, so long as the placements meet the substantive requirements of the CWS program. The fact that a student is receiving both academic credit and financial assistance through CWS in no way violates any provision of law. Indeed, the Higher Education Amendments of 1986 reinforce the long-standing requirement that, to the extent practicable, CWS placements be related to a student's academic or vocational goals. In addition, there is now a program that allows institutions, on a limited basis, to use CWS funds to subsidize off-campus employment in the for-profit sector. Notably, such placements must be related to a student's course of studies (Higher Education Amendments, sec. 443(c)

(4), 1986). Thus, the opportunity to combine CWS with cooperative education has now become a very powerful tool that should not be ignored by program administrators.

Liability and Risk of Loss

The conduct of a cooperative education program, like any activity carried out by an educational institution, carries with it certain risks. These can be divided into two major categories: (1) injuries to or damages sustained by the participating student; and (2) injuries to or damages sustained by others as a result of the conduct of the participating student.

Generally, those responsible for the administration of co-op programs tend to concentrate on the former. It is, after all, their students who may be at risk, and therefore it is only natural that first attention be paid to protecting their interests. But a comprehensive risk-management program must look not only to protecting the participating students but also to protecting those for or around whom they are working, as well as protecting the interests of the institution itself.

It is important to note at the outset that the question of liability and risk of loss is not a function of who can sue whom in a court of law. Under our judicial system, it takes precious little to bring a cause of action in court. What is important, however, is identifying who may be responsible for a particular course of conduct which results in injury or loss and, secondarily, who may ultimately be held financially accountable for the damages that arise from that course of conduct. These are quite often separable issues, the determination of which depends on rather independent elements. Simply put, the party that is ultimately financially accountable may not necessarily be the party whose conduct caused the loss. Indeed, the entire concept of insurance is intended to provide a loss-shifting mechanism that protects the insured party from actual financial consequences.

It would seem self-evident that the responsible party for damages caused by the student is the student. However, while the proximate cause of the loss may indeed be the co-op student's conduct, it is most frequently the case that he or she will not be held financially accountable for damages. As a general principle, responsibility for the consequences of such conduct lies with the employer, not the employee. In truth, this makes eminently good sense: the employee is assumed to be acting on behalf of and carrying out the instructions of the employer, and it is the employer who benefits from the work performed by the employee. Thus, it is almost always the case that the employer will be held responsible for loss occasioned by a co-op participant in the conduct of his or her work assignment. But the use of the term "almost" recognizes that there are exceptions to this rule. For example, the student may be an independent contractor. Where this is found to be the case, and the mere declaration of such status by the employer and the student is not dispositive, and where it is determined that the student was authorized to and did exercise considerable independent judgment in the conduct of his or her work, the employer may escape liability, which instead may fall directly upon the student participant.

Further, the student's college may have so contributed to the circumstances surrounding the loss that it is held accountable for the resulting damages. If, for example, the cooperative education administrator at the college was aware of a particular characteristic of the student that should have excluded him or her from specific types of activities but nonetheless placed the student in an assignment where he or she would have to perform those activities, losses arising from the occurrence of the potential event might be shifted back to the institution itself. An illustrative example may be useful to put this concept in proper perspective. A particular student is known by the institution to suffer from seizures. Despite this knowledge, the student is placed in a position which will require the operation of dangerous machines (of which a motor vehicle is unquestionably one). The employer is not advised of the student's problem. The student is assigned to drive a motor vehicle, has a seizure, and injures third parties. Who is accountable?

Obviously, the injured parties would file a claim against the employer as well as against the student, under the theory discussed above. But the employer, learning after the fact of the student's limitations, would doubtless seek to shift both responsibility for the injuries and the burden of loss to the institution for failing to act reasonably in light of the information available to it. The employer would argue that the institution should have reasonably foreseen the loss that did occur, yet it did nothing to prevent its occurrence, even though it knew, or should have known, the risk involved. If in fact the institution, knowing of the student's limitations, proceeded to make the placement, knowing or having reason to believe that the student's conduct of the work could be hazardous to others, then it is altogether possible for liability to accrue back to the student's college. Note that in the above example, it is not merely responsibility for the financial loss that is being shifted to the institution. Rather, the institution is being held accountable for the loss because of its conduct, in this case, arising both out of its action in placing the student and its lack of action in warning the employer.

Therefore, it is clear that the first and most important question that must be answered in any risk-management discussion of co-op programs is an analysis of to whom a certain duty of care is owed. Second, it must be determined what the nature of that duty of care is. Finally, it must be ascertained who will be financially responsible if a breach occurs. The relative rights and responsibilities of the student, employer, and institution are closely intertwined. As noted in the above example, the employer may have the right to rely on the institution with regard to the quality of the students placed with it or at least may rely on it enough to expect to be advised when such a student has a potentially hazardous limitation. Similarly, while the employer clearly has the obligation to employ students in a safe place, the school may have a parallel obligation not to place them in a situation known to be unreasonably hazardous. The case of *Wuerffel* v. *Westinghouse* [*Wuerffel* v. *Westinghouse* 372 A.2d 659 (N.J. Super 1977)] is instructive in this regard. In that case, the student was employed under a work-experience program administered by his college, Drexel University. The student was injured as a result of the negligence of the employer, Westinghouse. As expected, the student brought suit against Westinghouse. But, because recovery might be limited under the state Workmen's Compensation law, the student also sued the university and the co-op coordinator, alleging that he was owed a duty of care by the institution and its employees not to place him in a situation likely to result in his injury. The student argued that the school and the cooperative education coordinator owed him an affirmative duty to determine that the workplace was safe before exposing him to the risk of working there.

The court dismissed the action against the university on an interpretation of the "charitable immunity" statute of the state. More to the point, the court dismissed the action against the co-op coordinator, but on a rather novel theory. The judge ruled that since the coordinator's job description did not require him to investigate the safety of a particular assignment, he was not under any obligation to conduct such inspections and therefore could not be held responsible for the conditions the student found when he reported to work. Both the school and the coordinator escaped without liability, but neither could take much comfort in the ruling. For the school, its victory was based on the thinnest legal protections. The escape of the co-op coordinator was even more perilous, since the implication of the decision was that if the job description had even suggested responsibility on the part of the coordinator to determine whether a placement appeared safe, the case could have gone otherwise. Given the lack of precision in the drafting of institutional job descriptions and, indeed, the penchant for adding responsibilities that might not in fact ever be implemented, the risk of a different outcome is very real.

What *Wuerffel* does point out, however, is the degree to which the actions of the institution may be considered in a determination of whose conduct caused a particular adverse outcome. Summarizing the above examples, it is clear that the institution owes a duty of care to the other parties in the co-op relationship—the student and the employer—to use the information it has available, or which it reasonably should have had available, to prevent harm to any of the parties or to the public at large. If the institution fails to do so, it is at its own considerable peril. Thus, both the employer and the institution may be responsible for losses or injuries sustained by students or caused by them in the conduct of their employment.

Techniques of Risk Management

The Waiver. Many schools and co-op employers have asked—and not infrequently demanded—that their co-op students/employees execute a "waiver of liability" for injuries or damages arising out of the co-op placement. The ostensible purpose of requiring the signing of a "waiver" is to preclude the student from bringing an action against the school or the employer if he or she is injured or otherwise damaged. However, unless the terms of the so-called waiver are extremely artfully drawn, the value of such a document may be negligible or non-existent.

It is a fundamental principle of the law that a person cannot waive another's negligence. A student's declaration that he or she absolves the parent institution (or the employer) of all liability for all courses of conduct on the part of the employer (or the institution), no matter how egregious, will not serve to protect the institution (or the employer) if the student, in the conduct of his work assignment, is injured as a result of the negligence of his or her employer or institution. Indeed, the use of blanket waivers can be extremely dangerous, because it may lull the institution (or employer) into a sense of complacency and, in doing so, expose the college and the employer to even greater risks by making more prudent actions seem unnecessary.

Assumption of Risk. While a person cannot, even voluntarily, waive in advance the consequences of someone else's negligence, under certain circumstances a person may assume the risks of a course of conduct and therefore absolve another party of potential liability. For example, it is common for participants in hazardous recreational activities, such as white water rafting, to be required to sign an "assumption of risk" form before being allowed to venture out into the river. By so consenting, the participant assumes the ordinary and reasonable risks attendant upon the sport. If the raft capsizes and the participant is injured, he or she will not be able to sustain an action against the operators of the trip.

Similarly, a student participating in a cooperative education program could reasonably be asked, as a condition of a particular placement, to assume certain specified risks ordinarily attendant upon the work to be undertaken. To be effective, however, an assumption of risk must meet certain minimum requirements: (1) it must be specific to the risks involved, specifying the type of activity out of which the risks may arise; (2) the risks must be reasonable and foreseeable; and (3) the student must have the requisite knowledge and maturity to have willfully assumed the risks.

The application of this approach to cooperative education students is straightforward. A student may be asked to agree to assume certain risks attendant upon a particular co-op placement as a condition of the placement. If the risks are set forth with reasonable specificity, if the risks are reasonable and foreseeable, and if the student has sufficient knowledge, experience, or expertise to understand the extent of the risks involved, then the courts will probably construe an assumption of those risks as effective. But, if any of the key elements are missing, the assumption of risk is likely to be entirely ineffective. Such omission may be entirely inadvertent, as where an institution refers an asthmatic student to a placement in a flour mill. The school may assume that the student, in signing an assumption of risk, knows that the air in such facilities is heavily laden with dust. But, if the student is not aware of that fact or does not relate it to his or her medical condition, the assumption of risk may not protect the school against liability for harm to the student arising out of his or her exposure to the atmosphere at the plant.

The question of maturity is perhaps the most difficult to quantify: what a senior engineering student might be expected to know about the risks of working in a chemical plant is quite different from what can be expected of a freshman. It is particularly important not to lose sight of the "reasonableness" factor when dealing with college students. While an experienced adult may indeed assume the risk of climbing into a cage full of tigers, a college student with limited experience cannot be asked, with impunity, to assume comparable risks. Further, some states restrict the legal authority of minors to waive any rights through an assumption of risk, absent the concurrence of a parent or guardian.

There are certain risks one cannot assume. These are primarily risks arising out of the negligence of another party. Thus, in the white water rafting example, had the operator of the trip issued defective life vests, the waivers signed by the participants would not have protected him from liability had an injury arisen as a result of that negligent act. Similarly, even if the student in *Wuerffel* had signed a waiver in favor of his employer, he still would not have been barred from recovery on the basis of the company's negligence.

Finally, it is important to note that an assumption of risk should always be in writing, setting forth each of the elements described above. Proving an oral assumption of risk can be extremely difficult and in some circumstances impossible.

Indemnification. A third commonly used technique in the management of cooperative education programs is the indemnification agreement. Through this device, one of the parties contractually agrees to "indemnify" one or more of the other parties against any losses it may sustain as a result of its participation in the program. If the indemnity is unlimited, then the indemnified party is protected regardless of whose conduct causes the loss, including its own. Often, however, the indemnification agreement is limited, usually excluding from coverage losses arising out of the negligence or willful misconduct of the indemnified party.

Indemnification is a useful mechanism for shifting the burden of loss. As such, it is comparable to an insurance policy in that it does not render any party's conduct any less actionable but either transfers accountability for that action to another party or requires a party to remain accountable for its own actions. The analogy with insurance is important for several reasons. First, the value of an insurance policy is entirely contingent upon the ability of the insurance company to pay its claims. Similarly, the value of an indemnification agreement is dependent upon the ability of the indemnifier to assume the burden of any loss covered by the agreement. If the indemnifier lacks the financial ability to handle the loss, the indemnification agreement is worthless. Thus, it is of primary importance to ascertain that an indemnifier has the financial capacity to make good on any likely loss. This is particularly important if an institution requests an indemnification agreement from employers with whom it places co-op participants. If the employer is a small community organization or similar impecunious entity, the fact that it signs such an agreement has little actual value in protecting the interests of the institution. Of course, it is for just this reason that students should never be required to indemnify anyone as a condition of their participation. Illusory indemnification is far worse than none at all.

A second essential element of indemnification involves the legal capacity of the indemnifier to respond to the claim. Employers sometimes agree to take co-op participants if the school agrees to indemnify the employer for any loss. But if the school is a public entity, it may be barred under state law from entering into any such agreement. If a problem occurs and the employer seeks protection from the school under the indemnification agreement, an interesting lawsuit may arise, with the school defending on the basis of a lack of capacity to enter into the agreement and the employer arguing that the school, having induced it to accept the student with the promise of indemnification, cannot now hide behind the statute. This creates the real possibility of shifting liability to the individuals responsible for the school's signing the indemnification agreement. Likewise, indemnification agreements with employers may be unenforceable if the employer has statutory protection, as is usually the case with public agencies.

Finally, even if the indemnifier has the resources and the legal capacity to protect the indemnified party, public policy may render the agreement ineffectual. If the conduct of the indemnified party is egregious, the courts may determine that the public good forbids the shifting of accountability to another. This is particularly common when the loss is caused by the willful neglect of one party.

As indemnification agreements are contractual in nature, they are narrowly construed, and in most jurisdictions they must be in writing to be enforceable. As with any contractual commitment, and particularly in this case, because of the financial risk, an indemnification agreement should always be subject to appropriate review and signature only by a duly authorized official.

Insurance. The simplest form of protection against losses arising out of the conduct of a cooperative education program is the provision of adequate insurance coverage. To be complete, an insurance program should cover all potential risks: injuries or losses to the participant students or those caused by their participation. The insurance should cover losses arising out of the direct conduct of the insured party or attributed to that party.

Some employers decline to accept co-op placements because they claim their insurance does not cover them in such cases. This is rarely correct: certainly, compensated co-op students are, for virtually all purposes and certainly as to inclusion under business liability insurance, employees of the entity where they are working. In most cases, students who are working without compensation would still fall within the scope of general liability insurance with respect to either their own losses or their actions on behalf of the employer that cause loss to others.

However, unpaid co-op students are generally not covered under state Workmen's Compensation statutes. This poses a problem for employers, since, if a student is not within the scope of the Workmen's Compensation statute, he or she has the right to seek unlimited damages for injury or loss arising out of the negligence of the employer, a right that is severely limited under Workmen's Compensation statutes. This, of course, is a double-edged sword: a student who is covered by Workmen's Compensation does not have to prove negligence to recover medical expenses and any loss of earnings.

Whether the conduct of a student assigned to a co-op placement is covered by his or her institution's liability insurance raises an interesting set of questions. Generally, an institution is not responsible for the conduct of its students beyond the confines of the campus. But, there are ample cases where an institution was held responsible for the conduct of or losses to students arising out of off-campus activities, where it could be shown that the institution had a direct relationship to that activity. The degree and extent of the relationship drives the liability issue and sets the threshhold question of whether a school's liability insurance will apply.

At one extreme, there is the co-op program, where the only involvement of the institution is to grant after the fact academic recognition. The school is not involved in developing placements, evaluating in any way the qualifications of a given student for a particular job, or matching students to jobs. In such a case, it is doubtful that there would be sufficient contact to create institutional liability for the conduct or safety of the student, and therefore any insurance issue. However, if the college screened prospective placements, evaluated the compatibility of students and placements, and made appropriate matches, then it is entirely likely that losses arising out of those placements could be attributed back to the college, provided it could be shown that the institution was negligent in the conduct of its responsibilities.

In most cases, it is a relatively simple matter to have an institution's general liability policy amended to expressly incorporate the activities of co-op participants. It is important to recognize that in doing this the institution is in no way changing its own liability: it is not somehow assuming the liability of the employer by virtue of bringing co-op participants within its insurance umbrella. What it is doing is ensuring that if the institution's conduct creates liability, its insurance carrier will pay the bill, rather than the institution itself. Insurance therefore differs from indemnification in that it only shifts financial accountability from the party itself to a separate entity, not to one of the other parties to the cooperative education agreement.

Entirely dependent upon the terms of the individual policy obtained by the college, the student health insurance may not be in effect during the co-op period, particularly where the student is not officially enrolled in a cooperative education course but rather simply documents his or her experience at the end of the period. Even where students register for a co-op course, their health insurance may be written so as to exclude such periods or to exclude injuries obtained while at work and not attending classes. The solution is to ensure that the insurance policy covers co-op participation or to provide students with access to a special policy during such periods.

Faculty and administrators frequently become concerned as to their personal liability for the conduct of their institution's cooperative education program. Generally, this fear is misplaced. If the college employee is carrying out the duties of his or her employment, any losses arising out of the conduct of those duties will be imputed to the institution, not to the individual. For example, in the *Wuerffel* case, had the court held against the co-op director, it is clear that his college would have been the financially responsible party. Of course, if the college employee steps outside of his or her duties, and it is clear that such action was not subsequently expressly or implicitly embraced by the institution, then personal liability could attach where such action causes a loss. The risk of this happening, however, is so remote that the insurance that has been made available is extremely inexpensive. As it is a fundamental truth of the insurance industry that the level of premiums is directly correlated to the degree of risk, low premiums for "educator professional liability insurance" are a rather good gauge of the very small risks involved. Indeed, one major carrier reported never having to pay a claim arising out of such a set of circumstances. Insurance for the individual faculty member or administrator is far more for the comfort it affords than for protection against any real risks.

Cooperative Education and Civil Rights

Virtually without exception, because they are beneficiaries of various federal aid programs, colleges and universities that offer cooperative education are covered under several civil rights laws. With regard to discrimination based upon race, color, or national origin, the statutory authority is Title VI of the Civil Rights Act of 1964: "Sec. 601. No person in the

United States shall, on the grounds of race, color, or national
origin, be excluded from participation in, be denied the benefits
of, or be subjected to discrimination under any program or activity receiving Federal financial assistance" (U.S.C., title 42,
sec. 601, 2000d, 1964).

Sex-based discrimination is proscribed under the provisions of Title IX of the Education Amendments of 1972: "Sec.
901(a). No person in the United States shall, on the basis of sex,
be excluded from participation in, be denied the benefits of, or
be subjected to discrimination under any education program or
activity receiving Federal financial assistance" (U.S.C., title 20,
sec. 901(a), 1681, 1972).

Age-based discrimination is similarly proscribed under the
provisions of Title III of the Age Discrimination Act of 1975:
"Sec. 303. . . . [N]o person in the United States shall, on the
basis of age, be excluded from participation in, be denied the
benefits of, or be subjected to discrimination under, any program or activity receiving Federal financial assistance" (U.S.C.,
title 42, sec. 303, 6102, 1975).

Finally, discrimination against the handicapped is dealt
with under the provisions of Section 504 of the Rehabilitation
Act of 1973: "No otherwise qualified handicapped individual in
the United States . . . shall, solely by reason of his handicap, be
excluded from participation in, be denied the benefits of, or be
subjected to discrimination under any program or activity receiving federal financial assistance" (U.S.C., title 29, sec. 504,
794, 1973).

The sanction for violating any of these provisions is the
termination of federal funding to the institution (U.S.C., title
20, sec. 1683, 1986; title 42, sec. 200d-1, 1986; title 42, sec.
6104(b), 1986). It is unsettled whether the termination is for all
federal funding or only for that of the particular agency enforc-
ing the statute, and whether it is only for the particular "program or activity" in which the discrimination has occurred. The
legal definition of "program or activity receiving federal financial assistance" is not spelled out in the law and is only imper-
fectly defined in the implementing regulations. It has been left
to the courts to define the scope of this term. Regardless, the

conduct of a program supported in any respect by the federal government, and more particularly access to its benefits, must be guided by the nondiscrimination requirements of the several acts.

The application of these rules to cooperative education programs raises a host of rather complex issues, since it is not only the conduct of the institution that may affect compliance. If one defines "participation in" the program to include access to placements, then the conduct of the employers in accepting (and in the case of the handicapped, accommodating) cooperative education students must be considered by the institution, for if a student is denied access to a particular placement because of his or her race, sex, age, or handicap, it is altogether possible for that denial to constitute a violation of the statutes on the part of the institution. This is particularly so if the institution is a party to the action, but it can be the case even where the institution's role is passive. The regulations of the Department of Education that implement Title VI speak quite specifically to the issue of second-hand discrimination (C.F.R., title 34, sec. 100.3(b), 1986).

> Sec. 100.3(b). Specific discriminatory actions prohibited—(1) A recipient [institution] under any program to which this part applies may not, directly *or through contractual or other arrangements,* on ground of race, color or national origin:
>
> (i) Deny any individual any service, financial aid, or other benefit provided under the program;
>
> (ii) Provide any service, financial aid, or other benefit to an individual which is different, or is provided in a different manner, from that provided others in the program;
>
> (iii) Subject an individual to segregation or separate treatment in any manner related to his receipt of any service, financial aid or other benefit under the program;
>
> (iv) Restrict an individual in any way in the enjoyment of any advantage or privilege enjoyed

by others receiving any service, financial aid, or
other benefit under the program;

(v) Treat an individual differently from others in determining whether he satisfies any admission, enrollment, quota, eligibility, membership, or
other requirement or condition which individuals
must meet in order to be provided any service, financial aid, or other benefit provided under the
program;

(vi) *Deny an individual an opportunity to
participate in the program through the provision
of services or otherwise or afford him an opportunity to do so which is different from that afforded
others under the program* . . . . (2) A recipient [in-
stitution], in determining the types of services, financial aid, or benefits, or facilities which will be
provided under any such program, or the class of
individuals to whom, or the situations in which
such services, financial aid, other benefits, or facilities will be provided under any such program, or
the class of individuals to be afforded an opportunity to participate in any such program, may not directly or through contractual or other arrangements utilize criteria or methods of administration
which have the effect of subjecting individuals to
discrimination because of their race, color or national origin . . . . [C.F.R., title 45, sec. 80.3(b),
1986; italics added].

The basic problem arises in the following context: a prospective employer informs the institution that it would be pleased
to accept co-op placements, but it is seeking only a particular
class of student. Certainly, if the employer said it would only
accept white males, there is little doubt that the representatives
of the institution would decline to have anything to do with the
company, quite independent of any legal compulsion. But, what
of the case where the employer only wants to interview minorities and women? What if the employer justifies this request by

explaining that the company is seeking to meet its affirmative action requirements?

Under such circumstances, the institution is in a serious quandary. If it complies with the request, and if a white male student, for example, applies to be referred to the employer and is refused referral by the institution, that student would be well within his rights to file a complaint that the school is violating Title IX by denying him access to participation on the basis of his sex. The same would be true if the school, knowing that the student would not be accepted, nonetheless went through the motions of making the referral. Even if a comparable placement were to be offered, the fact that he was excluded from the particular placement may be sufficient to find against the institution. On the other hand, if the school declines to comply with the request, it chances losing access to the placement site.

Of course, the simplest solution is for the institution to convince the employer to interview and consider all applicants, regardless of race, sex, age, or handicap. The institution certainly may agree to make a special effort to encourage minorities and women to apply for the placement. This is not only entirely acceptable conduct, but it is consistent with public policy.

However, it is all too often the case that the employer remains adamant: minorities and women only or no one at all. The prudent solution is to forego the placement. This is not to say that race or sex cannot be taken into account in employment, as that is frequently done in the conduct of affirmative action programs, whether voluntary or under governmental mandate. But the right of an employer to so discriminate does not extend to the ability of an institution to exclude any of its students from full participation in an institutional program because of their race or sex. The risk of liability arising out of a discrimination complaint is far too great, relative to the value of retaining one employer (even if that employer happens to be a federal agency, as is, regrettably, sometimes the case). Further, if the school ignores the limitation imposed by the employer and refers students without regard to race and sex, and then finds a pattern of overt or covert discrimination in the conduct of the employer, it would be well advised to cease making referrals to that employer until the employer changes its policy.

In dealing with equal opportunity, it is important to recognize that, with the notable exception of Title VI, the anti-discrimination statutes are somewhat less than absolute. Although the general language of each of the four acts is quite similar, they diverge in a very important respect. While Title IV of the Civil Rights Act is essentially devoid of any exceptions, the Congress not having contemplated any circumstances which would justify racial discrimination, each of the other statutes allows for both general and specific exceptions. With regard to sex, the general exception is the "bona fide occupational qualification" (BFOQ), which affords an affected entity the opportunity to demonstrate that a facially discriminatory policy (that is, one that appears to favor one sex over the other) is founded in the legitimate necessities of the work to be performed. Perhaps the most common example is the requirement for certain activities that the applicant be able to lift a heavy load, effectively disqualifying most women. Where such lifting is, in fact, a normal requirement, such a test is allowable. But, where it is used as a subterfuge for discriminating against women, it is not. Thus, if a co-op employer were to require the school to screen applicants, sending it only those who could lift 100 pounds, it would not violate Title IX to do so, if the institution was satisfied that the requirement was legitimately related to the work. But, if the co-op placement was for office work, such a requirement would clearly be a subterfuge to exclude women, and therefore would be impermissible.

On the other hand, there are cases where a declared sex requirement is in fact within the law. An employer who is seeking students to work in a rape counseling program would certainly be within its rights to specify women only, and that would not be offensive to the requirements of Title IX. However, the courts have viewed the BFOQ as a limited exception to the non-discrimination rule, and the burden has frequently been placed on the entity claiming the exception to demonstrate that a particular action does not have the effect of discriminating.

Responding to the needs of handicapped students is perhaps the greatest challenge to the cooperative education administrator. Again, Section 504 of the Rehabilitation Act makes clear that a handicapped person cannot be discriminated against in his or her ability to participate in a program or activity in which there are federal funds. Here, however, the concept of BFOQ is joined by the parallel concept of "reasonable accommodation." A covered institution is required to make "reasonable accommodation" to the needs of its handicapped students. This may entail the provision of interpreters, special equipment, and, most commonly, assuring reasonable physical access. In the case of a cooperative education program, it also means dealing with special needs of handicapped students in their access to and placement in work assignments.

Once again, the institution may find itself in a situation where its obligation exceeds that of the prospective employer. A particular employer may not be covered by Section 504, but that does not relieve the institution from the obligation to afford a handicapped student reasonable access to all programs and benefits, including co-op. Thus, an employer might be unwilling to build a ramp to afford wheelchair access to its offices and may not be under any compulsion to do so. However, if a wheelchair-bound student applies for that position, and he or she is qualified but for the access limitation, it may be seen as an obligation upon the school to either secure from the employer a commitment to afford physical access or to strike the employer from its referral list. However, an employer need not remake its operations to accommodate to the needs of a handicapped student: the same wheelchair-bound student would not be considered a qualified applicant for a position which required as a regular duty climbing upon equipment to make adjustments.

A major problem in dealing with handicapped students is the need to strike a balance between accommodating their needs and protecting their rights of privacy. The Family and Student Educational Rights and Privacy Act, commonly known as the Buckley Amendments, forbids an institution from releasing all but the most rudimentary information about a student to most third parties without the student's consent (U.S.C., title 20, sec. 1232g, 1986). As discussed earlier, a student with a physical ailment may require special consideration in being placed, as would be the case with the student with a history of seizures. Section 504 mandates the school to seek to accommodate his or her needs in affording access to its programs. But the Privacy Act limits the ability of the school to divulge information about the student's infirmity without his or her consent. If the student will not consent to the release of information about his or her physical limitations, and if the school considers divulging that information essential to protect the student's health and welfare, as well as that of others around him or her, then the only prudent course of action is to decline to make any placement of the student where there is any likelihood that the student will be required to perform hazardous work.

Finally, there is the question of whether a school can limit participation in its cooperative education program to students with more than a specified grade point average. Does excluding certain students because their grades were not high enough violate any civil rights law? As a general rule, the answer is in the negative; a school has the right to set whatever academic standards it deems appropriate. However, like the BFOQ test discussed above, the academic standard must be fair, not only in its purpose but in its effect, and must not unreasonably burden any protected class. If setting a 2.5 grade point average as the minimum to participate in the school's cooperative education program can be defended as ensuring that only those students with a reasonable grasp of the academic process should take the time for co-op, that standard will not be found defective. But if the same standard is found to have the effect of excluding a disproportionate number of students in a particular ethnic category, and if the standard is not clearly and closely related to the reasonable academic needs of the program, then a violation could be found to exist.

Conclusion

Cooperative education does indeed operate in two legal worlds. While the conduct of any educational program should be guided by what is proper and appropriate to enable it to accomplish its academic goals, by what should be done, rather than by what is prescribed by law or what must be done, the latter inevitably constrains and directs the former. It is therefore the obligation of administrators of cooperative education programs to understand the broad sweep of the legal obligations under which such programs must function. It is also important to recognize that co-op is generally a low-risk enterprise, so that abiding by the requirements of law ought not to impose any undue burden upon the program or the institution. The emphasis should be on preventive law, rather than upon reacting to crises. A periodic "legal audit" of the program should be conducted by the institution's counsel to ensure that the program does comply with all the legal requirements, and to assist the program administrators in making the program as effective and problemfree as possible.

References

"Beware of Volunteers." *Collective Bargaining Reporter,* Nov.-Dec. 1981, p. 2.

Jennings, E. "Breach of Contract Suits by Students Against Postsecondary Education Institutions: Can They Succeed?" *Journal of College and University Law,* 1980-81, 7, 191.

Nordin, V. "The Contract to Educate: Towards a More Workable Theory of the Student-University Relationship." *Journal of College and University Law,* 1981-82, 8, 141-144.

Opinion Letter, No. 927 CCH W-H Admin. Rul. Nov. 1966-March 1969, sec. 30,939 (May 29, 1968).

Ray, L. "Toward Contractual Rights for College Students." *Journal of Law and Education,* 1981, *10,* 163.

Reidhaar, D. "The Assault on the Citadel: Reflections on a Quarter Century of Change in the Relationships Between the Student and the University." *Journal of College and University Law,* 1985, *12,* 343.

U.S. Department of Education. *The Bulletin.* Washington, D.C.: Office of Student Financial Assistance, U.S. Department of Education, Jan. 1981.

U.S. Department of Labor. *Wage and Hour Division: Field Operations Handbook.* Washington, D.C.: U.S. Department of Labor, n.d., secs. 10(b)11 and 10(b)14.

Ten

The Employer's Role
in Program Development

Bruce T. Evans

The growth that cooperative education has experienced since its inception in 1906 could not have occurred without strong employer support. There are a number of sound business reasons why, nationally, an estimated 75,000 to 85,000 employers participate. Objectives to be met through participation vary, and one company's objectives may or may not be appropriate to those of another. It is certain, however, that benefits derived from participation in a co-op program must complement an employer's business concerns if that employer is going to participate in the program in a significant way over an extended period of time. Simply stated, in order to justify participation, an employer's cooperative education program must make good business sense.

Cooperative education by its very name implies a cooperative effort among employer, co-op student, and educational institution. This chapter has been written to present the program from the employer's point of view. It explores and identifies many issues and procedures to be considered by an employer when establishing and operating an effective co-op program. To operate effectively, some employers will need to carefully formalize their programs and perhaps even publish a cooperative education policy and procedures manual, while other employers may be able to structure their programs much less formally. This chapter will consider the following four components of the implementation and management of an effective employer program: advance planning for implementation of a cooperative education program; the operational plan for a cooperative education program; developing the cooperative education student; and monitoring program effectiveness.

Advance Planning for Implementation of a Cooperative Education Program

Proper advance planning for the implementation of a cooperative education program will include the six steps that follow.

Identifying Benefits to be Realized. Proper identification of benefits to be realized will provide the basis by which participation in the program can be successfully sold to top management and throughout the organization. Identification of appropriate benefits will also help establish an overall tone and direction for the program. It may only be possible to secure top management's commitment to the program if management is willing to accept and support those benefits which have been identified and presented.

Employers have come to realize the following benefits from participation in cooperative education programs.

- A ready source of motivated and qualified employees to fill temporary positions and to staff special projects
- A ready source of motivated and qualified employees to fill long-term positions
- A cost-effective method of meeting both immediate and long-term human resource needs
- An opportunity to identify, train, and evaluate potential full-time employees without making long-term commitments to them
- Reduced employee turnover
- An opportunity to establish productive relationships with academic institutions

- A more direct opportunity to influence academic curricula
- An opportunity to contribute to society
- An increased recognition of the employer on campus, which may assist in recruiting other non–co-op graduates

Recognizing Co-op Student Objectives. It is important to understand that students participate in cooperative education programs because they have high expectations that they will personally benefit from that participation. The ultimate student motivator must be more than just earning money, because in many instances it would be easier for students to simply work at part-time jobs while attending classes. In addition to income, students participate in co-op programs to gain first-hand insight into business and to gain related professional experience. Many students explore career fields through co-op to confirm interest and commitment to a given profession and to identify how they might best fit into that profession. Co-op gives students the opportunity to test strengths and weaknesses in career-related settings while still in school. Some students will be seeking opportunities to make pregraduation contacts for future full-time employment. Finally, the program can help students make better decisions when selecting classes based upon feedback and counseling provided by their co-op employers.

It should be apparent that cooperative education students are serious about their work assignments. They seek meaningful positions to test professional abilities, confirm career decisions, gain business experience, and make future contacts for full-time positions after graduation. They expect to be paid fairly for their work. The successful co-op employer will recognize the student's itinerary for participation and will structure the program to assure that both student and employer objectives will be served.

Responding to Initial Issues. There are a number of concerns an employer must resolve during this planning phase. Steps must be taken to create student work schedules that are complementary to both the academic calendars of participating schools and the employer's business requirements. Cooperative education schools operate under a variety of calendar and scheduling options, so it should not be difficult for an employer to identify programs that will complement their unique scheduling needs. If a number of students are to be hired from a number of schools, it will be important to coordinate the various co-op schedules. The important issue of student productivity versus short- and long-term training should be addressed. How much should students be paid? Will salaries be billed directly to the customer, or will they be carried by the employer as an overhead expense? What is the relationship to be between student productivity and compensation? Will they be accepted as productive members of the work force? Steps must be taken to assure that students will be accepted by full-time employees and customers alike. Should they be viewed as professionals in training? What position will the union take regarding cooperative education students? Many unions support co-op programs as a vehicle by which members' children are able to earn an education. Other unions may resist the program. Should students hold high-profile positions, or would low-profile, behind-the-scenes positions be more appropriate? How many students should be hired? What credentials should they possess, and how will they be selected? What benefits will they receive? Who pays for transportation and relocation expenses, and how do students find housing?

Developing a Preliminary Policy and Procedures Plan. The development of a preliminary policy and procedures plan will be important to assure program continuity as well as to resolve potential conflict. A primary purpose for the plan will be to avoid possible confusion which may develop within the employing organization. Personnel from cooperative education schools can be of great assistance in the development of a preliminary plan.

Employers have suggested that it is also appropriate to include the personnel office and user departments in the development of initial program guidelines. The personnel office will be particularly helpful in designing a candidate screening and selection process. It can help identify appropriate credentials expected of student applicants. It will be able to advise regarding administrative issues, such as wages and benefits to be paid, student/employer evaluation procedures, guidance and counseling, and housing and relocation policy. User departments, along with the personnel office, should cooperate to develop program content, including scheduling, orientation procedures, development of job descriptions, and supervisory responsibilities. In some companies, student assignments may be administered centrally through the personnel office. Other employers may decentralize program administration and training by assigning students directly to the user department.

Marketing the Program Within the Organization. Step five represents the first real marketing effort undertaken to gain commitment from an employing organization to implement the cooperative education program. Ideally, top decision makers will accept the program proposal and will communicate that endorsement down through the chain of command to all levels within the organization. To be most effective, to eliminate possible confusion, and to secure real commitment at all levels, the program should be thoroughly explained throughout the organization to general management, department managers, supervisors, and finally, to all affected employees.

It is important, however, to realize that it may not be possible to even present the program to top management, let alone secure its endorsement. If that is the situation, it should be recognized that many successful programs have been initiated at the departmental level and later, because of documented positive results, have been sold up through the company to management.

An effective presentation must identify results expected from participation in the program. It should clearly explain the program's purpose and objectives and how they complement the organization's mission and goals. It will be advantageous if benefits can be illustrated in a qualitative and quantitative fashion. Hard-dollar and soft-dollar program costs should be identified. Co-op program costs should be compared to traditional methods used by the organization to meet stated goals and objectives. The presentation should be prepared to respond to initial program concerns that may be expressed by management and that may include the preliminary operational plan. After approval has been earned to implement the program, it will be time to proceed to the sixth step.

Identifying an Individual Within the Organization to Be Responsible for the Program. Integral to this planning phase, the employing organization should identify a person who will have total responsibility for coordination of the program. Ideally, this person will have been a part of the entire program identification and early planning process.

The Operational Plan
for a Cooperative Education Program

The second component of an effective cooperative education program is the development of the operational plan. The operational plan should define as clearly as possible how the program will function. Its development can eliminate a great deal of confusion about the program that may develop over a period of time. It will address the following issues.

Program Coordinator Responsibilities. The program coordinator will be responsible for overall administration and will be accountable for the success of the co-op program. The coordinator will identify the who, what, when, why, and where issues and will manage the day-to-day operations and coordinate activities of all people involved in the program. The coordinator will identify those schools participating in the program and work to cultivate a satisfactory relationship with them. A successful relationship with the co-op schools can be extremely important to the operation and effectiveness of a program. The coordinator will interview and select those co-op students to be employed. The coordinator will identify work stations and assist in the development of job descriptions. The coordinator will develop and coordinate student learning programs. The coordinator will be responsible for monitoring student academic and co-op progress, as well as that of participating departments, to assure that program objectives are achieved. The coordinator will resolve conflicts that may develop. In addition, this person will maintain necessary records, conduct exit interviews, evaluate student performance, and counsel students, and may extend job offers to graduating students. In other words, the coordinator will assist the overall program as appropriate.

Student Supervisor Responsibilities. The day-to-day management of the cooperative education program is handled by the student's immediate supervisor. Supervisors must cooperate with the co-op coordinator and fully support the program to assure its success. Selection of a student's supervisor is critical to the program. That person must be willing to accept responsibility to supervise the student and must not look upon the student merely as someone to be tolerated. The supervisor should understand that the cooperative education student can provide support required to accomplish the work of the department. He or she should understand that the student can and should be productive and contribute to the department. The supervisor is the interface between the co-op student, co-workers, and management.

The supervisor must take time to understand the student's educational background, previous experience, and interests to form a basis for designing specific work assignments. He or she will handle the day-to-day development and supervision of the student. He or she will provide technical assistance, tutor as appropriate, and evaluate student performance. Together, student and supervisor will identify individual and departmental goals to be realized during the work period. The supervisor must allow the student to learn and to experience a realistic overview of the profession. Additionally, the supervisor will have the following responsibilities: to explain the department's specific objectives and to learn about the student's previous academic and professional experience; to give the student a variety of assignments, provide a broad experience, and develop a range of skills; to explain what is to be learned from an assignment and establish specific and measurable learning objectives relative to the project; to assess throughout an assignment the student's progress and review his or her plans; and, finally, to regularly confirm that the student is progressing toward stated learning objectives that have been associated with the assignment and, periodically, review and discuss with the student his or her progress and development. Objective and accurate assessment is to everyone's advantage. In many instances, the supervisor will interpret company policy and even administer discipline as needed.

In a small employer program, the coordinator and supervisor may be the same person and may even be a principal or partner in the firm. The importance of excellent student supervision cannot be overemphasized and is absolutely critical to the success of a program.

Budgeting. Many employers establish a centralized budget that is assigned to the training or personnel group. They believe a centralized budget assures control of the program over and above that of individual training stations and departments, so that program objectives may be better realized. Other employers believe that there are at least two disadvantages to a centralized budget. The first disadvantage is that individual departments may take advantage of the program without making a reasonable commitment to it. The second disadvantage is that the co-op budget may become so highly visible that during an economic downturn it may be tempting for the employer to reduce or eliminate that budget item, especially if the alternative is to lay off full-time employees.

A decentralized approach places the budget within the user departments. Some employers believe that this strategy encourages departmental commitment to the program and that it may be more difficult to eliminate the program during lean economic times, as managers fight to protect their budgets. A disadvantage to a decentralized budget may be a loss of control by the co-op coordinator, which may be demonstrated by a manager's reluctance to permit students to be moved into cross-departmental assignments.

Many companies combine approaches, maintaining some of the budget centrally to provide overall program administration and control, while placing the rest within user departments.

Recruiting Cost and Ongoing Cost. Recruiting cost includes expenses for staff salaries; recruiting literature; promotion materials; recruiter visits to campus; candidate visits to the employment site; and miscellaneous expenses, including phone, postage, and supplies. Training cost includes expenses for student orientation and on-the-job training. Ongoing cost includes expenses for wages, benefits, administration, ongoing training, and overhead.

Student Salaries and Benefits. Student value to an employer is determined by both the immediate ability to contribute and the potential to contribute over the long term, including after graduation. Salary decisions may reflect the following: the rate at which co-op services are billed to customers, salaries offered regular full-time employees, student academic levels, student majors, the competition, market conditions, student expectations, and employers' expectations regarding job performance. A rule of thumb indicates that co-ops often start at 60 percent or 65 percent of the salary paid entry-level, non-co-op college graduates. During the final work period, they typically earn about 85 percent to 90 percent of the salary paid to non-co-op college graduates. Co-op graduates normally receive starting salaries that are appreciably higher, perhaps 10 percent or more than those paid to non-co-op graduates.

Student fringe benefit packages should be limited by what is offered regular employees. It is important that co-ops not accrue special benefits. Consider whether students should be classified as part-time employees, with benefits accruing only during co-op work periods, or as full-time employees on leave while attending classes.

A few employers elect not to pay fringe benefits, while others offer complete benefit packages and even allow students to earn seniority while they are on co-op and while they are attending classes. Compensation packages should be reasonable and competitive with market standards. Co-op schools can provide assistance regarding these issues.

Staffing Levels. An employer should review overall staffing requirements to establish immediate employment needs to be met through co-op, while projecting full-time needs to be staffed by hiring students graduating from the program. The coordinator must consider the time frame required to bring students through the program to graduation in order to establish final staffing requirements.

Selection of Schools. The employer's selection of co-op

schools to participate in the program is important. The coordinator should identify those schools presumed to have effective programs in appropriate disciplines. The coordinator should try to determine the reputation of those schools, the reputation of their co-op programs within the industry, and the quality of students participating in the program. Is a specific institution committed to cooperative education? Has the employer's previous experience with that school been favorable? Does the institution support the program by assisting employers with student recruitment, by making regular site visits, and by evaluating and advising both its students and employers? State, regional, and national cooperative education associations provide excellent resources to answer these questions.

Recruiting Students. The coordinator should communicate his or her needs to the selected school's co-op office and create a working relationship whereby the school's faculty will support the program. He or she should carefully coordinate recruiting procedures in advance to be sure to attract appropriate candidates. Many schools will prescreen a number of applicants for the coordinator. To do this effectively, the school should be well informed of the employer's objectives and department requirements and should be provided accurate and meaningful job descriptions. Only those applicants meeting immediate needs and/or long-term objectives should be considered. Students often interview with several employers, so the coordinator should be prepared to sell the company's program. The coordinator should develop appropriate literature about the company and, if the students will be required to relocate, about the community and geographic area where they will be working.

Work Assignments. Generally, student training programs should include technical training, process training, and personal development. Technical training allows for the application of theory and skills learned in the classroom, along with learning new skills and techniques necessary for career proficiency. Process training includes establishment of objectives and time frames, problem identification, development of courses of action and follow-up, data analysis, and experience to develop the abilities to formulate conclusions. Personal development refers to the ability to assess one's capabilities, set goals, exercise time-management skills, and relate effectively with co-workers.

Specific assignments are best developed by staff members and students in each department with co-op. The department should identify "permanent" co-op jobs available each work period. Appropriate positions should challenge students and provide a variety of exposure with increasing levels of responsibility. Good assignments will provide opportunities for independent and group work, along with the chance to address individual career goals. They should provide time to experiment with tools and techniques and should provide opportunities to strengthen essential skills such as planning, interpersonal relationships, and analytical abilities. Assignments should increase in complexity and responsibility and develop one to another in building-block fashion. Job rotation can help develop a variety of skills associated with a student's field of study and, accordingly, departments should be willing to participate in cross-departmental assignments. Finally, a co-op position must provide a student the opportunity to do meaningful work. For the co-op student, employment is a regular, continuing, and essential element of the educational process. It is a basic requirement that the student be given assignments that yield educational as well as experiential value.

It is very important to carefully assess each student before giving the first assignment, as the student's performance the first time out will make a lasting impression. At its conclusion, the coordinator should assess the student's performance and developing career interest before assigning subsequent responsibilities.

Job Descriptions. Well-written job descriptions assist faculty coordinators to prescreen student applicants, thereby aiding the employer in recruiting students and in matching candidates with positions. Well-written job descriptions are clear, concise, and accurate. They establish the overall scope of a project. They must list specific responsibilities and duties. Job descriptions guide students and supervisors in meeting project objectives.

A typical format for a job description should include the company's name, department's name, department's objectives, job title, job grade, a brief statement explaining the purpose of the job, a list of major duties and responsibilities with emphasis on the most important and regularly performed duties, job specifications, equipment to be used, required skills, and unusual physical requirements. It should include the salary range. It should identify what is to be learned from the assignment, the date requested, and the requester's signature.

Departmental Responsibility. The day-to-day management of the co-op program takes place at the departmental level. Department members must cooperate with the coordinator if the program is to be successful. The student's immediate supervisor will assign the work, provide on-the-job training, define department and/or employer objectives, interpret company policy, and administer discipline and evaluate student performance.

The success of a cooperative education program is directly related to the establishment of enforceable program guidelines, incorporating enough flexibility to ensure that individual needs will be met. Policy should be capable of addressing unusual situations without compromising either basic program principles or format. Of the many issues identified that need to be resolved, perhaps the single most important issue is effective student supervision because, in the eyes of the student, the line supervisor is the co-op program.

Developing the Cooperative Education Student

This component of an employer cooperative program concerns the development of the cooperative education student.

Student Selection Process. The student selection process is similar to that used when recruiting full-time employees. Most initial interviews are coordinated through a school's cooperative education office and occur on campus. During the student interview, the recruiter should thoroughly present the company and its co-op program, including its goals, objectives, and procedures. The recruiter should be prepared to provide accurate descriptions of co-op assignments. Candidates should understand why the position is to be filled by a co-op student.

After the campus interview, some employers make it

their policy to invite promising candidates to their business office or plant location to be screened by several other members of the management staff. The co-op supervisor may be involved at that time. A luncheon with each candidate will continue the selection process in an informal atmosphere. Many employers give considerable importance to how well the student may fit into the employing organization. After the final selection has been made, many recruiters feel it appropriate to notify all applicants in writing that they were or were not selected for the position.

Orientation to Co-op Life. Student orientation to co-op life begins during the interview process. At that time, the nature of the employer's business and typical student responsibilities and work assignments are presented. General information, such as working hours, lunch periods, and pay policy, may also be covered during the selection process.

It is important to maintain open lines of communication. Once the job offer has been accepted, the coordinator will want to keep in extremely close contact with the student. The co-op student should have access to someone who can answer questions and solve problems. Perhaps that contact could be with a student who is presently employed.

If the newly employed student will be required to relocate, a packet of information suggesting potential housing accommodations, expected cost, proximity to work and to other co-op students, the names of potential roommates, and information on public transportation would be helpful and appreciated. Upon arrival at the worksite, the student should be introduced to key people within the organization and given the grand tour of the facility. The student should be thoroughly informed of pertinent company policy. Students are interested in community information, such as educational opportunities at the local college, social and cultural opportunities, shopping locations, medical facilities, and intramural sports activities. They want to know about company-sponsored social events. Invitations to departmental picnics, Christmas parties, and other special get-togethers will help give them a secure sense of belonging.

Students like to have a mentor to whom they can go with questions. When a number of students are working, it may be appropriate to appoint an experienced student responsible for the group. It would be that person's responsibility to serve as spokesperson and to act as an advisor to incoming students. Among other activities, that spokesperson could compile a list of each student's interests and hobbies to facilitate interaction.

Work Environment. A co-op student is a special employee by nature: he or she does not work full-time, attends classes, and is generally younger than most employees. The cooperative education position may provide the first opportunity for professional exposure to his or her chosen career field. Co-workers need to thoroughly understand and support the student and the cooperative education program to avoid jealousy, conflict, or misunderstandings that may arise over specific work assignments or procedures.

The staff should work to place the student in a productive environment that will be supportive, and the student should be made to feel a part of the group. Encouragement should be offered as appropriate. Every effort should be made to treat the student like any other employee. For example, the student's work station should be similar to others in the department. The student should attend and be encouraged to participate in department staff meetings, group meetings, problem-solving sessions, meetings with clients, monthly technical meetings, and project review meetings with senior management. Further, the student should be expected and prepared to give staff presentations.

Work Assignments. Assignments must be important to the work of the employer. Make-work assignments are inappropriate. Positions that are mundane and totally repetitious are to be avoided. A realistic work experience will, however, include some of the day-to-day routine experienced by regular employees. Students should be made to realize that some routine work is to be encountered on any job.

Co-op students should be expected to adhere to work rules and safety regulations. It is important that students develop realistic standards of conduct. An employer should not be obligated to co-op students who refuse to meet company standards.

The initial assignment should be given as soon as possible.

Because of a lack of previous experience, beginning responsibilities must be kept fairly simple. Responsibility should increase on subsequent assignments as the student gains work experience, additional academic training, and maturity. Therefore, the supervisor should establish productive goals commensurate with each student's increasing abilities. A quality assignment will have realistic expectations and will force the student to stretch to fulfill it. Assignments should be varied to expose students to different aspects of the profession while stimulating personal growth. It would be thoughtful to provide at least one assignment each work period which would be appropriate to be included in the student's portfolio or listed on his or her resume. The level of responsibility in the final assignment should be equivalent to that of other employees having a similar length of service.

Ineffective work experiences may lead to shallow learning. Worse, poor work experiences discourage students, leading to unusually high rates of student turnover. Further, students talk about their experiences when they return to campus, and comments by dissatisfied students can severely damage a program's reputation, making it difficult for the employer to attract other qualified students and graduates.

Supervision. The supervisor should understand that effective management of the co-op student is an assigned responsibility. In addition, the co-op program will give an inexperienced supervisor the opportunity to develop and demonstrate overall supervisory skills. Management should insist upon and reward good supervision and provide training opportunities to improve supervisor effectiveness. Supervisor training should stress how to develop quality work assignments, how to integrate the student into the department, and how to supervise. The supervisor must learn to discuss professional goals, assess performance and potential, and present students with career alternatives as appropriate.

In the eyes of the student, the supervisor is the co-op program. The supervisor holds the real key to determining the success of the co-op program and to determining the student's future success in the company.

Ten Checkpoints to Effective Supervision

1. Orient the student to the company, including its purpose/philosophy, position relative to the competition, status, organization chart, opportunities for advancement, and salaries and benefit policy, and why it has a co-op program.

2. Orient the student to the specific department, including departmental organization, working hours, record keeping, time sheets, overtime and sick leave policy, holidays, parking, public transportation, dress codes, lunch and break times, office supplies, and safety equipment and procedures, and provide an office tour, with appropriate introductions.

3. Orient the student to the city, including housing, recreation, shopping, churches, medical facilities, and cultural opportunities.

4. At the beginning of each work period, review the student's professional and academic development, review previous work experience, discuss interest and concerns, and identify several concise and quantifiable learning objectives to be completed during the work period that complement both student and company interests and needs and relate to the work at hand. Tell the student how those objectives will be evaluated.

5. Provide a thorough explanation to the student at the beginning of each assignment. Explanations should include a statement about the overall project, its status, its timetable, the student's specific responsibilities and tasks, and how they relate to the project. The description should outline the quality and thoroughness of work expected, give specific instructions, and identify to whom the student reports and who will direct the student throughout the work period. It should tell when the work is expected, how it will be evaluated, when it will be evaluated, and by whom it will be evaluated. It should relate learning objectives to the assignment and identify supplemental learning opportunities. It is important to maintain careful communication throughout the work period to assure the assignment is effectively accomplished.

6. Evaluate student performance throughout the period as appropriate.

7. Evaluate student learning objectives throughout the work period as appropriate.

8. Review the work period with the student at its conclusion. Identify job performance issues requiring additional development, as well as those skills which have been mastered. Seek student input and identify student likes, dislikes, and concerns. Counsel the student regarding job performance and career development issues. Review and suggest academic opportunities that may be appropriate to the student's development.

9. Based upon anticipated work available during the next work period, project learning opportunities and develop a preliminary action plan.

10. Maintain communication with students while they are attending classes.

Assessment. Assessment begins with the interview/selection process and should continue throughout the student's career with the employer. Opinions developed during the interview process have bearing upon the formulation of the student's initial training, while opinions developed throughout the co-op experience affect the student's ongoing program. A final decision to offer or not to offer full-time employment should be based upon student performance and potential as demonstrated over the significant period of time during which the student participated in the cooperative education program. Naturally, both guidance and assessment given to the student throughout that period will have significant impact upon the employer's final decision regarding a long-term relationship with the company.

Periodic evaluation gives the employer an effective mechanism both to evaluate the student's overall work performance and to judge potential for assuming additional responsibility. Communication established through the assessment process should result in improved job performance. It should identify for the student how he or she is viewed by others. The assessment process provides another vehicle for advising the student and offering suggestions for improvement and increased effectiveness, in addition to providing information to the supervisor useful in making planning decisions.

Assessment should take place throughout each work period. The evaluator must be consistent and give a fair but straightforward evaluation. It should be realized that a student's downfall may be a reflection of an organization's inability to interact effectively with the student. Student and evaluator should review the evaluation together. It is appropriate to identify and discuss both strengths and weaknesses and to recommend courses of action to help the student improve immediate performance as well as long-term potential. If necessary, the evaluator should supplement appraisal forms provided by the school with company forms if they are more appropriate to the situation. At the completion of the work period, the employers will want the cooperative education student to be their employee returning to campus, rather than a student returning to school from just another work assignment. Effective assessment of the cooperative program will provide hard data and general information to improve program performance. Information developed through the assessment process will be beneficial to both student and company.

Monitoring Program Effectiveness

The purpose of monitoring the program is to provide hard data to improve its effectiveness. Ability to demonstrate effectiveness is necessary to justify continuing participation in a cooperative education program, and it is essential when requesting additional human and/or financial resources to improve upon or expand a program. Documented co-op successes make it much easier to explain and, if necessary, defend a program's value to top management as well as to other company employees.

Most successful cooperative education employer programs require a strong commitment to clearly identify goals and objectives. Program policy and procedures should be reviewed periodically to assure that they address stated concerns of current importance. A number of reasons to participate in a program have already been identified. Information gathered through periodic monitoring can help management, coordinators, and supervisors make refinements as appropriate to better direct energy and resources.

Participating employers are usually strongly committed

to cooperative education, and most believe that their programs are effective in meeting accepted goals and objectives. They point out clearly identified goals, and objectives statements have been written and accepted throughout the organization, indicating that the program is well supported. They note that their programs have well-defined policy and procedure manuals, adequate budgets, and that departments are appropriately staffed. They insist upon efficient program administration and supervision. These kinds of comments and observations serve only to indicate that the employer perceives that the program is operating effectively and that it has taken the necessary steps to administratively support it for the time being. But, one question remains unanswered: Is the program meeting stated objectives effectively and at reasonable cost?

Few employers are able to statistically document the effectiveness of their programs. For example, if an objective for participation in a cooperative education program is long-term human resource development, the employer should have a system to track its co-op graduates. To be truly effective, that system should be able to compare co-ops to other employees who did not participate in the program. The employer will want to systematically monitor job performance, job satisfaction, and career progress over a continuing and significant length of time. Systems should be able to compare retention rates. Employers will want to know if co-op graduates are promoted faster and higher and if they earn more money and stay with the company longer. A system should be able to determine if co-op graduates are better contributors. It will be easy to defend the co-op program if it can be demonstrated that it is cost-effective in both the short and long term and that the performance of co-op students and co-op graduates is significantly better over a long period of time than that of employees hired through other methods.

A co-op coordinator must be able to demonstrate that the program meets stated objectives at reasonable cost. He or she must be able to show that the system consistently provides qualified and effective employees to fill short- and/or long-term staffing needs. The coordinator must be able to document that students fill only positions of demonstrated need and that co-op recruiting and training costs compare favorably with other methods of bringing employees on board. Has the co-op program increased the employer's ability to recruit females and minorities? Is the student's salary and benefit package more favorable to the company than that for other employees? The co-op coordinator should be able to compare student performance to that of other employees. It is absolutely imperative that the coordinator be able to graphically demonstrate that the cooperative education program is producing sufficient return on assets involved.

Summary

Since 1906 many employers throughout the country have experienced the significant advantages to be gained by participation in and commitment to cooperative education programs. Regardless of the many valid reasons why employers establish programs—and all employers do not have the same objectives for participation—all programs must operate in a cost-effective manner. Cooperative education coordinators should be able to graphically demonstrate the effectiveness of their programs to management. During difficult economic times, it is essential that top management understand the benefits gained through participation in cooperative education to justify continued strong program support when difficult decisions concerning company operations must be made.

This chapter has presented material developed over several years by numerous employers recognized for having quality cooperative education programs. It has been divided into four components for implementation and management of an effective cooperative education program from an employer's point of view. Adherence to the issues identified through these components will assure employers that their programs meet the desired goals, objectives, and benefits for participation in a cooperative education program in a cost-effective manner.

Eleven

Enhancing the Student's Cooperative Education Experience

Patricia T. van der Vorm

Cooperative education provides students with a host of learning opportunities in addition to hands-on experience. A co-op assignment is more than arriving at work on time and performing well on the job. Cooperative education is an educational concept, a philosophy that must be attended. The co-op work component should not be perceived as just another job. The most obvious learning is, of course, the development and improvement of skills required in performance of the job. But the broader learning implications for a co-op assignment include students' personal, social, and career development, as well (Wilson, 1971). Academic supervisors and staff can greatly enhance students' learning by providing a broader context in which to experience and assess the co-op assignment. With proper guidance, students can learn ". . . to define and solve problems, to recognize different value systems, to test theory against practice and to appreciate knowledge both for its utility and for its own sake" (Davis, 1971, pp. 140–141). In addition, students develop interpersonal skills. When asked to analyze the co-op experience, one of the most common benefits cited by students is "learning to deal effectively with other people." Interpersonal competence is important in all professions and, in the broader context, in virtually every aspect (social, economic, and political) of living (Cooperative Assessment of Experiential Learning, 1975).

There are a number of methods that may be used in guiding students through a cooperative education assignment. This chapter will discuss (1) preparing students for the co-op experience, (2) getting the most from a co-op assignment, (3) synthesizing the co-op experience, and (4) preparing academic supervisors (faculty, staff, or both) for their role in co-op. (The term *academic supervisor* is defined in the next section.) Specific techniques described include preplacement programs, specially designed courses, learning contracts, evaluations, postplacement programs, and faculty development. These educational methods are intended to enhance students' cooperative education experiences and may be used by centralized or decentralized, credit or noncredit, mandatory or nonmandatory programs. Introducing a combination of a few or all of these techniques will make the cooperative education experience more meaningful to students and will reinforce the true educational philosophy of cooperative education.

Preparing for the Co-op Experience

Orientation to Co-op and Its Purpose. The first activity essential to all cooperative education programs is an orientation session. Students receive a thorough briefing on the philosophy and procedures of the programs to which they are applying. The supervision of students provided by the academic institution may be done by staff members (with or without faculty rank) or by teaching faculty from academic units. The term *academic supervisor* is used in this chapter to refer to faculty or staff members providing oversight and guidance to students on the job.

Orientation may be provided to individuals or groups of students as a verbal presentation, a videotape, or as written handouts. Orientations should be consistent in content and should define the appropriate roles for all participants—students, faculty, staff, and employers. A good preparatory session will increase students' commitment to the cooperative education concept and reduce the potential for problems and confusion as they progress through the program.

Guidance given to students participating in cooperative education should begin prior to the actual work assignments. The majority of students who enter a cooperative education program are considering several career options and have not yet made a decision. Even those students who have chosen a specific professional field often lack a clear and accurate picture regarding positions available and appropriate career goals for their selected profession. Career education services assist students in preparing for cooperative education and provide students with skills they will use throughout their lifetimes.

Life Career Planning Prior to Co-op. Depending on students' particular needs, some or all of the following career education activities will be appropriate in preparing for a cooperative education assignment.

Skills Assessment. It is important for students to decide which skills they perform best, which skills they prefer to use, and which skills they need to develop. For many students this requires a serious assessment of prior experience and of successful and enjoyable activities. For others, who are less confident about their preferences and priorities, aptitude testing may be useful to get them started. Tests, such as Holland's Self-Directed Search (Holland, 1984) and the Strong-Campbell Inventory (Hansen and Campbell, 1985), are popular instruments for initial self-assessment. The Myers-Briggs Type Indicator (Myers, 1985) is often used to assist individuals in determining personal qualities and environmental preferences.

Resource Review. Research is an essential component in making career choices, as well as in choosing a cooperative education assignment. Students should become familiar with self-help resources that assist with self-assessment, resume writing, and interview skills. Students should also understand how to use specific resources such as guides and directories to professional fields and annual reports. (References such as those listed in the sample bibliography at the end of this chapter can assist in putting together job search services for co-op students.)

Networking. Once students have conducted research and

begun to focus on particular professions, they should identify people in the fields that interest them. The names of helpful professionals may be identified by talking with staff, faculty, family, and friends. Some schools are able to provide names of alumni volunteering career assistance to students of their alma mater.

Information Interview. Gathering first-hand information directly from the field is an important career research tool. Students should be taught the distinction between interviewing for information and interviewing for a job. Then students should be encouraged to talk with professionals in their fields of interest. The information interview helps students determine their personal preferences as well as the necessary skills and qualifications for a particular field.

Life Career Planning Courses. Some schools have designed an optional course for students early in their academic programs, sometimes called a "life career planning course." Generally, such a course includes help with decision-making skills, and with looking at academic majors and their implications for career choices. The course should also help students choosing field experience options (van der Vorm and Jones, 1985).

Getting a Co-op Assignment. While some cooperative education programs use only positions developed by staff and faculty, other programs are based on the philosophy that a valuable part of students' experiential learning is developing their own co-op positions. For students in the latter type of cooperative education program, assistance with job-hunting techniques is particularly important.

Job Search. Job search techniques are lifetime career development skills and are valuable for all cooperative education students. Learning to network, target a job search, use the appropriate resources, and develop the right personal presentation package are all strategies which can lead to more and better opportunities, whether for cooperative education assignments or for permanent employment in the future (see sample bibliography).

Resume Writing, Standard Form 171 Preparation, and Cover Letters. The resume is an essential part of job seeking in the United States and one of the most difficult steps to accomplish. Writing a resume is easier for students who have done self-assessment, because they have explored their interests and have a better understanding of why they would be a valuable asset to an employer. There are many good reference materials available (see sample bibliography) to help students get started. Once a draft has been completed, students should seek an objective critique from others.

It is also important to determine the purpose of the resume being written. Some professional fields have an established protocol that dictates a particular length and format for a resume. For example, employers considering candidates with a master's degree in business administration prefer resumes limited to one page, with education and experience listed concisely, including dates. For other professional fields and for individuals seeking a change of profession, a more extensive description of skills and previous responsibilities is appropriate.

Some hiring authorities require a listing of experience according to their own exclusive format. One example is the federal government. The Standard Form 171 (SF171) is used in addition to or in place of the traditional resume. There are specific guidelines used to complete a SF171. Students should understand the purpose of these and other traditional application forms in order to use them to the best advantage.

Cover letters are often the most important and least understood component of an employment application package. Cover letters can be used to describe employment objectives and to target individual skills and interests to a particular position or employing organization.

Resumes, cover letters, and special applications are job-seeking tools used to secure cooperative education assignments. Instruction and assistance with these tools will make students better cooperative education candidates.

Job Interview. Again, there are many written resources to assist students with interview skills (see sample bibliography). Objective feedback, through such methods as role playing and videotaping, is also helpful for students developing interviewing proficiency. In this case, practice becomes an important teacher. Most students perform better when they have prepared for their cooperative education interviews.

Preplacement Seminar. Once students have obtained their cooperative education assignments, it is important to prepare them for the work experience prior to their first day on the job. Group preparation sessions are often most effective and should include pointers on the obvious and the not-so-obvious realities of the working world. A discussion of the obvious might include tips on proper dress, the importance of arrival and departure times, and office protocol. It is a mistake to assume that these topics are already "obvious" information to students.

A discussion of the not-so-obvious should always include students' expectations for the co-op experience. Clarifying expectations will help to ensure that they are both realistic and appropriate. Understanding one's expectations can also promote heightened and more effective on-the-job observations by students (Ramsey, 1979). For example, an accounting student may look forward to an assignment in a government agency in order to enhance the accounting skills taught in the classroom. However, a co-op placement may also be an opportunity to compare public versus private sector accounting programs, to study the hierarchy of a public organization, or to observe management styles and the role of office politics. These learning opportunities can be easily overlooked if they are not discussed as appropriate expectations.

However, it may not be possible to hold group sessions due to staffing or time limitations. Alternatives for preplacement preparation might be viewing a series of audio or video materials made available in a central resource center or attending certain sections of courses already being taught in the general curriculum (Angus, 1974). Some form of pre-placement preparation for students immediately prior to the co-op is essential.

Getting the Most from a Co-op Assignment

Learning Objectives and Academic Requirements. Statistical data on cooperative education programs in the United

States indicate that in the majority of co-op assignments, some form of academic credit is earned. Academic supervision is a powerful method of quality control and is therefore a very important component of the co-op experience. Some type of academic supervision should be provided, even for noncredit programs. The following discussion of academic supervision refers to guidance provided by the students' academic institutions, in addition to the employers' on-site supervision. Academic supervision may be provided by staff coordinators, teaching faculty, or both.

There are a number of tools that may be used, individually or in combination, to effectively supervise cooperative education assignments. Whatever type of supervision is provided, it is important to remember that the ultimate goal is to enhance the students' experience. The guidance offered through academic supervision should provide a breadth of knowledge that would not be gained by students simply finding part-time jobs for the semester. The cooperative education experience should be examined from many perspectives. These might include:

1. Self-development: looking at skills, and even attitudes, which are being developed or newly acquired.
2. Career development: recognizing insights gained in planning future careers. This may include gathering information from people at the worksite, analyzing personal preferences regarding an organization or a working environment, or rejecting a particular field as a result of experience gained in the co-op assignment.
3. Relevance to classroom learning: relating first-hand work experience to the theoretical base being acquired in the classroom. This may enhance both students' work on the job and classroom discussion upon return to campus.

Some of the most typical and popular academic supervision tools are described as follows.

Manuals. Written guidelines for both academic supervisors and students are extremely useful in guiding them through co-op assignments. An academic supervision manual should in-

clude the institution's cooperative education program procedures and examples of the various forms and how they are used.
The student manual should include sample documents and instructions, as well as a general discussion of the academic component and appropriate expectations.

Syllabi. Students should understand the academic requirements of cooperative education assignments. No matter
what methods are used to promote learning for students, they
should be described in writing. Since the academic component
is really a teaching-learning situation, the traditional syllabus
can be a useful format to follow.

Learning Agreement/Contract. As the name implies, this
is a formal written document outlining the academic component of a given cooperative education assignment. The agreement is usually drawn up by students and academic supervisors.
It is useful to have job supervisors sign the documents as well, so
that all parties are aware of what is expected of the co-op students.

The learning contract generally includes an outline of
those things students hope to learn from their particular co-op
assignments. It will list tasks to help students achieve these objectives (reading lists, papers, journals, portfolios), deadlines,
and the method of evaluation to be used in assessing students'
achievement of these objectives. Academic supervisors should be
prepared to assess learning objectives with students periodically
during the work term, since these objectives often change as students become more involved in their assignments.

Academic Requirements. A diversity of academic requirements should be considered, depending upon the job assignment. For some assignments, a portfolio may be an appropriate
requirement. Journals, kept by the day or the week, are popular
academic tools. Journals can be required for a special purpose,
such as analyzing decisions made on the job. Written assignments may include a series of short papers or one final extensive report. These assignments can also be used for a specific
purpose. Short papers may be targeted to critical incidents that
influence students' decisions or behavior. For example, students
may write about "... specific situations or actions which dem-

onstrate a use of cross-cultural skills" (Angus, 1974, p. 80). Longer papers may include research topics, either of students' choice or decided on in collaboration with job supervisors. Some excellent topics have been developed from employers' back-burner projects.

Monitoring the Experience. There should be ongoing and regular communication between students and their academic supervisors. This may be accomplished through periodic conversations in personal meetings and by telephone. Such communication is essential in order to reconfirm or modify students' expectations (see above discussion of learning contract) and to resolve potential problems that may arise during placements. Additional monitoring techniques include those discussed below.

Seminars. Group sessions are an important tool for cooperative education programs with large numbers of students assigned to each academic supervisor. These sessions can be more cost-effective than contract and site-visit methods of supervision (Seeman, 1984).

Topics for these seminars may range from the general to the specific, while still being applicable to a number of different types of jobs. General topics might include readings and discussions on organizational dynamics or public versus private sector employment. Specific topics might address on-the-job interpersonal skills or a guest speaking from personal experience about what to do when one is blackballed in an organization.

Some schools use a formal course to accompany the cooperative education assignment. One example of such a course would be a study of the classical versus modern thinking about work, followed by focusing on the students' co-op experiences, for example, ". . . how their jobs are organized and administered, how work affects the quality of their lives, and how they (the students) affect the workplace" (Levine, 1984, p. 21).

No matter what the topic or the format, any discussion will be enlivened by students' co-op experiences. These group sessions can also establish an informal support system—by sharing experiences verbally, students often discover how to help one another.

Site Visits. A visit to the worksite by the academic supervisor is an important supervisory tool for a number of reasons. It gives all parties—students, academic supervisors, and job supervisors—an opportunity to discuss assignments together. This discussion may uncover potential problems that can be immediately resolved, or it may facilitate the identification of a special project to be incorporated into students' academic assignments. A site visit can also give students a boost in morale at a crucial time. Finally, it gives the academic supervisor a better understanding of a particular work assignment and organization. Direct affiliation of academic supervisors with cooperative education employers has been known to lead to special projects or consulting opportunities for the supervisor, as well. If it is not possible for the academic supervisor to make a site visit, it is important to communicate with the job supervisor by telephone or written correspondence at some point during each assignment. However, if there are recurring problems raised by either students or employers during any assignment, it is extremely advisable to arrange a site visit.

Assessing the Learning and Job Performance. One of the most challenging responsibilities for the academic supervisor is assessment, especially if it is for academic credit and a grade. It is very important to use measurable criteria in formulating learning objectives. Part of the assessment can be based on the work products produced in demonstrating that learning. However, there are other factors that must be taken into consideration. Elements of student assessment should include skill development, knowledge, experience acquisition, and work accomplished. Site visits and periodic academic supervisor-student meetings are important to evaluation, both in assessing the above elements and in providing intermediate feedback to the student (Angus, 1974). Formal evaluations are also a useful tool for the academic supervisor.

Employer Evaluation. Assessment of students' work performance on the job by their immediate supervisors is essential. Evaluation forms provided by the school can facilitate employers' assessments. Forms should include elements that academic supervisors will be considering and should specifically request employers to review the evaluations with students.

Student Evaluations. Students should have an opportunity to evaluate the work assignments, the academic supervisors, and the cooperative education program staff. Some major as well as minor program flaws can be uncovered through students' evaluations. Students' evaluations may also reveal information regarding learning and the success of placements.

Synthesizing the Co-op Experience

Finally, in bringing proper closure to a cooperative education assignment, it is helpful to conduct a debriefing session for students. The debriefing can assist students in bringing ". . . to a certain level of consciousness . . ." the learning which has taken place in a work assignment (Ramsey, 1979, pp. 146–147). These sessions may be conducted by the academic supervisors one-on-one with students or with groups of students in a formal seminar.

Postplacement Seminars. Seminars are most successful when conducted in small groups with a facilitator who can ask thought-provoking questions to stimulate discussion. For example, What was the atmosphere of your workplace? How did this atmosphere affect your performance? What would be your ideal workplace? What kinds of rewards motivate you? What supervisory qualities are important for leadership?

The discussion should prompt students to share insights regarding their experiences and to offer verbal evaluations of their assignments. They may also want to discuss, in retrospect, what they would do the same or differently on their next work assignment.

Most importantly, a debriefing of co-op placements should assist students in planning for the future. Has the co-op assignment helped them to determine their choice of career field, courses they should add to their academic program, whether to do another co-op in the same or a different field, how to use this experience in their search for permanent employment, whether to pursue graduate education, and what kind of organization they will look for in the future? The individual conducting the debriefing should try to facilitate discussion for the students' future planning.

This session is also a good time to get students' written evaluations of the program and to determine whether they would recommend their work placements to other students.

Preparing Teaching Faculty as Academic Supervisors

When they first begin, teaching faculty who play an active role in a cooperative education program often do not feel comfortable or confident about field experience supervision. Many ask, "Are they professors, guidance counselors, policemen, or all three?" (van der Vorm and others, 1979, p. 27). Providing services to the faculty can make them more effective and helpful supervisors to students, and these services can add a whole new dimension to their role as postsecondary educators.

Development Activities. One of the most intimidating responsibilities for many faculty is addressing students' career development and personal skill-building as part of the academic component. Special training sessions for faculty, preferably conducted by other faculty with expertise in organizational development and interpersonal skill-building, can be extremely helpful (van der Vorm and others, 1979).

Orientations. Bringing inexperienced and experienced faculty supervisors together to discuss the academic component is a good first step. The faculty session might be prefaced by recommended readings, such as publications from the Council for the Advancement of Experiential Learning (Columbia, Maryland) or *Cooperative Education Across the Disciplines: A Faculty Perspective* (van der Vorm and Jones, 1985).

Publications. Since written publications are an important component of most college professors' job responsibilities, cooperative education should be urged toward the top of their lists. The cooperative education community needs more research to forward the cause of this important academic model. Faculty who are already involved in cooperative education as teachers and supervisors should consider utilizing that knowledge and experience for publication purposes.

Co-op Assignments. First-hand experience, of course, is the best way to instill confidence and competence. So, why not send faculty out for their own cooperative education experience? Many organizations are very interested in having someone with experience and expertise work for them on special projects. And faculty may be looking for a change of pace for the summer or for part of a sabbatical year. Those who take advantage of a field experience opportunity for themselves are bound to gain invaluable insight for their role as cooperative education student supervisors.

Summary

Authors of the recent national education document entitled *Nation At Risk* (Gardner, 1983) recommend that United States educators focus on the creation of a "learning society" (p. 13). The basis of this learning society is ". . . the idea that education is important not only because of what it contributes to one's career goals, but also because of the value it adds to the general quality of one's life" (p. 14). And at the heart of such a society are ". . . educational opportunities extending far beyond the traditional institutions of learning, into every place where the individual can develop and mature in work and life" (p. 14).

The techniques described in this chapter for expanding the cooperative education experience respond directly to this future vision for education in America. Cooperative education provides a clear linkage between education and work. Assisting students to use this linkage in developing life skills as part of their educational experiences can only maximize their learning opportunities. Decision-making techniques such as goal setting, conflict resolution, long-range planning, and interpersonal and organizational skills are essential to the workplace and are most often learned in that setting.

Students who have the opportunity to gain theoretical knowledge and cognitive skills from the classroom concurrently with personal, social, and career development skills from the workplace will be better prepared to meet the demands of the future. These skills are the essential elements of a "learning society." They are the resources for a more fulfilling and purposeful life.

Sample Bibliography for Job Hunters

Suggested Readings

Bolles, R. N. *The Quick Job-Hunting Map.* Berkeley, Calif.: Ten Speed Press, 1977.

Bolles, R. N. *The Three Boxes of Life.* Berkeley, Calif.: Ten Speed Press, 1978.

Bolles, R. N. *What Color Is Your Parachute?* (Rev. ed.) Berkeley, Calif.: Ten Speed Press, 1981.

Catalyst Staff. *What to Do with the Rest of Your Life.* New York: Simon & Schuster, 1980.

Figler, H. *The Complete Job-Search Handbook.* New York: Holt, Rinehart & Winston, 1980.

Michelozzi, B. N. *Coming Alive from Nine to Five.* Palo Alto, Calif.: Mayfield, 1980.

Powell, C. R. *Career Planning Today.* Dubuque, Iowa: Kendall/Hunt, 1981.

Resumes and Cover Letters

Catalyst Staff. *Marketing Yourself—The Catalyst Guide to Successful Resumes and Interviews.* New York: Bantam Books, 1980.

Gray, E. *Successful Business Resumes.* Boston: EBI Publishing, 1981.

Jackson, T. *The Perfect Resume.* New York: Anchor Press/Doubleday, 1981.

McDaniels, C. *Developing a Professional Vita or Resume.* Garrett Park, Md.: Garrett Park Press, 1978.

Powell, C. R. *Career Planning Today.* Dubuque, Iowa: Kendall/Hunt, 1981.

Job Search

Figler, H. *The Complete Job-Search Handbook.* New York: Holt, Rinehart & Winston, 1980.

Irish, R. *Go Hire Yourself an Employer.* (Rev. ed.) New York: Anchor Press/Doubleday, 1978.

Jackson, T. *28 Days to a Better Job.* New York: Hawthorne Books, 1977.

Jackson, T. *Guerrilla Tactics in the Job Market.* New York: Bantam Books, 1978.

Powell, C. R. *Career Planning Today.* Dubuque, Iowa: Kendall/Hunt, 1981.

Salmon, R. D. *Job Hunter's Guide to Eight Great American Cities.* Cambridge, Mass.: Brattle Publications, 1978.

Zehring, J. W. *Careers in State and Local Government.* Garrett Park, Md.: Garrett Park Press, 1980.

Interviewing

Amsden, F. M., and White, N. F. *How to Be Successful in the Employment Interview.* Dubuque, Iowa: Kendall/Hunt, 1977.

Martin, P. *Martin's Magic Formula for Getting the Right Job.* New York: St. Martin's Press, 1981.

Medley, A. H. *Sweaty Palms—The Neglected Art of Being Interviewed.* Belmont, Calif.: Lifetime Learning Publications, 1978.

References

Angus, E. L. "Evaluating Experiential Education." In J. Duley (ed.), *Implementing Field Experience Education.* New Directions for Higher Education, no. 6. San Francisco: Jossey-Bass, 1974.

Cooperative Assessment of Experiential Learning. *The Learning and Assessment of Interpersonal Skills: Guidelines for Students.* CAEL Working Paper no. 5. Princeton, N.J.: Educational Testing Service, 1975.

Davis, J. R. "Cooperative Education: Prospects and Pitfalls." *Journal of Higher Education,* 1971, *42,* 139-146.

Gardner, D. P. *Nation at Risk: The Imperative for Educational Reform.* Washington, D.C.: U.S. Government Printing Office, 1983.

Hansen, J. C., and Campbell, D. P. *Strong-Campbell Inventory.* Palo Alto, Calif.: Consulting Psychologists Press, 1985.

Holland, J. P. *Self Directed Search.* Palo Alto, Calif.: Consulting Psychologists Press, 1984.

Levine, A. E. "The Bradford Plan: The Story of a Liberal Arts College." *Journal of Cooperative Education,* 1984, *20* (2), 18-23.

Myers, I. B. *Myers-Briggs Type Indicator.* Palo Alto, Calif.: Consulting Psychologists Press, 1985.

Ramsey, W. R. "Strategies for Enhancing Learning from Work Experience." *Alternative Higher Education,* 1979, *4* (2), 140-147.

Seeman, H. "Training for On-the-Job-Survival and Promotion: An Inductive Co-op Seminar." *Journal of Cooperative Education,* 1984, *15* (3), 22-29.

van der Vorm, P., and Jones, N. (eds.). *Cooperative Education Across the Disciplines: A Faculty Perspective.* Washington, D.C.: University Press of America, 1985.

van der Vorm, P., and others. "A Close Encounter of the Co-op Kind." *Journal of Cooperative Education,* 1979, *15* (3), 22-29.

Wilson, J. W. "Historical Development." In A. S. Knowles and Associates (eds.), *Handbook of Cooperative Education.* San Francisco: Jossey-Bass, 1971.

Twelve

Overseas Program Development and International Student Placement

Robert E. Vozzella
Robert R. Tillman

Cooperative Education for International Students in the United States

As the predicted demographic decrease in the number of college-age men and women affects institutions of higher education in the United States, schools will be seeking potential students from nontraditional areas. One probable outcome of declining enrollments will be an increase in the number of international students admitted to American colleges and universities, including those with cooperative education programs. Although an influx of international students benefits the institution by providing an expanded applicant pool, cultural diversity, and financial support, consideration should be given to the impact on the cooperative education program.

International students enrolled in cooperative education programs present unique and often complex problems. Issues such as communication difficulties, cultural differences, and legal considerations can complicate the cooperative education process and present challenges to both the cooperative educator and the employer. However, with an understanding of the problems, strategies can be developed for successfully integrating international students into a domestic co-op program.

International students are a heterogeneous population including non-U.S. citizens whose first language is not English, U.S. citizens whose first language is not English, and U.S. citizens whose first language is English and who may be permanent residents, immigrants, or refugees.

Communication

Adequate verbal and written communication skills are required for success in the world of work. However, many international students who speak, understand, or write the English language well enough to succeed in school may still lack the sophisticated level of communication necessary for participation in the co-op program. In school, a student with limited English language skills can tape lectures, read and translate at his or her own pace, and speak English only when required. Friends with stronger bilingual skills can help students who struggle with the English language.

The world of work, however, has a much lower tolerance than academia for inadequate communication skills. For example, international students may ask supervisors and colleagues to speak slowly or repeat instructions or, conversely, speak with an accent that co-workers have difficulty understanding. Common professional jargon may not be in the student's vocabulary. Under the pressure of business deadlines, the student's written communication may not meet the standards of the employer.

Problems with communication vary among cultures and students. Some students simply cannot speak or understand English. Others speak haltingly, using incorrect grammar and pronunciation, or with accents that impair communication so that students are unable to make themselves understood. Some cannot easily comprehend rapidly spoken American English. Most lack the technical vocabulary used in their respective professional fields. To compound the problem, international students tend to socialize with others who share the same language and culture so that they do not take the opportunity to practice speaking and listening to English. Furthermore, some students can speak and understand English adequately but have poor English writing skills.

Communication problems hinder international students in every step of the co-op process. Writing resumes and interviewing can be major obstacles. Because they have difficulty communicating their background, interests, goals, and needs to the co-op advisor and to the co-op employer, their potential for co-op employment may be underestimated or misunderstood. Consequently, in spite of adequate professional skills, international students may be unemployed or underemployed only because of communication problems.

During the referral process, many communication barriers become apparent. Some students are afraid to interview because the procedures seem so overwhelming. For example, they must write a resume, use the telephone to arrange an interview appointment, find their way to the interview, and discuss their qualifications in an uncomfortable language. If they are hesitant and uncertain in expressing themselves, they may be perceived as unqualified or uninterested in the job. They simply do not sell themselves well in an interview.

Because students with communication problems do not always understand directions and either cannot or are reluctant to reveal their confusion, they require more intensive training and closer supervision on the job. They may have trouble with routine job-related activities, such as using the telephone, writing reports, contributing ideas to projects, and working with groups. Social isolation results when communication hinders interactions with co-workers and supervisors.

Language proficiency is assessed prior to admission by the TOEFL (Test of English as a Foreign Language) exam. Administered routinely to international students applying to American colleges and universities, TOEFL consists of three parts measuring mastery of English grammar, listening comprehension, and reading comprehension. The exam was designed to assess language proficiency relative to school, not work.

Therefore, TOEFL alone is an inadequate screening device for cooperative education because the communication requirements of school and work are not the same. While a student may succeed in school with limited English language ability, work demands diverse and sophisticated communication skills. Therefore, some students are accepted into co-op programs without the communication skills necessary for successful participation.

Culture

Student Expectations. International students have a variety of preconceived notions about America. When students try to interpret American culture from the perspective of their native culture, misunderstanding, confusion, frustration and anger may result.

Problems often start with the admissions process. International students who apply to American colleges and universities are primarily interested in the academic program and may overlook or misunderstand information about cooperative education. They may have little or no interest in or commitment to the concept of cooperative education. Consequently, once they are enrolled and are made aware of the co-op program, some students fail to seek information or attend co-op orientations and, instead, try to circumvent mandatory co-op programs or ignore requirements to participate in optional co-op programs.

International students may be reluctant to participate in the cooperative education program for a variety of reasons. First, they either want or need to finish their education and return home as soon as possible because of family or military obligations, postgraduation employment commitments, financial support, or scholarship constraints. Second, they want to remain in the United States to take advantage of the practical training option, which is at least partly precluded by participation in a cooperative education program, or continue on to graduate school. Third, they rely on the advice of other international students, who may have had discouraging experiences with the co-op program, without exploring their own options for cooperative education, sometimes out of fear of losing their only source of social support.

International students who do participate in the co-op

program often have unrealistic early expectations of the program. For example, many do not expect to perform entry-level jobs in spite of their background and level in school. They also tend to overestimate the salary they will be offered and attempt to bargain for an unrealistically high wage. Many are unwilling to relocate for a co-op job because they will be cut off from their social support group.

In addition, international students sometimes expect the co-op program to respond to immediate needs, such as a financial emergency precipitated by changing personal, family, or political circumstances. In this case, the unprepared student may expect more than the program is designed to deliver within the student's compelling time frame. For example, political upheavals in the students' home country can cause unprepared international students who formerly eschewed the co-op program to suddenly need jobs because they have lost financial support at home.

It is important to recognize that other cultures do not necessarily share the American work ethic. Most American students expect to start at the bottom, develop professional skills, and then assume increasing responsibility in the employing organization. But many international students expect a higher-level position more consistent with their social status at home. Consequently, they are surprised to be asked to consider entry-level positions that provide necessary skills and experience.

Social Customs. Some social customs that are acceptable or even rewarded in the student's own culture are misunderstood or discouraged in American culture. Cooperative education forces international students to engage in a social group outside their protected circle in school. Although the students' customs are different, they must adapt to the customs of the American employer in order to succeed in the co-op program. Just as the international business community recognizes the importance of mediating cultural differences abroad, so too must the co-op educator be aware of the difficulties faced by international students trying to adapt to the American business culture.

Although there are many examples of customs that can be misinterpreted, some cause problems for international students in a co-op program more commonly than others. For example, while many Americans believe that each individual must succeed on his or her own merit, students from other cultures may feel responsible for helping others from their own society. Consequently, students behave in ways that surprise Americans, such as "helping" each other with exams and papers, sending a substitute to work or class when the student is unavailable, or sending or taking a friend with better language skills for a job interview. And while some cultures accept gift giving as a method of opening doors and securing favors, most co-op educators and employers would, at best, be amused by the suggestion.

Time schedules are another common source of cultural misunderstandings. For example, employers may find that international students, unaware of expectations, do not report for work, go to lunch, and go home at the prescribed times. While in some cultures "tomorrow" is soon enough to undertake a project, students in other cultures will come in early, work through lunch, and stay late to complete a project. Because the students' behavior is culture-based, they may not understand criticism and may be reluctant to change or adapt.

In addition, customs regarding religion, health and hygiene, the status of women, or behavior towards those in authority all contribute to the potential for cultural conflict.

Interpersonal Relationships. Because culture dictates to a large extent the way in which people relate to each other and because interpersonal relationships are so important to success on the job, cultural misunderstandings can prevent international students from developing the interpersonal relationships necessary for successful participation in the co-op program. For example, international students who enjoy high social status in their home country may have difficulty accepting direction and guidance from supervisors or working cooperatively with colleagues. Yet, if they do not develop professional ties with colleagues or mentoring relationships with superiors, participate in organizational functions, or develop on-the-job friendships, they feel isolated and alone at work.

Another potential problem area relates to gender. Working with and being supervised by women can be a new and disquieting experience for international students, especially male students, from some cultural backgrounds. For example, students may refuse to interview with a woman, cooperate with female colleagues, or work for a female supervisor because of the lower status of women in the students' own culture.

In addition, international students frequently encounter real or perceived prejudice among supervisors and colleagues. Students' relationships may be influenced by shifting political winds or international incidents, such as hostage crises, which are beyond the control of the students.

Legal Considerations

While a complete discussion of the laws and requirements regarding the employment of international students is beyond the scope of this chapter, there are a number of legal considerations pertinent to the participation of international students in a cooperative education program.

With respect to federal regulations governing the placement of foreign students (F-1 visa holders) on co-op assignments in the United States, the section on curricular practical training programs states that, "An F-1 student enrolled in a college, university, conservatory, or seminary having a curricular practical training program (such as alternate work/study, internship, or cooperative education) as part of the regular curriculum may participate in the program without obtaining a change of nonimmigrant status" [U.S. Department of Justice, Immigration and Naturalization Service Regulations Governing Nonimmigrant Classes, F-1 Academic Students, 8 CRS Part 214.2 (f)(10)(i)(D)]. It is important to note that the co-op program need not be mandatory as long as it is an integral part of the curriculum. The new Immigration Reform and Control Act, which went into effect in June 1987, impacts the aforementioned regulations by requiring documentation of the student's eligibility to be employed on co-op.

Legal Status. In order for international students to work on co-op in the United States on a full-time basis, the educational institution must apply to the United States INS (Immigration and Naturalization Service) for permission for attendance by nonimmigrant students. According to INS requirements, international students on F-1 visas must be registered in a degree program as full-time students (minimum of twelve credit hours per academic term) and they must work in major-related co-op positions. International students in cooperative education programs are fully protected by federal laws against discrimination in employment.

Practical Training. International students on F-1 visas are usually eligible to work in their professional field in the United States for a maximum of twelve months after graduation. However, students who participate in a cooperative education program lose all or part of their eligibility for practical training according to the number of months of co-op experience accrued.

Social Security and Taxes. International students who participate in a cooperative education program must have a social security number for employment purposes, although they are exempt from social security taxes. They are also required to file federal, state, and local tax returns.

Security Clearance. Most international students are not eligible for routine security clearance, required for some co-op positions. Accordingly, in majors in which the majority of the work involves government contracts, there are many jobs for which international students cannot even be considered.

Federal Government. The federal government does not hire international students. Some state and local governments also restrict the employment of international students.

Strategies

Strategies for working with international students may involve the students, co-op employers, and the educational institution.

A complete exploration of work in America is too ambitious a project for a series of workshops. A career development course for international students offered during the students' first year on campus is a useful adjunct to co-op orientation and workshops. Such a course can help students compare American culture with their own culture, understand the world of work in the United States, and improve job-seeking and job-survival skills. As additional benefits, the course can help students improve oral and written English language skills prior to participation in the co-op program and provide a forum for international students to explore and discuss issues of special interest to them.

Co-op Employers. Special information, both written and verbal, regarding international students should also be available for cooperating employers. Employers need information about types of visas and their scope and limitations, taxes, social security, and practical training. They should also be made aware of cross-cultural issues to improve the receptivity of the employer to international student candidates.

Because written information is effective only for practical information and not for employer education, workshops are an important part of the strategy. Two different approaches are available. The co-op educator may design and present an on-site workshop to one co-op employer, involving supervisory personnel and other staff. Or, as an alternative, several co-op employers may be invited to a workshop on campus. Like students, co-op employers who have had positive experiences with international students are usually willing to share their insight and expertise through presentations, discussions, and panel participation.

It is important to identify and work closely with co-op employers who are supportive of international student participation in the co-op program and therefore routinely hire international students. However, in the face of employer reluctance to hire international students, each co-op employer should see a mix of qualified students that includes both American and international students.

Just as co-op employers sometimes need priming when faced with a domestic student with problems, they may prefer to know in advance that they are about to interview a student who speaks English with difficulty. It is wise, therefore, to communicate closely with co-op employers when referring international students.

Educational Institution. The co-op staff should include an international student specialist to act as an intermediary both within and outside the educational institution, to assess the needs of international students, counsel the students, assist co-op staff with international student problems, assist with documentation such as social security numbers and visas, and design and conduct special co-op orientations and workshops for international students. Other than co-op staff, other institutional resources may be available to address the unique needs of international students. For example, specialists in teaching ESL (English as a second language) can assist students with technical language or with professional jargon. International student counselors can help students to adjust to living and working in America and assist with bureaucratic or political problems.

Educational institutions with a commitment to participation of international students in the cooperative education program may decide to charge an appropriate student fee to offset the additional expense of providing necessary support services.

The influx of international students into schools with cooperative education programs can mean the addition of unique and often complex problems for co-op educators. Unaddressed, these difficulties become on-the-job problems for both students and employers. However, several strategies for addressing these issues have proven successful, including the appointment of a co-op liaison, special co-op orientations and workshops, a career development course for international students, and the development of workshops and seminars for co-op employers.

Home Country Co-op Placement

Despite the plethora of problems associated with the placement of foreign students on co-op assignments in the United States, the fact remains nonetheless that thousands of these students continue to enroll in co-op institutions each year with the expectation, and in some cases even the requirement, that they will participate in the traditional co-op program. Clearly, if these institutions are to remain true to their mission and to provide equal opportunities for these students to derive the benefits inherent in cooperative work experience, then a viable institutional policy regarding foreign students and co-op must be developed within the context of and directly related to their basic educational mission. Within the framework of the policy, new strategies must also be devised to address the issue. One such strategy that appears to offer promise in facilitating the professional development of foreign students is that of arranging to have the students return home for their co-op assignments.

The primary reason why the concept of home country co-op placement holds a good deal of promise lies in its beneficial impact on all of the various constituencies involved and the manner in which it addresses the needs of each. With respect to potential multinational employers, these organizations have in recent years faced increasing pressures to nationalize the professional staffs in their overseas operations. Indeed, this nationalization requirement is often stipulated as a provision in engineering construction and design contracts.

Thus, there exists a felt need on the part of the multinationals for a cost-effective recruiting mechanism to access qualified foreign talent being educated in the United States who are interested in returning home to work. From the vantage point of a corporation, a home country co-op program could provide a ready source of company-trained manpower who have developed a familiarity with both the corporate culture and company equipment and whose performance will have been assessed in the actual home-country work setting prior to the offer of permanent employment. Moreover, such a program would eliminate the need for costly language and cultural training programs and could establish linkages with young professionals who might well represent the future business and governmental leaders of their countries.

With respect to its impact upon foreign students, a home country co-op program would address many of the critical co-op problems currently confronting them. In the face of these problems that beset the students in their quest to obtain co-op employment in the United States under the aegis of traditional domestic programs, the fact nonetheless remains that there is a dire need for such practical experience, especially on the part of students from developing nations.

In a major national research project undertaken by the National Association of Foreign Student Affairs in conjunction with the Agency for International Development (Lee, 1981), it was found that the needs for practical experience among such students were among the least met, and a key recommendation at the conclusion of the study called for the inclusion of such training in their programs. Moreover, the ever-present financial problems arising out of spiraling tuition rates and the increased cost of living in the United States have only served to be exacerbated by the unemployment or underemployment that is often the lot of these students.

In turning the focus of their employment search back to their home country, those factors such as language, culture, and work ethic that had heretofore been viewed as liabilities in the American labor market are suddenly transformed into assets. The most tangible benefits accruing to students under a home country co-op program would, of course, be the acquisition of experience in the site of prospective permanent employment and the opportunity for postgraduation employment potential. Within the context of certain cultures, the opportunity to re-establish family ties might serve as an equally important consideration as well.

Although the needs of students and employers are of course paramount in the development of any co-op program, it is nonetheless important to note that a co-op program based in a student's home country would also help meet certain important needs, as well as providing significant benefits to the country itself. Those nations that send out large numbers of sponsored students to be educated in the United States are constantly seeking to develop a more effective student selection policy. Participation in a home country co-op program could provide an additional viable criterion to the selection process.

Developing countries in particular are also very much concerned with improving methods for the transfer of technology and securing the cooperation of multinationals in the efforts to move forward with indigenization. A fully developed home country co-op program would help, at least in part, to address these concerns. Perhaps most important from the perspective of many Third World countries, this program, by periodically re-immersing its youth in the home culture, provides a greater potential for the return of its Western-educated talent and thus an effective response to the critical issue of "brain drain." Finally, the participants in the program might well serve as the foundation for the emergence of a cadre of managerial and technological leaders in the country's infrastructure.

A decision to establish a home country placement program should take into consideration the institutional resources, especially those of the co-op department, necessary to support such an endeavor. Obviously, a project of this nature must be viewed as an integral component of the college or university's total international program and commitment. Thus, it is essential to have a strong degree of support from the institutional leadership, as well. The latter is especially crucial in this instance since, as we shall see, the cooperation and coordination between the co-op department and other areas, notably the admissions office, is key to its success.

The first step in the development of a home country placement program involves the conducting of an economic risk analysis of those countries from which an institution desires to attract increasing numbers of students and in which it hopes to develop such programs. The information provided by these analyses can help determine which of the targeted countries are better able to economically sustain and support the programs. One possible approach, adopted by Northeastern University, entails sending a co-op representative to certain selected countries to explore the feasibility of initiating home country co-op programs with prospective employers, both multinational and indigenous.

Close on the heels of these visits would be those of a representative of the admissions department who would concentrate recruiting efforts in those countries wherein the prospects for developing co-op programs appeared to be optimal. Obviously, such an approach involves close collaboration between the admissions and co-op departments, and it is crucial that there be direct input from those coordinators most directly involved with the placement of such students, as well as from the international student office on campus. Of paramount importance in this effort is the development of appropriate literature, at least some of which should be in the native language of the country, geared to both the students and the prospective employers. Finally, interaction with the various educational ministries, both with the U.S.-based offices as well as with the home-country-based ones, is also essential in enlisting their cooperation and support of the concept, with respect to both their student clientele (especially government-sponsored students) and their government and the private sector.

In marketing a home country co-op program to multinational corporations, contact may be made to either the U.S.-based headquarters or to the overseas operation directly. Each approach offers certain inherent advantages and disadvantages and, in the final analysis, perhaps a combination of both might be most effective, depending on the individual company and specific country involved. Certainly, dealing directly with U.S.-based headquarters is a much less costly endeavor. If the interviewing and selection process is to be carried out in the United States, logistics are much easier to coordinate as well. Moreover, if the corporation desires that the student obtain some degree of experience with certain of its U.S. facilities prior to assignment back in the home country, then direct communication with U.S.-based headquarters appears to be the most feasible route to follow.

However, the overseas operations are certainly more cognizant of their own human resource needs, and ultimately the student will be expected to function in that setting. Further, it is not unusual for communication problems to arise between U.S. and overseas offices of the same company; therefore, if a company's plan calls for a student to begin work immediately in the home country facility, a direct approach to the latter may well be in order. Finally, there is increasing sensitivity on the part of the U.S. headquarters of multinationals to the local management prerogatives of such home-country operations.

For the past several years, many co-op institutions with sizeable foreign student enrollments have sought to develop new career models in an effort to meet the practical training needs of this growing element of their student body. A home country placement program represents one such viable model to better address these needs. At the same time, however, a program of this nature would impact on co-op personnel by necessitating certain significant changes in their modus operandi, including a modification of expectations regarding foreign students, a need for cross-cultural sensitivity training, and the acquisition of expertise in the home country employment scene.

On balance, the implementation of an effective home country placement program could prove to have significant benefits for the co-op department, including new and improved ties with the international components of business and industry, as well as increased levels of student satisfaction. Most important, it could enable an institution to truly fulfill its commitment to provide the maximum opportunity for the professional growth and development of these young people.

Overseas Placement of American Co-op Students

While students at traditional academic institutions have often used their summer vacation periods to travel throughout Europe and to seek employment in the various service industries, it is not surprising that increasing numbers of co-op students in recent years have expressed interest in obtaining overseas co-op assignments related to their major fields of study. In view of the economic interdependency that exists in today's world and the significance being accorded the transfer of technology, such requests are not only to be expected but are generally justifiable. However, as noted in the previous section, those forces and factors that have influenced multinational organizations to employ foreign nationals rather than American expatriates in their overseas operations have made it increasingly difficult for young American professionals to avail themselves of meaningful international experiences. Thus, for those students whose career plans would stand to benefit from the experience of an overseas assignment, obtaining the latter while on co-op takes on additional significance.

The decision to establish an overseas co-op program should be carefully considered in light of an institution's mission and resources and the interests and goals of its students. While an overseas co-op program can properly serve as an integral component within the overall international schema of an institution and may certainly enhance its presence abroad, the program should relate appropriately to the stage of development of the domestic program. For just as there is a critical need for an institutional commitment on behalf of the domestic co-op program, so too does this need exist for the international component.

Given the unique problems, cross-cultural issues, and often excessive time demands associated with the development and administration of an overseas co-op program, an institution would be well advised to consider appointing to its co-op staff qualified individuals whose primary or sole responsibility would focus on the overseas program. Indeed, if the program were to include exchanges with non-English-speaking countries, then language competence of the coordinator(s) should be taken into consideration as well. In addition to the institutional support in the form of personnel and financial resources, assistance and cooperation must also be forthcoming from those who are responsible for conducting the domestic program. Indeed, it is absolutely essential to enlist the support of the latter before embarking on any overseas venture.

In establishing an overseas co-op program, it is of the utmost importance to take into consideration the needs and goals of the students as they relate to their personal and professional development in addition to their academic programs. In general, an overseas co-op experience will serve to meet such needs and goals by providing students with an international component to their overall work experience, a cross-cultural awareness, personal growth and development, and an opportunity to improve language fluency where applicable.

Similarly, determining the focus of the program with respect to the countries and disciplines to be involved will be influenced in great measure by the interests and needs of the students, as well as by the institution's academic offerings and particular strengths. However, it must be recognized that marketing considerations also play a key role in such determinations. Those academic fields of study that have traditionally served as the bulwark of co-op programs in this country, that is, engineering, business administration, and certain of the health-related disciplines, are also those which are most in demand in overseas markets. Thus, the ultimate configuration of a viable overseas co-op program will be one that is employer driven as well as student driven and attuned to the marketing considerations of the individual countries targeted for development.

Unquestionably, the greatest challenge that confronts an institution in the establishment of an overseas co-op program is how to go about developing the overseas assignments. The resolution of this problem, at least in part, relates back to considerations of the program's size, projected number of participants, and issues of cost-effectiveness that subsequently must be addressed. If the number of students desiring overseas placement is minimal and internal resources are still not adequate to service their needs, it may be in the institution's and students' best interests to consider the feasibility of working with a reputable international organization such as IAESTE, the International Association for the Exchange of Students for Technical Experience (Columbia, Maryland), which provides international work experience for college and university students in engineering, agriculture, architecture, math, and science; AIESEC, the Association Internationale des Etudiants en Sciences Economiques et Commerciales (New York), which provides similar practical training opportunities for students of economics, business, and commerce; and CIEE, the Council on International Educational Exchange (New York), the largest organization responsible for administering programs that enable students to work abroad, generally in nonrelated, service-type positions. In the case of working with certain of these organizations, an institution is expected to provide a placement for a foreign exchange student in reciprocity for one of its own students being placed, while other external programs require the payment of substantial fees for use of their placement services.

If an institution determines that the degree of student interest in overseas co-op assignments, combined with its overall international objectives, would best be served by the development of its own overseas co-op program, then the internal resources must be examined for potential use in marketing the program and developing placements. A university's alumni relations office could be of assistance in providing a network of contacts, both of foreign alumni in targeted countries and American alumni working abroad. In addition, faculty who have recently taught, consulted, or worked abroad might also prove to be helpful in this effort.

Unquestionably, however, the most valuable resource in the cultivation of overseas placement remains those co-op employers that have operations, subsidiaries, and contacts in the countries of interest. Enlisting their support can be instrumental in the success of the program. It should also be noted that students who have worked in such companies are often desirous of securing experiences with the overseas affiliates of these organizations. Such students can be extremely helpful in developing their own co-op assignments and thereby providing the necessary opening wedge for future students.

Despite the best efforts of all concerned in developing overseas co-op programs, however, there exist certain inherent problems over which the institutions can exercise no control and which often stand in the way of success. First and foremost among these problems is the attitude of many foreign governments toward the employment of nonnationals in any capacity other than entry-level service positions. This attitude most often stems from the inordinately high unemployment rate that frequently exists among the youth of the country and is not very dissimilar to that reflected by the U.S. government during similarly difficult economic periods. Employers, including multinationals, especially those in smaller countries, likewise express nationalistic sentiments and concerns with respect to the impact of hiring American co-op students in the face of severe unemployment among their own youth.

In addition to the unemployment issue, another major obstacle involves an excess of bureaucratic red tape and prolonged waiting periods in order to secure a working permit in certain countries. Such delays can often render the best-laid plans futile. Programs such as IAESTE and AIESEC, however, are granted special authorization for work permits and visas in some countries.

One of the most effective strategies for dealing with the aforementioned problems is to establish a reciprocal work exchange program with an appropriate institution in the country where placements are desired. The key factor here is that of reciprocity, which, according to Sprinkle (1981), is "perhaps the single most difficult issue to be faced and the one most crucial to the long term future of co-op exchanges" (p. 105). It is incumbent upon the U.S. co-op institution to provide appropriate placements for the students of the schools with which it becomes affiliated in return for similar services rendered to its own students. The necessity for support in this endeavor by those who are responsible for the domestic co-op program thus becomes readily apparent.

It is important to note at this juncture that although the provision of placements for the exchange students is of the utmost importance, so too is the securing of appropriate visas (type J-1) to enable them to work in the United States. Perhaps the most effective way of addressing the latter issue is to apply to the USIA (United States Information Agency) for approval by that organization as an "Exchange Visitor Program." Such approval enables the institution to issue IAP-66 forms to exchange students who then are able to secure the J-1 visas from the American consulates in their home country. However, having an approved Exchange Visitor Program entails certain specific obligations and a degree of accountability, as outlined in the *Regulations Governing Designated Exchange-Visitor Programs* (United States Information Agency, 1983). Some of the key responsibilities outlined are as follows: "The sponsor . . . shall ensure that the practical training experience in the United States is suitable and appropriate for the individual's level of career development. The sponsor must assume full responsibility for the selection of trainees, regardless of the extent to which cooperating organizations in other countries may be involved" (p. 13). In addition to the foregoing, each program sponsor is expected to arrange an equivalent number of appropriate work experiences for U.S. students in other countries. Accountability is ensured through an annual report that must be submitted to the USIA.

In selecting an appropriate overseas affiliate, there are several important considerations to be borne in mind. One of the most critical involves the institution's co-op "track record" and its demonstrated linkages with business and industry. It is also generally advisable to seek out those institutions that are similar in terms of their basic nature and mission, academic calendars, majors to be serviced, and the marketability of their students. As Allen (1976) has wisely observed, all of the preceding factors should be considered, but the final selection should be made on the basis of personal trust and compatibility of the individuals most closely involved with the exchange.

After the selection of an exchange program partner has been made, it is highly advisable that an institutional agreement be drawn up that delineates the objectives of the exchange and enumerates the essential components. The following items should be incorporated in any such agreement:

- number of students to be involved in the exchange
- level and major of the students
- application and selection procedures
- length of work periods
- time frame for placements (including critical cutoff dates)
- provision of visas and work permits
- housing arrangements
- supportive services by host institution (including nature of information to be provided in orientations)
- evaluation procedures
- language capability, if applicable

If the institutions deem it advisable to have an academic period precede the work placement, then any financial arrangements regarding the tuition involved for both parties should be spelled out in the agreement, as well. Finally, provision should also be made for a liaison system that will effectively service the needs of the exchange.

Unquestionably, the most difficult aspect of carrying out

a reciprocal exchange agreement involves the placement of exchange students. As previously noted, the cooperation of the domestic co-op staff is essential in this process. Indeed, it would certainly be to the advantage of the international program if specific individual coordinators/advisors were designated as official liaisons to the program. Such an arrangement would not only serve to facilitate the placement process but would enhance the credibility of the program, which may well be perceived as diverting attention and resources from the domestic program. It would also be highly desirable whenever possible to involve members of the domestic co-op staff in activities such as meeting international visitors and visiting the exchange students on the job.

Although fortuitous timing and the unavailability of qualified domestic co-op students may sometimes make it possible to place exchange students in ongoing co-op jobs, most assignments will need to be individually developed. Since candidates will be prescreened by the overseas institution liaison, it is essential that a thorough accord be reached on the nature, qualifications, and marketability of proposed applicants. In addition, considerable care should be taken to ensure the uniform high quality of the dossiers, since the students' acceptability will in great measure be decided on the basis of such documentation. If at all possible, those responsible for the exchange should attempt to meet any prospective candidates during visits to the overseas institution.

In developing new placements for the exchange students, it is advisable to enlist the cooperation of the domestic co-op staff in approaching long-standing employers, particularly multinationals or companies that either have overseas affiliations or who themselves are subsidiaries of foreign firms. If the overseas institution also has an ongoing co-op program with the same company, it may be possible to work out a quadrilateral agreement, wherein a U.S. student would have a position set aside in the foreign operation in return for a similar arrangement for the exchange student in the U.S. firm. In approaching co-op companies, however, it is well to bear in mind Sprinkle's observation (1981) that "employer motivation for supporting domestic co-op programs does not necessarily extend to support for international experience for co-op students" (p. 102). Indeed, those employers who see fit to provide opportunities for foreign exchange students may do so for an entirely different set of reasons than those which motivate domestic co-op employers. Such reasons often bear upon public relations considerations, with respect to both their domestic clientele and their international presence. Thus, marketing strategies should be formulated that emphasize the latter advantages in addition to the individual qualifications of the students.

Even after appropriate positions have been secured and attentive care given to the placement process, it is not unusual for minor adjustment problems to arise as a result of cultural differences and their impact on both students and employers. These difficulties can be minimized by providing the employer, particularly the immediate supervisor, with as much background information as possible on the candidate, his or her institution, and the expectations set forth in the program. Similarly, the student should also receive information on the company even prior to arrival in the United States and be fully informed as to the employer's expectations during the orientation session preceding the work period. Although refinements and adjustments to the program are sometimes necessary to ensure its well-being and to promote mutual satisfaction, the presence of a support system at the host institution to which the student can turn as needed can prove to be of significant benefit in facilitating the adjustment process.

Just as it is essential to have complete and highly presentable dossiers on the foreign exchange students, so too is it equally incumbent upon American students to prepare the same. Northeastern University's Reciprocal Exchange Program has found it advisable to include in the complete application packet a general application form, one-page statement from the student as to his or her motivations and objectives in applying for an international co-op experience, transcript of grades, description of relevant course work, personal health statement, resume, and three letters of recommendation. If language proficiency is a consideration, appropriate certification of competency is also required.

While the application packet or portfolio stands to serve

as the primary marketing device in promoting American students to prospective foreign employers, it may be advisable to supplement this device whenever possible by arranging for telephone interviews between the student and employer. This direct communication often serves to alleviate any possible misunderstandings concerning the job description and/or expectations on either side. In addition, consideration may also be given to having the students enroll in coursework for an academic period preceding the work experience. Although the latter arrangement can introduce other potential problems into the exchange, such as tuition factors and the necessity of placement guarantees, it does nevertheless guarantee the student's availability for personal interviews.

In selecting students for participation in an international exchange program, certain factors must be kept uppermost in mind. Obviously the marketability of the students is a major issue and therefore, their academic performance, major fields of study, and previous records of successful co-op work experience are key determinants. Just as critical as these criteria, however, is the exchange program advisor's assessment of the student's overall maturity and ability to function independently and effectively in a totally different cultural milieu. For this reason, it is essential to have advisors on the staff who have themselves experienced such isolation and culture shock.

In those countries where English is not the primary language, this issue, along with that of language proficiency, becomes even more critical. It is therefore advisable to consider the introduction of special language courses specifically geared to students preparing for overseas co-op assignments and to arrange for intensive language training at special overseas schools, accompanied by home stays, prior to the beginning of the work period.

Although an entire chapter could well be devoted to the legal, taxation, and insurance issues involving the placement of students on overseas co-op assignments, there are at least a few key points that should be stated here. Students would be well advised to secure their work permits for certain countries through appropriate official, intermediary organizations with offices in this country, such as BUNAC (British Universities North American Club) and USIT (Union of Student Ireland Travel). For a minimal fee, these organizations, which also make presentations on campuses, provide not only the work permit but sound advice and can serve as excellent points of contact for the students through their home offices. It should be noted, however, that the normal work permits, at least in Ireland and the United Kingdom, are only valid for four and six months respectively. Arrangements must be made to secure extensions for longer co-op work periods, and extensions are often difficult to arrange.

With respect to taxation issues, it is incumbent upon the exchange office of the host institution to provide as much information as possible. The home offices of the intermediary organizations previously cited can also be most helpful in this regard. Foreign exchange students working in the United States under a J-1 visa are required to pay both federal and state income taxes on earned wages but are exempt from social security deductions. The International Exchange Program Office at Northeastern University provides the students with a letter that clarifies their tax status to their employer upon their arrival. In addition, arrangements are made for them to secure their social security numbers.

In view of the exorbitant costs of health care in the United States today, it is most prudent to require foreign exchange students to be covered by a health and accident policy prior to their arrival. Should their own policy not cover them while they are working in the United States, they would be well advised to enroll in the NAFSA (National Association for Foreign Student Affairs) International Accident and Sickness Program (Washington, D.C.). American students should, in turn, review the coverage limits of their own policies and make the necessary arrangements to ensure their protection while they are overseas. Those students in certain of the health care professions should also consider the feasibility of securing professional liability insurance, which is often available through their individual professional associations.

No chapter dealing with the placement of students in foreign countries would be complete without reference to the vital role that well-planned orientations can play in the ultimate success or failure of the endeavor. While the importance of such orientations has long been recognized by those responsible for study-abroad programs, the issue is far more critical in preparing those to work abroad. Indeed, the USIA's *Regulations Governing Designated Exchange-Visitor Programs* (United States Information Agency, 1983) also require that sponsors provide each participant with an orientation that is suitable to the length and nature of the assignment. Carefully planned and executed orientations can be instrumental in minimizing culture shock, facilitating adjustment, and helping to optimize the benefits that a student can derive from the work experience. Perhaps more than any other single element, the one factor that can contribute to the effectiveness of such orientations is the inclusion of former participants, as well as those foreign exchange students working in the immediate geographic area. In fact, the development of a student support group from among the latter can immeasurably assist in the promotional efforts, smooth functioning, and ultimate success of any overseas co-op work exchange.

References

Allen, D. R. "Foreign Exchange and Cooperative Education: A Blueprint." *Cooperative Education Association Journal,* 1976, *12,* 75–82.

Lee, M. Y. *Needs of Foreign Students from Developing Nations at U.S. Colleges and Universities.* Washington, D.C.: National Association for Foreign Student Affairs, 1981.

Sprinkle, R. M. "International Work Assignments for Co-op Students: Some Issues to be Considered." *Cooperative Education Association Journal,* 1981, *17,* 99–107.

United States Information Agency. *Regulations Governing Designated Exchange-Visitor Programs.* Washington, D.C.: United States Information Agency, 1983.

Thirteen

What Students Gain from Cooperative Education

James W. Wilson

Were you to ask a cooperative education advisor, a faculty member, a work supervisor, or anyone who has observed co-op students for any length of time just what it is that the cooperative experience does for students, you would surely get one, or more, or most likely all of the following kinds of responses.

1. It makes them more mature.
2. It motivates them to work harder on their studies, and they are more likely to graduate.
3. It gives them greater self-confidence.
4. It helps them to better know where they are going.
5. It makes them more responsible.
6. It makes them more realistic.
7. It makes them more aware of the expectations of the workplace.
8. It helps them develop important interpersonal skills.
9. It helps them to find greater relevancy in their studies.
10. It helps them to become effective members of their communities and the society of which they are a part.

These propositions constitute much of the accumulated wisdom regarding the values that accrue to co-op students. During the early years of co-op, the principal source of this wisdom was the observations and reflections of those who have worked closely with co-ops. For example, Ayer (1931) stated, "Another interesting by-product of cooperative training is the effect upon the student of his contact during his formative years with mature men. A freshman comes in to complain to the coordinator about his work and its lack of educational opportunities. His whole conversation is a striking example of kiddishness. Sometime between two and three years later, he comes in again, and the coordinator realizes at once that this immature student had evolved [sic] into a man. When we remember that the full-time student has very little contact with men, beyond his associations with his instructors, and that he lives almost entirely in a somewhat secluded world of immaturity, it is not surprising that he gets an erroneous idea of life as it is actually lived. . . . The cooperative method teaches by experience life in a highly competitive society and hastens manly development through contact with adults" (pp. 625–626).

To illustrate further, Disque (1931) advanced two reasons, based on his twelve year experience with cooperative education, for his conviction that co-op stimulates analytic proficiency: (1) after fourteen years of almost continuous study, students tend to become stale and the change to work experience gives them renewed interest and vigor; and (2) the cooperative work experience provides students with opportunities to visualize the practical results of their theoretical training. Finally, in the twenty-first yearbook of the Society for the Study of Education (Morgan, 1932), we find this statement about the influence of cooperative education on students by the then President of Antioch College, Arthur E. Morgan: "In their industrial experience, which is carefully selected and is supervised and interpreted by faculty members appointed for that purpose, the students develop practical judgment, self-reliance, responsibility, and a knowledge of men and affairs" (p. 186).

One might be tempted to dismiss these "undocumented" contentions of the impact of co-op upon participating students as little more than the biased and unsupported remarks of professional enthusiasts. That would be a mistake. First, an accumulation of empirical research lends support to their accuracy. Second, they have served and continue to serve as "hypotheses to be tested" and thus guide research. This chapter will examine the research that provides the empirical base for our current beliefs about the influence of the cooperative education experience on students. The information to be presented will be organized under the following sections: student motives for participating, developmental outcomes, academic outcomes, and other outcomes. Within this organization, however, research findings bearing on each of the alleged values noted above will be presented.

Student Motivations for Participating in Cooperative Education

The question is often asked, Why do students choose to co-op in the first place? It is assumed just about as often that the principal reason is to earn money. A second question usually follows: "Are there differences to begin with between students who co-op and students who do not?" This question is significant for two reasons. First, if there are differences and they can be used to predict who will be attracted to co-op, then admissions officers and cooperative education staffs would be better able to focus their recruitment efforts. Second, if such differences exist, then they might account for some of the subsequent differences that research finds.

Unfortunately, however, there has been relatively little research into possible differences between students choosing the cooperative plan and those not choosing it, and neither of these factors has been the focus of any research. For the most part, reported information indicates that students who participate are similar to those who do not. Cohen and others (1978), for example, hypothesized eight precooperative experience variables to be associated with choosing to participate. Six of these were confirmed through a statistical procedure known as discriminant analysis; however, when they were used to actually predict participation, they yielded only chance results. The hypotheses for which they found support are as follows.

1. The greater the amount of parental support received by a student, the less likely he or she is to co-op.
2. Minority students are more likely to co-op.
3. Students who receive greater amounts of tuition assistance are less likely to co-op.
4. Male students are more likely to co-op.
5. Married students are more likely to co-op.
6. Veterans are more likely to co-op.

Wilson and Lyons (1961) and Wilson (1974) found a relationship between social class membership and participation in co-op. In both studies, co-op students were found distributed across all social strata, but with noticeable skewing toward the lower-middle and working classes. This suggests, and is generally interpreted as evidence, that students attracted to co-op tend to use higher education as a means of upward mobility and thus seek career-directed and practical education. In this connection, it is interesting to note that in the same study noted above (Wilson, 1974), freshman liberal arts students who had expressed their intention to co-op were less sure of their career goals than a like group of freshman liberal arts students indicating they would not co-op. It appears that cooperative education may have a particular attraction to students for whom the principal purpose of education is to prepare for a career, but who are not sure of their career goals.

A number of researchers have examined students' reasons for participating in cooperative education (Pitcoff and Brodsky, 1965; Cohen and others, 1978; Perry, 1981). The most typical reasons cited include the following:

- To explore and clarify career goals
- To acquire skills and experience related to career goals
- To gain practical experience
- To make educational experience more rewarding
- To make postgraduation job contacts
- To gain financial assistance

Among these, the most frequently cited reasons relate to educational gains that might be achieved, not financial or postgraduation employment. It is clear that students opt for co-op because they perceive that it will provide them with skills, information, and insights essential to their futures.

Outcomes

Over the years, a substantial body of empirically derived knowledge of cooperative education outcomes for students has accumulated. The substantive thrusts of this research have been career development, academic progress, personal growth, and financial assistance.

Career Development. As noted above, a major motivation for student participation in cooperative education is to clarify career goals and to better prepare for a career. There is abundant evidence that this occurs. Wilson and Lyons (1961) reported that 88 percent of their sample of 614 senior cooperative education students perceived that both their educational and career goals were clarified as a consequence of their work experiences. Brown (1976) conducted a study of co-op and non-co-op alumni and found a significantly greater proportion of the co-op graduates felt, at the time of graduation, that they had received adequate career information during their college careers. Weinstein (1980) found that a significantly higher proportion of seniors who had had cooperative work experience were more confident of their career choices than their counterparts without co-op. More recently, Brown (1984) found that recent co-op graduates have more realistic job expectations on their first job after graduation than non-co-op graduates. This was especially true for those who had gone to work for their former co-op employer, but it was also the case for those co-ops who went to work for a different employer. Interestingly, her research showed that nonsponsored work, regardless of the amount, did not influence job expectations as much as participation in cooperative education.

Several additional studies (Smith and Beckley, 1946; Baskin, 1954; Fram, 1964; Wilson, 1974), conducted with local samples, also indicated that co-op students had more frequently decided upon a career after graduation and were more confident of their decisions than students who had not co-oped. One of these (Wilson, 1974) also provided strong evidence that one outcome of cooperative work experience is more realistic and practical (and less idealistic) career expectations. Although the methodology of this research was cross-sectional, it simulated a longitudinal study by sampling students from each of five sequential undergraduate classes. The results showed that for co-op students, as opposed to non-co-ops, there was a clear trend away from anticipating careers in service and humanitarian fields and toward careers in business and business-related fields, with successive classes from the freshman to the senior year.

A number of the studies cited above on career clarification also provide support for the proposition that cooperative education contributes to career preparation. In all instances (Wilson and Lyons, 1961; Brown, 1984; Cohen and others, 1978), the data consisted of students' or graduates' reports of their own perceptions. For example, the Wilson and Lyons (1961, p. 107) study observed that 84 percent of their sample of senior co-op students reported that their work experiences "demonstrated the application of theory to practice" and that 77 percent reported that it "provided training in an occupational area." For their sample of non-co-op seniors, these percentages were, respectively, 67 and 56. Cohen and others (1978) reported that 55 percent of their co-op sample, in contrast to 38 percent of their non-co-op sample, rated their improvement of job skills by the end of their college program as above average or excellent.

Another element of preparation that has been reported upon is that of co-op graduates going to work full-time with a former co-op employer. Wilson and Lyons (1961) found that 38 percent of their total co-op graduate sample went to work for a former co-op employer. They also reported differential rates of return among the curriculum areas represented in their sample, with engineering graduates being the largest, business second, and liberal arts third. These differential rates were better explained by Cohen and others (1978), in terms of length of student co-op service with the firm. This same study also found an overall co-op employer retention rate of 38 percent. It was found that 27 percent of students returned if they worked for the firm co-op between one and six months; 40

percent returned if they were with the company seven to twelve months; and 53 percent returned if they worked thirteen months or longer as co-op students. Typically, engineering students are more likely to remain with a single employer for all co-op terms and liberal arts students are more likely to change employers each co-op term. In a very different but related study, Weinstein (1980) found, for a sample of engineering students, that cooperative work experience of any amount helped students to clarify their career goals, but successive work terms with a single employer also promoted assurance of the job they would take after graduation.

Academic Progress. Wilson and Lyons's national appraisal of cooperative education in 1961 investigated a series of claimed advantages and disadvantages of the plan. One of the presumed disadvantages about which data were collected was that scheduled interruption of academic study with periods of work would be distracting, would disrupt student learning efforts, and consequently result in achievement loss. Contrary to this concern, the research found no loss, as measured by results of the Graduate Record Examination area tests. In fact, cooperative students scored somewhat higher on these standardized achievement tests than did noncooperative students. In subsequent research (Smith, 1965; Lindenmeyer, 1967; Yencso, 1970; Gore, 1972; Davie and Russell, 1974; McNutt, 1974), small but statistically reliable differences in grades between groups of co-op and non-co-op students were found to favor the co-op students. Typically, these gains were somewhat less than one letter grade.

Research has also compared the retention rates of co-op and non-co-op students. In separate studies, Smith (1965), Stark (1965), and Lindenmeyer (1967) compared otherwise comparable groups and found that, once the co-op experiences began, a larger proportion of cooperative students continued their programs to graduation than did the non-co-ops. Brightman (1973), on the other hand, found no difference between co-ops and a control group in terms of the proportion of students starting a semester and completing that semester or continuing on to the next semester. He did find, however, that during a given period, co-ops carried and completed more credits than non-co-ops.

→   *Personal Growth.* Research into the influence of cooperative education on the individual growth of participants has generally examined such matters as improving interpersonal relations, developing autonomy and self-confidence, applying theory to practice, and finding greater meaning in one's studies. For the most part, data have been obtained from current cooperative students (Smith, 1944; Mosbacker, 1957; Brightman, 1973; Keith, 1974; Peart, 1974; Wilson, 1974; Cornelius, 1978). However, data have sometimes been obtained from graduates of cooperative programs (Brown, 1976), from both students and graduates, and from faculty and employers, as well (Wilson and Lyons, 1961; Cohen and others, 1978).

A number of the studies simply asked current co-ops to respond to questions about the perceived effect of their cooperative work experience. Thus, for example, Keith (1974) asked students the extent of their agreement with the statement: "My co-op experience helped me develop greater understanding of interpersonal relationships in a work environment" (p. 7). Eighty-four percent of the respondents either agreed or strongly agreed with this statement. Other researchers, for example, Cohen and others (1978), compared responses of co-op and non-co-op students to personal growth items. They reported that a significantly greater proportion of co-op students found the following two statements to reflect important advantages of holding a job while in college than did non-co-op students: (1) "Provides an opportunity to apply the things I study to actual work situations"; and (2) "Gives me a chance to assume real responsibility" (p. 133).

Wilson and Lyons (1961) obtained questionnaire responses from current freshmen and senior co-op and non-co-op students and from co-op and non-co-op alumni from five graduating classes. For each of the seven comparison groups, the co-ops assessed their college opportunities to apply theory to practice more favorably than did their noncooperative counterparts. Wilson (1974) sought to simulate a longitudinal study by comparing student responses across classes for samples of co-op and non-co-op students. He found that a significant number of co-op students, from freshmen to seniors, reported change (and presumably growth) in the variables that follow; whereas non-co-op students did not report such change.

- Development of social skills
- Development of an interest in new fields of learning
- Development of friendships and loyalties of lasting value
- Efficiency as a student
- Tolerance and understanding of other people and their views
- Freedom to express thoughts and feelings
- Development of an identity and sense of self-confidence
- Appreciation of individuality and independence of thought and action

Two studies (Brightman, 1973; Cornelius, 1978) used a pre- and postsurvey design in which they administered a survey instrument to co-op students before they commenced a work term and then again upon the completion of that work term. Brightman, who also used a pre- and postsurvey control group of non-co-op students, found a statistically reliable and positive change in attitudes toward education on the part of the co-ops, but not among the non-co-ops. Cornelius used only a cooperative education sample, but examined the possibility of change among a number of subgroups based on demographic characteristics: race, sex, age, course of study, whether or not the students had had prior work experience, and whether or not the students had had a formal career education course. Although some subgroups did not exhibit change on some variables, she found statistically reliable post–work term gains, for the sample as a whole, in terms of career awareness, self-confidence, and the need for coursework outside normal major requirements that would be important or helpful to career success.

The thrust of research findings in the area of cooperative education and personal growth is that cooperative work experience does contribute to individual development. It appears to have a positive impact on how students feel about themselves— their self-confidence and level of independence; it seems to make them more conscious of the importance of good human relations and helps them in developing interpersonal skills, it affects their sense of responsibility and their work habits; it impacts positively on their attitudes toward education and learning; and it aids in developing skills of application.

Financial Assistance. To the consternation of many professionals in the field, the single value of cooperative education that most often attracts attention and generates excitement is the financial assistance it provides students. They believe, correctly so, that cooperative education was initially conceived as an educational strategy, that years of evolution have proved it to be an educational strategy of considerable merit, that it continues to provide today's students strong educational enhancement, and that the financial values that result are too much emphasized. Nonetheless, the fact remains that over 87 percent of all cooperative education programs in the United States place most or all of their students in paid positions. Wages and salaries vary widely, depending upon the business, industry, or agency in which students work, the geographic region of the country, and where the students are in their academic program. Hence, an average wage may not be particularly meaningful, but the current best estimates for the Northeast and Midwest (Dailey, 1986; Crusoe, 1986) place it in an hourly range of $6.80 to $7.20. What this translates to in annual co-op income is further dependent upon the number of weeks students actually work. The typical range is from one semester to two quarters, or seventeen to twenty-six weeks, of co-op work in a year. Using the extremes of both the wage range and the weeks of work range, an average annual range of from $4,600 to $7,500 is obtained.

Total annual 1986 costs are estimated at $5,700 at public four-year colleges and universities and at $10,300 at private institutions (Evangelauf, 1986). Because co-op students pay taxes on their earnings and incur living expenses during their work terms, it would be an infrequent occurrence for a student to be able to meet college expenses completely in a public institution and next to impossible in a private one. Nonetheless, co-op earnings can be and are used to offset some portion of college costs. Unfortunately, there are no recent national data available to indicate what that portion is. Two earlier studies, however, reported relevant information. Wilson and Lyons (1961) found that 50 percent of their sample of senior students paid 70 percent or more of their college expenses, presumably from co-op earnings. In contrast, only 16 percent of their noncooperative senior sample met that proportion of expenses. Smaller proportions of their graduate samples contributed that much to their college expenses. But for each class sampled the co-ops contributed significantly more than the non-co-ops. Yencso (1970) also surveyed graduates and found a large proportion, 76 percent, contributing three-quarters or more of their college costs, again presumably from co-op earnings.

However, it should be noted that while the potential for financial gain is obviously present and is, just as obviously, a motivation for participation, it is not the only motivation or necessarily even the greatest one. For example, 70 percent of Wilson and Lyons' (1961) sample agreed or strongly agreed with the proposition that the educational benefit is the ultimate value of cooperative education. Cohen and others (1978) found that only 34 percent of their student sample chose the cooperative program because the additional income was essential to their continuing college. This was the fifth most frequently given reason for participating, behind such reasons as the acquisition of skills related to career objectives and making educational experience more meaningful.

An Interpretation of Research Findings

The body of research studies examining the impact of cooperative education on students clearly indicates that participation contributes to clarification of career goals and greater assurance in deciding upon a goal; developing autonomy and self-confidence; increasing awareness of the need for and skills involved in interpersonal relations; and increasing motivation for studies, as manifested in increased academic achievement and perseverance. The obvious question is Why? Why is it that these values are associated with student participation in cooperative education?

To suggest an answer, the essential nature of the cooperative experience must be examined. It has several characteristics. First, and most important, it is work. Hence, the student becomes productively involved in whatever functions and responsibilities are dictated by the assignment. Student involvement is a critical element of the experience. It is a well-established principle that learner involvement in the tasks of learning contributes strongly to the effectiveness of learning. Too frequently in learning situations, students are put in the position of being passive recipients.

Second, the work experience and the environment in which that experience occurs provide the student with many direct opportunities to explore career possibilities, to test the appropriateness of choices already made, and to check requirements and conditions against aptitudes and interests. A very important part of the work environment is that it gives students an opportunity to observe what professionals in the field do and, thereby, to know better what will be expected of them. Tyler (1981) observed that this process of observation is an important mechanism for students to clarify their learning goals. He further noted that many students, even those preparing for professions, have little contact with professionals in the field and, thus, do not have appropriate role models for their learning efforts.

Third, the cooperative experience is, and is perceived by students to be, a formal and integral part of their total college education. This is not casual, part-time employment. Because of this, the work experience and the academic experience become linked and a student perceives job learning, job performance, and "getting along" on the job as vital elements of the total educational experience. This view of the co-op experience is supported by the previously cited study by Brown (1984), in which she found that in their first year and first job after graduation, both co-op graduates who went to work for a co-op employer and co-op graduates who went to work for another employer had more realistic career goals than graduates who had worked during college but were not co-op students. It is not work alone that leads to the reported results. It is the total experience, which necessarily includes work but also includes institution sponsorship and guidance and assistance by a coordinator or advisor.

Fourth, performance in the work situation is assessed, and the student is apprised of that assessment. This occurs formally at the end of the work term, but it occurs informally along the way. What is important is that students get feedback on the success or failure of work performed and on how they interact with supervisors and co-workers. This feedback comes quickly. In school, students often get no clear feedback on their learning efforts or, when they do, it is often delayed so that there is no opportunity to correct errors quickly. In the work situation, there is such opportunity, and the result is typically one of student incentive to achieve and to view that achievement as reward for the effort.

Fifth, students are paid for their work. The importance of this as financial assistance has already been discussed. There are, however, two other reasons why paying co-ops is important. It is acknowledgment that their efforts are worthy and that they are a contributing part of adult society and are being compensated as are other contributing adults. And when employers pay for work to be done they are more likely to hold employees to high standards of responsibility and performance. In turn, this contributes to more realistic, challenging, and meaningful cooperative experiences for students.

Thus, the cooperative experience places responsibility on students for productive work, furnishes them with a rich environment for exploring and testing career choices, provides professional role models, gives them feedback on the adequacy of their efforts, reminds them that they are productive adults through the mechanism of wages, and formally links the work experience to the academic experience to create a synergism. Each of these elements of the co-op experience entails a sound learning principle. It seems only reasonable that the experience would stimulate students to clarify goals, develop greater confidence in themselves, become more responsible, and relate more effectively with others—in short, to become more mature. It is equally reasonable to understand that as students clarify their goals and are assured of them, as they better understand where their studies will likely lead, as they become more sure of themselves, their motivation for study will increase and their learning will be more effective.

References

Ayer, F. E. "Some Unsung Aspects of Cooperative Training." *Journal of Engineering Education,* 1931, *22,* 625-626.

Baskin, S. "The Graduate of the College Work-Study Program: A Study of His Career Planning and Later Work Adjustment." Unpublished doctoral dissertation, New York University, 1954.

Brightman, R. W. "Attitudes, Persistence and Performance of Cooperative Work Experience Students." Unpublished paper, Coast Community College District, 1973.

Brown, S. J. *Cooperative Education and Career Development: A Comparative Study of Alumni.* Boston: Cooperative Education Research Center, Northeastern University, 1976.

Brown, S. J. *The Influence of Cooperative Education on First Job After Graduation.* Boston: Cooperative Education Research Center, Northeastern University, 1984.

Cohen, A. J., and others. *Cooperative Education—A National Assessment: Final Report.* Vol. 1. Maryland: Applied Management Associates, 1978.

Cornelius, C. P. "Florida Community College Student Self-Perceptions Related to an Initial Semester of Participation in a Cooperative Education Program." Unpublished doctoral dissertation, University of Florida, 1978.

Crusoe, J. A. *Student Employee Salary and Benefits Survey.* Detroit, Mich.: Midwest Cooperative Education Association, 1986.

Dailey, T. G. "Analysis of Cooperative Student Wages, 1986." Memorandum, Northeastern University, 1986.

Davie, R. S., and Russell, J. K. "Academic Performance and Work Experience: An Australian Experience." *Journal of Cooperative Education,* 1974, *10* (2), 26-34.

Disque, R. C. "Education for Analysis in the Cooperative Plan." *Journal of Engineering Education,* 1931, *22,* 523-524.

Evangelauf, J. "Colleges and States Devising New Ways to Help Families Pay High Tuition Fees." *The Chronicle of Higher Education,* 1986, *32* (20), 23.

Fram, E. H. "An Evaluation of the Work-Study Program at the Rochester Institute of Technology." Unpublished doctoral dissertation, State University of New York at Buffalo, 1964.

Gore, G. "New Evidence of Co-op System Relevancy." *Journal of Cooperative Education,* 1972, *8* (2), 7-14.

Keith, N. R. *Student Evaluation of Cooperative Education Experience.* Research and Evaluation Report no. 6. Park Forest South, Ill.: Governors State University, 1974.

Lindenmeyer, R. S. "A Comparison of the Academic Progress of the Cooperative and Four-Year Student." *Journal of Cooperative Education,* 1967, *3* (2), 8-18.

McNutt, D. E. "A Comparison of Academic Achievement Between Cooperative Education Students and Non-Cooperative Education Students at College of the Mainland." Unpublished doctoral paper, Nova University, 1974.

Morgan, A. E. "Learning through Experience: Antioch College." In *Liberal-Arts Education,* Part 2. Twenty-first yearbook. Chicago: Society for the Study of Education, 1932.

Mosbacker, W. "Women Graduates of Cooperative Work-Study Programs on the College Level." *Personnel and Guidance Journal,* 1957, *35,* 508-511.

Peart, G. "A Survey of the Cooperative Work Experience Education Program, Fresno City College." *Journal of Cooperative Education,* 1974, *10* (2), 55-68.

Perry, A. M. "Non Traditional Student Participation in Cooperative Education: Report of a Survey." *Journal of Cooperative Education,* 1981, *17* (2), 43-48.

Pitcoff, J., and Brodsky, F. "Highlights of Cooperative Student Opinion Survey." *Journal of Cooperative Education,* 1965, *2* (1), 21-27.

Smith, L. F. "Cooperative Work Programs." *Journal of Higher Education,* 1944, *15* (4), 1-3.

Smith, L. F., and Beckley, D. K. "What Do Students Think of Co-operative Education?" *Industrial Arts and Vocational Education,* 1946, *33,* 295-296.

Smith, S. H. "Influence of Participation in the Cooperative Program on Academic Performance." *Journal of Cooperative Education,* 1965, *3* (1), 7-20.

Stark, M. H. "An Appraisal of the Work-Study Program at Wilmington College and the Cooperative Industry." Unpublished doctoral dissertation, Colorado State College, 1965.

Tyler, R. W. "The Values of Cooperative Education from a Pedagogical Perspective." *Proceedings of the Second World Conference on Cooperative Education.* Boston: Northeastern University, 1981.

Weinstein, D. S. *Cooperative Education Strategies and Student Career Development.* Cooperative Association Research Monograph no. 1. Boston: Cooperative Education Research Center, Northeastern University, 1980.

Wilson, J. W. *Impact of Cooperative Education upon Personal Development and Growth of Values.* Boston: Cooperative Education Research Center, Northeastern University, 1974.

Wilson, J. W., and Lyons, E. H. *Work-Study College Programs.* New York: Harper & Row, 1961.

Yencso, W. R. "A Comparative Analysis of Engineering Graduates from Cooperative and Regular Programs." Unpublished doctoral dissertation, University of Michigan, 1970.

Fourteen

The Impact
of Cooperative Education
on Employers and Graduates

Sylvia J. Brown

The principal focus of this chapter will be on the impact of cooperative education on employers and upon research findings regarding employer involvement in co-op. Since, however, some of the potential employer benefits occur as a result of the full-time employment of graduates who were co-op students, and since there is substantial correspondence in the values that may accrue to both employers and graduates, graduate outcomes will be assessed as well.

Employer Motivation to Participate

Cooperative education is an example of a joint venture be between two identifiably different but interdependent organizations and hence is subject to analysis in terms of the principles and theories of organizational behavior (Wilson, 1983). In the present context, the significant principle is that two organizations will enter into joint ventures only if they have compatible needs that cannot be satisfactorily met independently and the interactive venture is seen to have promise for fulfilling these needs (Tornatsky and Lounsbury, 1979; Wilson, 1980). In this instance, the college and university need is to attract students, and the employer need is for human resources.

The essential point here is that employers participate in cooperative education because it has the potential for addressing both their immediate and long-term employment needs. Wiseman and Page (1983) analyzed the responses of 141 employers of co-op students from a Western university. The employers came from both the private and public sectors. The students whom they employed were social science, humanities, and human services majors. They statistically reduced fifteen potential and generally recognized benefits to employer participation down to three general goals: increased productivity; reduction of overhead expenses; and a long-term training relationship with co-op faculty. Weinstein and Wilson (1983) reported a study of seventy-four large, high-tech corporations which, through three rounds of questioning, "described" a model cooperative education program. As viewed by the respondents, the principal objectives of a model program were, in rank order, (1) to retain students on graduation; (2) to provide challenging, interesting, and practical work for the students; and (3) to assess future employees before hiring.

For the reported sample of companies, and one might cautiously generalize to large corporations, a major motivation for participating in cooperative education is to meet long-range, full-time employment requirements. Even the second objective, to provide "good" work experiences for students, can be construed as having the intent of attracting students to postgraduation employment. To recruit full-time employees has been cited as a primary motivation to participate by others as well (Gore, 1973a; Arthur D. Little, Inc., 1974; Deane and others, 1978; Robbins, 1978; Pistler, 1984).

In contrast, in a replication of the study by Weinstein and himself, using a sample of employers with no more than 100 employees, Wilson (1985) found that the principal objective of their participation was to "increase cost effectiveness by using co-ops to release professional employees from subprofessional duties." Of course, these findings do not mean that small employers are never interested in recruiting co-ops for full-time employment, nor that large employers care nothing about meeting immediate employment needs. They do suggest, however, a basic difference between large and small employers insofar as what it is they principally seek to gain from taking part in cooperative education.

Costs to Participating Employers

It is obvious that employers who become co-op employers will incur costs: hiring costs, administrative costs, wages, supervisory costs, and evaluation costs. Estimates of these costs have ranged from high (Phillips, 1978) to negligible (Deane and others, 1978). Phillips, describing the program at the Georgia-Lockheed Company, reported that, based on an initial group of ten co-ops and taking in account attrition from that group, the total cost for three years of co-op culminating in full-time employment cost the company $23,100 (1973 dollars). The cost elements included by Phillips were: recruiting and travel, program coordination, administration, and unproductive labor.

In contrast, Deane and others collected cost-related data from approximately 250 co-op employers and concluded that, for the most part, the costs of participating in a co-op program are minimal. The discrepancy in these two analyses is due, in large measure, to the fact that Phillips reported actual costs incurred by the company and Deane and others reported, in effect, marginal costs attributable to the cooperative program. Specifically, Deane and others asked employers to judge whether particular cost items were more or less for co-ops than for regular employees, or the same. The cost items to which employers responded were start-up costs, compensation costs, training costs, supervision costs, evaluation costs, turnover costs, union negotiation time, and customer relations. Supervisory cost, measured in terms of expended time, was the only cost item which showed somewhat greater cost attached to co-ops. Other researchers have also found the actual costs of using co-ops to be essentially the same as using regular employees (Cunningham, 1972; Ehrlich, 1978).

Benefits to Employers

Based on seven case studies with diverse cooperative education employers, Arthur D. Little, Inc. (1974), developed a timeline model of when and what kind of benefits co-op employers might anticipate. Their summary of the model is reproduced here to provide a framework for examining potential employer benefits.

Table 14-1. The Phases of Cooperative Education
in Which Employer Benefits Occur.

Phases	Definition	Benefits
1. Preprofessional Employment	The period begins with the first workblock and extends up to the last workblock of the employed co-op student. Phase ends when the employee seeks and the employer considers permanent employment.	a. Provides good source of manpower (preprofessional or paraprofessional) b. Generates professional release time c. Improves the personnel selection process d. Enhances relations with colleges and other students
2. Recruitment, Selection, Orientation, and Hiring	The phase includes the last workblock of co-op student employment through completion of orientation to entry-level employment. The orientation can include either formal or informal training. Phase ends when the co-op student is hired full time *and* becomes "permanently" responsible to the supervisor for the quality of his/her work.	a. Facilitates entry-level recruiting b. Facilitates assessments of employee quality and promotability or advancement potential c. Improves access to and by minority employees d. Improves cost benefits in recruitment and training
3. Permanent Professional Placement	The period includes at least the first three years of employment. The end point of this phase is not clear from our study but	a. Improves average retention (decreases attrition b. Increases the quality of employees

Table 14-1. The Phases of Cooperative Education
in Which Employer Benefits Occur, Cont'd.

Phases	Definition	Benefits
	needs to be established. It extends to that time beyond which differences in value or performance of employees cannot be attributed to whether or not they are former co-op students.	c. Increases rapid advancement

Preprofessional Employment. This so-called phase of the Arthur D. Little, Inc., model obviously refers to the time when the co-op student is, in fact, a student. Their analysis of potential benefits that may accrue to employers corresponds with the primary motives of employers for becoming co-op participants, reported above. Employers seek cost-effective, productive workers who may have the potential, should the need exist, to become full-time employees after graduation. To what extent are these objectives realized?

One answer to the question may be inferred from the fact that over 200,000 U.S. students co-op with an estimated 75,000 to 85,000 participating employers. Ever since the time of rapid co-op expansion in the late 1960s, employers and co-op jobs have been found to meet the growing number of co-op students. Although no empirical data are available to document the claim, many cooperative education directors and coordinators of newly implemented optional programs have stated that they experienced greater success in their recruitment of employers than of students.

In the same study referred to above, Deane and others (1978) assessed employer perceptions of co-op student employees on eight performance variables. For each variable, employers were asked to evaluate the co-op student as better than, the same as, or worse than regular employees. Their findings are summarized below.

Additionally, Deane and his colleagues asked their sam-

Table 14-2. Employer Perceptions of Co-op Student Employees
Compared to Regular Employees.

Skill Category	Percentage of Co-op Employers Reporting Co-op Students as Better	Percentage of Co-op Employers Reporting Co-op Students as the Same	Percentage of Co-op Employers Reporting Co-op Students as Worse
Technical knowledge	46.5	26.3	27.2
Communication skills	47.0	38.4	14.6
Quality of work	44.7	37.9	17.4
Quantity of work	36.2	42.2	21.6
Cooperation, ability to work with people	51.6	45.7	2.7
Dependability	44.8	49.8	5.4
Ability to follow instructions	49.8	44.3	5.9
Motivation	67.3	28.6	4.1

ple of employers to provide an overall rating of the quality of the co-op programs with which they worked. Forty-eight percent rated the programs as excellent and 38 percent rated them as being above average. Only 3 percent judged them to be below average or poor. Ninety-six percent of these employers reported their intention to continue their co-op programs, and 41 percent indicated that they planned to expand their participation. Based upon these employer perceptions, and particularly in view of their findings that the marginal costs of participating are negligible, Deane and others (1978) concluded that co-op students were clearly productive and "earning their way" and that employers were satisfied that their purposes were being achieved. Other surveys of employers have yielded similar perceptions regarding the productivity of students and of employer support of cooperative education (Gore, 1973b; Ehrlich, 1978; Perloff and Sussna, 1978; Wright, 1980).

A number of studies compared the compensation of co-op student employees to that of regular employees, apparently making the assumption of negligible differences in employment costs. For example, in an assessment of Xerox Corp.'s cooperative program, Cunningham (1972) found that both wages and fringe benefits of co-ops were less than those for regular employees and concluded that the program was financially justified, provided that the co-ops perform meaningful work.

Wright (1980) assessed the co-op program of the Georgia Organization of Southern Bell in terms of its efficiency as a permanent employment source (its primary objective) and for its economic value to the company, as well. He compared the salaries of co-ops in their third through seventh quarters with the company to those of "fully productive" engineers. Before calculating the difference between the two, however, he adjusted the engineers' salaries by a "productivity factor" (0.75), which was a figure determined from questionnaire responses of supervisors of co-op students asked to judge how productive the co-ops were in relation to the engineers. (Initially, he had used "quality of work" as a second factor but found that supervisors judged co-ops and engineers to be equal in this regard and so eliminated it from his analysis.) This adjusted figure was taken to be the value of the co-ops to the company. The difference between this "value" figure and the co-ops' actual salaries was judged to be savings. He estimated (1980 salary data) that the company saved over $8,000 per co-op annually.

Wright's (1980) analysis was made only for co-ops who had worked for the company two or more quarters. He did note, however, that the productivity factor for first-quarter co-ops was 0.20 and for second-quarter co-ops was 0.50. Had his analysis included students at these levels of experience, the reported savings might well have been less. Even so, it seems likely that his conclusion that the co-op program has financial value to the company would hold true.

As part of the development and testing of a comprehensive employer benefit-cost model designed to apply to all three of the Arthur D. Little, Inc., phases, Wilson and Brown (1985) used Wright's analytic model to assess the worth of co-ops to employers. Their approach differed from Wright's in two ways. First, they interviewed supervisors to elicit their judgments of the relative productivity and work quality of co-ops. Second, the comparison group of regular employees were the persons who would perform the co-ops' tasks were there no co-ops. For the two companies that participated in their pilot study, the

average productivity factor was 0.90 and the work quality factor was 0.94. Although not as great as those of Wright, Wilson
and Brown also found employer savings in the use of co-op students. More recently, Klawitter (1986) used the same model
with thirty Canadian co-op employers and once again found
substantial savings associated with the employment of co-ops.

These savings seem to rest on four points. First, administrative costs associated with employing co-ops are marginally
negligible. Second, co-op employees are as (or nearly as) productive as the full-time employees with whom they are compared, and the quality of their work is as (or nearly as) good.
Third, the wages given to co-ops are generally no more and
often somewhat less than those given the regular employees
with whom they were compared. Lastly, fringe benefits to co-
ops are frequently less than those given regular employees
(Deane and others, 1978; Crusoe, 1983; Wilson and Brown,
1985).

There is one caveat regarding these findings that must be
noted. If co-ops were not used, they would not be replaced by
regular full-time employees in all instances. Wilson and Brown
(1985) reported that only 40 percent of the co-ops in their employer sample would be replaced. Klawitter (1986) reported
that 45 percent would be replaced by full-time employees. This
discrepancy raises questions about the necessity of those co-ops
who would not be replaced; in such cases, are there really any
savings associated with their employment? In both studies, the
employers stated that the work previously performed by the
dispensable co-ops would either be redistributed among existing
full-time employees or would simply delay the completion of
work. Both solutions would represent costs to the employers,
but whether they can be computed on the same basis used for
instances in which a full-time employee would be hired in place
of the co-op is undetermined. Hence, the conclusions of both
studies may stand, but with a more exacting analysis, the
amount of savings might be somewhat different.

In summary, available data indicate that while there are
clearly employer costs associated with the hiring of co-op students, they are marginally negligible. Some studies have shown

a comparative savings in the hiring of co-ops rather than regular employees. They further indicate that students are productive employees, comparing favorably with regular employees who would do the work were co-ops not there. Finally, it is apparent that employers perceive cooperative education to be of value, and support it with considerable enthusiasm.

Recruitment, Selection, and Hiring. As observed above, one of the major reasons for employers to participate in cooperative education is to identify and recruit potential full-time employees. This is particularly true for large corporations that annually hire substantial numbers of new graduates. Several studies suggest that the overall rate of hiring back former co-ops upon graduation approaches 40.0 percent. In a study of University of Cincinnati accounting graduates over a ten-year span, Lelievre (1960) reported that 40.5 percent remained with a co-op employer. In a national study of 1,200 cooperative graduates from five different graduating classes, Wilson and Lyons (1961) found that 38 percent returned full-time to former co-op employers. In a self-study of the Georgia-Lockheed co-op program, Phillips (1978) found that, for the twenty-two-year period from 1952 to 1973, 38 percent of their graduating co-ops returned. The University of Cincinnati (Howell, 1985), in a study of its 1985 graduates, found that 44 percent of its co-op graduates accepted offers from former co-op employers. Deane and others (1978) obtained an average estimate of 38 percent returning graduates from a national sample of 234 co-op employers. They, however, partitioned their data according to the number of months the graduate worked with the employer as an undergraduate co-op student. They found the length of co-op participation to be positively related to the rate of retention: a stay of six months or less resulted in 27 percent retention; seven to twelve months yielded 40 percent; and thirteen months or more, 53 percent.

These retention rates tell us the percentage of co-op students who remain with a co-op employer after graduation. They do not tell us the percentage remaining to whom offers were made but were unaccepted. There is not much published regarding the percentage of graduating co-ops who are invited to continue as full-time employees. Some data are available, though, and these give a somewhat different picture than "bare" retention rates. Phillips's (1978) data, for example, showed an average rate of 38 percent.

Further examination, however, shows that over the period studied, the company offered full-time employment to 60 percent of its graduating co-ops. The retention rate is raised from 38 to 65 percent when it is based on the number of co-ops to whom offers were made, rather than on the total number of co-op students graduating. Similarly, the University of Cincinnati's 44 percent retention rate is really 80 percent when it is based on the 55 percent of graduates who were tendered offers. Based on case studies of nine co-op employers, Hayes and Travis (1976) found an average 94 percent acceptance rate—166 offers of employment were made and 156 were accepted.

Despite the dearth of studies which show both offers and acceptances, the experience at Georgia-Lockheed is probably fairly typical of co-op employers who specifically seek to recruit and employ graduating co-ops.

There is another area for which published data are lacking—the comparative cost to a company of recruiting and employing one of its own co-ops as opposed to recruiting and employing a graduate who had not been a co-op employee with the company. The logic, however, is persuasive: It must be less costly to employ and place a co-op who has been with the company for some time than to employ a graduate without previous experience with the company through the customary practice of campus interviews, on-site interviews, hiring and placement decision making, and, finally, orientation of the new hire. It would appear, in any event, that many employers are persuaded that the assertion is true, since so many set the full-time employment of graduating co-ops as the principal objective of their cooperative program.

Full-time Employment. In this section, the benefits of the co-op experience for both the graduate and the employer will be examined. The two are to be linked here because many of the potential benefits for the one have their reciprocal benefits for the other. According to traditional accounts, the co-op experience helps the graduate to get a better job, get a job more quickly, get a better starting salary, and likely be promoted sooner. The same accounts assert that when employers hire co-op graduates they get better employees, more satisfied employees, and employees who stay longer. The purpose of this section will be to assess these interrelated assertions based upon findings from graduate follow-up studies.

Preparation for Careers. In assessing the impact of cooperative education on graduates, it is important to remember that they are the former students to whom the values discussed in the preceding chapter accrued as a result of their participation in co-op. Reported benefits to graduates often appear to be extensions of the same benefits ascribed to students. Thus, for example, comparative studies of cooperative and noncooperative alumni have shown that the co-op graduates were more certain of their career goals, believed themselves to be better informed about job opportunities, felt better prepared for their first job, and perceived those first jobs to be more closely related to their academic programs and to make better use of the knowledge and skills developed in college (Wilson and Lyons, 1961; Yencso, 1970; Gore, 1972; Brown, 1976; Frankel and others, 1977).

In a recent study, Brown (1985) compared three groups of graduates on their first job after graduation, all of whom worked for the same large corporation. The three groups were former co-op employees of this corporation; former co-ops who had not worked for this particular corporation; and graduates who had not been co-ops. She found that the group who had been co-op employees of the corporation had more realistic career expectations than either of the other two groups. She also found, however, that the co-op graduates who hadn't co-oped with this corporation specifically still had more realistic career expections than the non-co-op graduates. The collective evidence points to the superiority of cooperative graduates, in comparison with their noncooperative counterparts, in terms of possessing a clearer sense of career, more "savvy" about job hunting, greater ability to find permanent jobs related to their academic backgrounds, and more realistic career expectations.

The evidence also suggests that employers find these characteristics desirable. They want to hire co-ops because they are
serious and mature and not as likely to "job hop" as other candidates for employment (Gore, 1973a; Phillips, 1978; Kane,
1985). It must also be remembered that employers hire 40 percent of their co-op student employees. This, too, must be taken
as evidence that candidates for employment possessing these
qualities are perceived by employers to have value. Not only do
employers seem especially to want to employ co-op graduates
but, as one study of Australian engineering graduates has shown,
they also give them greater initial job responsibility (Gillin and
others, 1984). This difference in responsibility was even more
pronounced if the co-op graduates had fulfilled their co-op terms
at the employing company.

Financial Benefits to Graduates. The most comprehensive
assessment of cooperative education undertaken was done by
Congressional mandate and supported by federal funds. One of
the overall conclusions of that research (Frankel and others,
1977) was that cooperative education was, under most conditions, a good investment decision for students entering college.
They came to that conclusion after conducting a comprehensive
cost-benefit study of several mutually exclusive investment decisions, presumably made at the time of high school graduation.
The decisions were (1) to attend college or not; (2) to attend a
junior or community college, or a senior college or university;
(3) to major in liberal arts, engineering, business, or a health-
related field; and (4) to participate in co-op or not. A fifth variable with mutually exclusive values was also included in the
study but would seldom be referred to as an investment decision and that is the gender of the sampled students and alumni.
The researchers carefully collected, from a sample of college
students and alumni, all costs associated with attending college
(including wages they would have earned had they gone directly
to work after high school) and all income, both taxable and not
taxable. Using three-year earnings reported by their graduate
sample and census data, they also developed "streams of income" to age sixty-five for careers likely to be pursued within
each of the four fields of study.

Once all relevant cost and benefit data were collected, they were subjected to internal rate-of-return analysis. Their findings indicated, first, that an investment decision to attend college yielded significant benefits over the contrary decision. They also indicated that participating in co-op, particularly for senior college students in engineering and business, was a good investment, even if the program was five years in length. The advantage of the co-op decision was less clear for junior and community college graduates, females, or students in liberal arts and health-related curricula.

It seems a reasonable hypothesis that the advantage of choosing to co-op reported by Frankel and his colleagues is due to factors occurring at the beginning of their "benefit stream," because there is no way they could predict events along the way that would differentially alter the streams. To the advantage of the co-ops, two pieces of information collected from their graduate samples showed significant differences between co-op and non-co-op graduates, which would explain their cost-benefit results. The starting salaries of the co-op graduates were higher than those of the non-co-ops, and the co-ops had fewer and shorter periods of unemployment, when less or possibly no income would be recorded.

Other studies have also shown some starting salary advantage for the cooperative graduate, but the data on the subject are not totally consistent. Wilson and Lyons (1961) found a modest differential favoring the co-op graduates, as did Yencso (1970), Brown (1976), and Rowe (1980). The dollar differences have no meaning at this date but, in general, the reported differences were in the range of 5 to 8 percent.

On the other hand, Gore (1972) reported no difference in the starting salaries of a sample of University of Cincinnati co-op and non-co-op business administration graduates. Both Gore (1972) and Brown (1976), however, found starting salaries given graduates who had been former co-ops to be somewhat greater than those given to either non-co-op graduates or graduates who were former co-ops but with another company. In the same study, Gore (1972) found that, while the starting salaries of the co-op graduates were not greater than those of the non-co-op graduates, "current" salaries two to eight years after graduation were. Phillips (1978) also found initial salary grades of cooperative and noncooperative graduates to be the same. He further found that after three years on the job and continuing until at least the fifteenth year, co-op graduates were at a higher salary level than their non-co-op counterparts.

Employment Longevity and Promotion. Only a few available studies provide comparative information regarding either length of service with a postgraduation employer or job promotions of cooperative and noncooperative graduates. Wilson and Lyons (1961), collecting data from co-op and non-co-op alumni who had graduated two, five, seven, ten, and twenty years previously, found no differences in either the length of time they remained on their first full-time job after graduation or the number of jobs they had held since graduation. Similarly, Yencso (1971) found no difference between his samples of co-op and non-co-op alumni who had graduated five and eight years previously, in terms of the proportion still on their first job since graduation. Finally, Brown (1976) in her study of alumni graduating five and ten years previously also found no difference in the length of time graduates of co-op and non-co-op programs remained on their first job. While the belief is widespread that cooperative graduates do less "job hopping" than graduates of traditional college programs, and while data that would provide substantiation may exist (in either organized or unorganized fashion) within companies, the available literature does not support it.

Brown's data (1976) also show no difference in the promotion rates of cooperative and noncooperative alumni. On the other hand, Phillips' (1978) evaluation of his own company's experience shows a steady advantage in promotions to cooperative graduates over a fifteen-year period. One possible explanation of the discrepancy in these findings is that Phillips was reporting on the experience of one company with a highly structured cooperative program, the intent of which is to groom students for full-time employment, and the graduates studied were this company's own co-ops; whereas Brown's data constitute the reports of several hundred graduates whose co-op employers surely represented a range of practices and who were not, in probably 60 percent of cases, working for former co-op employers. In any event, existing literature does demonstrate that either employment longevity or promotion is a probable outcome of the cooperative experience.

Summary

There appear to be identifiable benefits associated with participation in cooperative education for students (see Chapter Thirteen), graduates of cooperative programs, and employers of cooperative students. The evidence suggests that employers become involved in co-op because they have human resource needs which they believe can be effectively met through employing co-op students. Principally, they seek either or both cost-effective student employees and full-time postgraduation employees. Findings from several studies indicate that to a substantial extent they achieve both these purposes. It is generally argued that one of the values of hiring former co-ops is that the process of doing so is less costly than the more traditional process. The point is reasonable, but there are no available data to confirm or deny it. This seems to be a topic for future research.

Employers also seek co-ops for full-time employment because they are perceived to be mature, serious, and stable. There is evidence to support at least some of these perceptions. Co-op students are realistic in their expectations, have clear career goals and seem to be very sure of them, and are confident of their ability to meet work requirements. Available data about employment stability do not support the notion that co-op graduates remain longer with employers than do non-co-op graduates. Neither do the available data fully support the contention that co-op graduates are promoted sooner and/or more frequently than their non-co-op counterparts. As was the case in one study cited, it is possible that if the sample of graduates were restricted to just those co-op graduates working for a former co-op employer, greater stability over other graduates, co-op or not, might be evidenced.

The values to graduates who were co-op students seem to

lie in the facts that they do have a clear sense of career and purpose, good career and job information, and good job contacts and job-seeking skills. The evidence is that they have fewer and shorter periods of unemployment than non-co-op graduates. This last phenomenon is open to various explanations. One explanation is that co-op graduates tend to come from working-class families for whom jobs and careers are especially important and are responding to internal and/or external pressures to "get on with it." Hence, they tend to rush into employment. While this is a tenable explanation and may well apply in some instances, other data (such as a large percentage being hired directly from their co-op jobs and at higher starting salaries) suggest a simpler explanation, namely, that their job experience and the other characteristics already described make them highly desirable and sought-after job candidates.

References

Arthur D. Little, Inc. *Documented Employer Benefits from Cooperative Education.* Report of a Study for Northeastern University. Cambridge, Mass.: Arthur D. Little, Inc., 1974.

Brown, S. J. *Cooperative Education and Career Development: A Comparative Study of Alumni.* Boston: Cooperative Education Research Center, Northeastern University, 1976.

Brown, S. J. "The Relationship of Cooperative Education to Organizational Socialization and Sense of Power in First Job After College." Unpublished doctoral dissertation, Department of Educational Research, Measurement, and Evaluation, Boston College, 1985.

Crusoe, J. A. "First Annual Cooperative Education Student Salary and Benefits Survey." Paper presented at the 19th annual meeting of the Cooperative Education Association, Inc., Toronto, Canada, Apr. 1983.

Cunningham, J. B. "Cooperative Education Program Study." Unpublished paper, Xerox Corporation, Webster, N.Y., 1972.

Deane, R. T., and others. "An Analysis of Co-op Students' Employment Costs and Benefits." *Journal of Cooperative Education,* 1978, *14* (2), 5-53.

Ehrlich, D. J. "Employer Assessment of a Cooperative Education Program." *Journal of Cooperative Education,* 1978, *14* (2), 74–87.

Frankel, S., and others. *Cooperative Education: A National Assessment—Final Report.* Silver Spring, Md.: Applied Management Sciences, 1977.

Gillin, L. M., and others. "Evaluating the Career Progress of Australian Engineering Graduates." *Journal of Cooperative Education,* 1984, *20* (3), 53–70.

Gore, G. J. "New Evidence of the Co-op System Relevancy." *Journal of Cooperative Education,* 1972, *8* (2), 7–14.

Gore, G. J. "Why Should We Get Involved?" *Journal of Cooperative Education,* 1973a, *9* (2), 46–52.

Gore, G. J. "Value of Co-op as the Graduate Views It." *Journal of Cooperative Education,* 1973b, *9* (2), 53–59.

Hayes, R. A., and Travis, J. H. *Employer Experience With Cooperative Education: Analysis of Costs and Benefits.* Detroit, Mich.: The Detroit Institute of Technology, 1976.

Howell, J. "Employment Decisions of 1985 Co-op Graduates." *Co-op Ed Digest* (University of Cincinnati), 1985, *15* (1), 2.

Kane, L. J. "The Synergy of Industrial Internship Programs." *Journal of Cooperative Education,* 1985, *21* (2), 32–35.

Klawitter, R. "A Cost Benefit Model for Employer Participation in Cooperative Education." Unpublished report, University of Waterloo, 1986.

Lelievre, T. "Survey of Cooperative Education—1950–1959." Unpublished paper, University of Cincinnati, 1960.

Perloff, R., and Sussna, E. "Toward an Evolution of Cooperative Education: A Managerial Perspective." *Journal of Cooperative Education,* 1978, *14* (2), 54–73.

Phillips, J. J. "An Employer Analysis of a Cooperative Education Program." *Journal of Cooperative Education,* 1978, *14* (2), 104–120.

Pistler, N. "Quest for Quality—Monitoring the Program—'Monitoring Efficient Use of Co-op Students.' " Paper presented at 20th annual meeting of the Cooperative Education Association, Inc., New Orleans, Louisiana, Apr. 26, 1984.

Robbins, D. M. "Cooperative Education and the Federal Government." *Journal of Cooperative Education,* 1978, *14* (2), 88-92.

Rowe, P. M. "Cooperative Programs: Especially Beneficial for Women?" *Journal of Cooperative Education,* 1980, *16* (2), 50-58.

Tornatsky, L. G., and Lounsbury, J. W. "Dimensions of Interorganizational Interaction in Social Agencies." *Journal of Community Psychology,* 1979, *7,* 198-209.

Weinstein, D. S., and Wilson, J. W. "An Employer Description of a Model Cooperative Education Program." *Journal of Cooperative Education,* 1983, *20* (1), 60-83.

Wilson, J. W. *Models for Collaboration: Developing Work-Education Ties.* Washington, D.C.: American Society for Training and Development, 1980.

Wilson, J. W. "Analysis of Cooperative Education as a Work/Education Joint Venture." *Journal of Cooperative Education,* 1984, *21* (1), 29-39. (Originally published in *Proceedings of the World Conference on Cooperative Education,* no. 3. Hawthorne, Australia: Swinburne College Press, 1983.)

Wilson, J. W. "Cost-Effectiveness of Employer Participation in Cooperative Education." Paper presented at Fourth World Conference on Cooperative Education, Edinburgh, Scotland, September 1985.

Wilson, J. W., and Brown, S. J. *A Benefit-Cost Model for Employer Participation in Cooperative Education.* Boston: Cooperative Education Research Center, Northeastern University, 1985.

Wilson, J. W., and Lyons, E. H. *Work-Study College Programs: Appraisal and Report of the Study of Cooperative Education.* New York: Harper & Row, 1961.

Wiseman, R. L., and Page, N. R. "Predicting Employer's Benefits from Cooperative Education." *Journal of Cooperative Education,* 1983, *20* (1), 45-59.

Wright, J. J. "Georgia's Cooperative Education Program." Unpublished report, Georgia Organization of Southern Bell, 1980.

Yencso, W. R. "A Comparative Analysis of Engineering Graduates from Cooperative and Regular Programs: Career Status

and Attainment of 1962 and 1965 Baccalaureate Graduates."
Unpublished doctoral dissertation, University of Michigan,
1970.

Yencso, W. R. "Comparing Engineering Graduates from Cooperative and Regular Programs." *Engineering Education*, 1971,
61, 816-818.

Fifteen

Meeting the Challenges
and Opportunities
of the Next Decade

Kenneth G. Ryder

The intent of this chapter is to speculate on the future of cooperative education. Such speculation, of course, has the inherent danger of becoming simply a flight into prophetic fantasy. One way to avoid that danger is to use the "lost horse" method of prophecy. According to this method, one simply asks the question, What direction was it heading when last seen? The question to ask here, then, is, In what direction does cooperative education currently seem to be heading? To this question must be added a second, What conditions or circumstances are likely to influence co-op, pushing it further along its present course or setting it off in some other direction? A second way to avoid prophetic fantasy is not to look too far ahead. Thus, this chapter will content itself with reflecting on cooperative education as it may develop over the next decade, until the arrival of a new century. Finally, rather than simply focusing on the shape of co-op in ten years, this chapter will focus on forecasting the challenges and opportunities that will face cooperative education and the effect these can have on the method if they are indeed met.

Current Direction of Cooperative Education

Understanding where cooperative education currently stands and the direction in which it seems to be moving requires briefly reviewing the path already traveled. The preceding chapters have provided a rich account of that path. From a single program with twenty-seven students, cooperative education has grown in its eighty-year history to a plan of education involving one-third of all the postsecondary institutions in America and about 200,000 students annually. This growth occurred, at least in part, because co-op was extended from its initial implementation, in undergraduate, baccalaureate-granting, engineering programs for men, to associate degree programs and graduate programs in virtually any curriculum offered by institutions and for all students, including female, minority, handicapped, and adult students. It grew, in part, because it responded well to the educational and career development needs of students and because institutions sought to increase the relevancy of the education they offered. It grew, too, because employers found significant benefits in the program. Finally, it grew because individuals, groups of individuals, professional societies, and specialized agencies—all committed to the validity of co-op—provided strong and effective advocacy on college campuses, in employing firms, and in both the federal government and numerous state governments.

Throughout its history, cooperative education has demonstrated its value to higher education in at least four significant ways. First, it has demonstrated that it is an educational method of considerable merit; it is pedagogically sound. Second, it has shown itself to be a cost-saving means to postsecondary education. Third, it has been found to be an effective and cost-efficient human resource strategy for employers. Fourth, it has proved itself adaptable to a variety of institutional settings and to the educational needs of diverse students pursuing diverse fields of study. These are not only accomplishments of cooperative education, they constitute its fundamental strength as an educational method and will carry it, as such, into the future.

Current Forces and Their Likely Impact
on Cooperative Education

In the opening chapter of this volume, it was noted that cooperative education was conceived and its initiation made possible in part because of environmental conditions in the early twentieth century. So, too, events and circumstances in the last decade of the century will almost surely present challenges and opportunities that directly or indirectly affect the future character and role of cooperative education in higher education. Several such conditions already exist and are exerting their impact. Those that seem to have the greatest potential for influencing cooperative education include demographic changes, the cost of postsecondary education, a need for educational reform, changing employment needs, and international competition and internationalism.

Demographic Changes. Since the beginning of the 1980s, many parts of the country have been experiencing a sharp decline in the numbers of young persons in the eighteen to twenty-two age range, the typical college-age years. The decline is expected to continue until the mid-1990s. The impact of this on the nation's colleges and universities is obvious. It is the same as that experienced by elementary schools in the early 1970s and by secondary schools in the late seventies and early eighties. Facilities and staffs, geared for larger populations of school children and students, were too large and too many for the new population. About the only viable solution for public school systems was retrenchment—abandoning, leasing, or selling school buildings and letting teachers go. Institutions of higher education are facing retrenchment decisions now and will continue to do so over the next several years. Obviously, retrenchment is as likely to affect cooperative education as any other program. The consequence for institutions, particularly in the absence of external support, would be severe program curtailment. For some programs, again, should they not have external support, it could mean total abandonment of cooperative education. At best, assuming no options other than retrenchment were available or exercised, the continued growth of co-op would be stalled. Nationally, there would be a contraction of cooperative education of considerable proportions.

Institutions of higher education, however, do have options not available to elementary and secondary school systems. They exist because college and university student bodies are voluntary and because geographic barriers to enrollment are not obligatory. Thus institutions can try to cushion the need for retrenchment by attracting students whom they have not attracted in the past or have not attracted in large numbers. There are two principal strategies for accomplishing this. The first is to invest in recruiting the same kinds of students that have typically enrolled but to try to get a larger proportion of these students from regularly recruited areas and/or to go geographically farther and farther afield, especially to parts of the country where college-age youth are available. This is a strategy of trying to capture a larger piece of a shrinking pie. Cooperative education can have an especially significant role in this effort. It can become, as suggested by Dubé and Korngold (see Chapter Six), an important focus of an institutional marketing plan. If such a plan were at all successful, then one would expect students to arrive on campus with the intention of participating in co-op. Hence, existing co-op programs could grow larger.

The second strategy, and one likely to attract more notable success, is to develop new markets of potential students. The two most likely markets appear to be foreign nationals seeking an American education and older students seeking to retrain or to upgrade their knowledge and skills. The impact on cooperative education of successful efforts to attract substantial numbers of either of these groups, were they to participate in the co-op program, would be not only to expand the program numerically but also to change its character. For example, either group may need additional and/or specialized counseling. Adult students might require a different pattern of co-op to accommodate their need for continuous work and steady income. New arrangements with employers, such as those described by Vozzella and Tillman (see Chapter Twelve), might also be needed to accommodate foreign nationals.

Changing demographics are not only the concern of colleges and universities; they are the concern of employers, who require a steady flow of professional employees. It is clear to them that if there are fewer young people entering college, there will be fewer coming out. To increase their opportunities to "get their share" of graduates, employers look to cooperative education as a means of identifying as early as possible those students to whom they want to offer full-time employment. This could, if it has not already done so, lead employers to encourage colleges to expand their co-op programs or even to establish such programs where they do not exist.

Costs of Education. The cost of a college education in America has climbed steadily over the years. With relatively fixed overhead costs and declining enrollments, this trend is likely to continue. For the past few years, tuition and board increases have exceeded the national inflation rate. During the same period, there has been a dramatic shift from grants to loans as the principal means of student financial assistance. This has raised the specter of a generation of college graduates beginning their adult lives in serious debt.

Cooperative education does not represent a total solution to the tuition debt problem, but it offers a substantial partial relief from the burden of college expenses and a viable alternative to heavy borrowing. This fact, if made part of an institution's effort to market itself through its cooperative education program, could have a decided impact upon projections for declining students.

Education Reform. Over the past few years, American higher education has been the target of a number of commissioned reports, each of which has been critical of the curriculum provided and of the standards of excellence adhered to. In calling for reform, these critics have concluded that the nation is in serious risk of pervasive mediocrity. Frequently, their solution is "get back to basics." This could pose a problem or an opportunity to cooperative education.

Traditionally, and despite evidence to the contrary, many people involved in higher education who have clung rigidly to a belief that true excellence can only be achieved by emulating classical universities like Oxford and Cambridge have considered that cooperative education is not really academically legitimate. They contend that it is too applied, too vocational, and that it is anti-intellectual. These contentions could be rekindled as faculties wrestle with the issues of strengthening the curriculum and raising standards of excellence. Should cooperative education fail to respond positively to such criticism, a serious problem of faculty support could arise. In light of the potential pressure to strengthen and expand cooperative education noted above, such lack of support could lead to damaging conflict within the institution and could very well blunt further development of co-op.

On the other hand, cooperative education could become an integral part of curriculum reform. Proponents could respond in two ways to the concerns of those who question co-op's academic soundness. First, as Heinemann advises (see Chapter Five), they could take the lead in finding ways to more closely coordinate co-op with the curriculum. Many programs already have close links with their schools' academic departments through their advising and crediting practices. At least one program (LaGuardia Community College) has involved its faculty and coordination staff in collaborative efforts to incorporate into beginning courses instructional units that explain what a particular field of study has to say about work. For example, beginning courses in sociology, psychology, and communications could include units on the sociology of the workplace, the psychology of work, and communicating in the workplace. These programs sought to truly integrate the two elements of their curricula. More creative ideas are needed that, while recognizing and supporting the unique responsibilities of the classroom teacher and the cooperative coordinator, will bring them closer together in their common function.

The second effort cooperative education must make if it is to meet the challenge of education reform is to more fully develop a persuasive, pedagogical rationale, and perhaps the first step in this is to explicitly recognize that more than one valid rationale is possible. For example, it could be argued, as in fact it has been, that co-op is an extension, albeit a very sophisticated extension, of the college laboratory. It has also been suggested that co-op is an effective bridge between the explication of principles and theory and the practices based on them as required in the workplace. Finally, the point has been advanced that cooperative education, rather than being narrowly conceived as vocational, is really a part of general education because it promotes understandings, mature attitudes, and social skills required of all students, regardless of their fields of study or after-graduation objectives. Obviously, it is not the intent here to develop a pedagogical rationale for co-op. What is intended, however, is to suggest that a more sophisticated and well-documented rationale is needed and that, if it is to explain all of the applications to which co-op has been put and might be put, it must be multidimensional. Current interest in examining and reforming higher education could well stimulate the development of a widely accepted rationale for cooperative education.

Changing Employment Needs. The phrase "changing employment needs" has two points of reference: (1) jobs today are considerably different than they were just a few years ago and require greater skill and more complex knowledge; and (2) jobs are changing ever more rapidly, demanding ever new competencies. The consequence of these changes is a vast need for training and retraining. In 1986, U.S. corporations spent over $210 billion on employee training, and it is estimated that some 75 percent of all current employees will at some time during their working years require retraining. Corporations and professional employers will continue to look to postsecondary institutions for qualified workers, but the evidence seems clear that the simplistic view of the academy as supplier and the workplace as consumer of trained and productive workers no longer holds. They now share and will continue to share responsibility and investment in training and retraining. Thus, the issue is not who is responsible, but who can do what best in order to achieve a goal of national productivity.

Sorting out who can do what best will need to be done collaboratively. It seems clear that the colleges and universities can continue to educate their students in principles and theories as they traditionally have. However, as knowledge and technologies evolve at accelerating rates, this role may become increasingly important. This means that there will be less time available to teach applications and to prepare students for immediate productive employment after graduation. Instruction in specific applications may well be a responsibility that falls to the employers. The notion of cooperative education as a bridge between the academy and the workplace could well have particular significance under these conditions. Interaction and joint ventures between higher education institutions and corporations or other professional employers, with cooperative education as the principal vehicle, could be strongly stimulated by these events.

Institutions also have a potentially important role in the upgrading and retraining processes. With cooperative education as a central component, institutions could provide specialized and specifically designed courses and programs of study, which might or might not lead to a degree and which could be offered at the institution or at the worksite. A cooperative work component may be organized very differently than it is today but to the worker-students of tomorrow will be just as beneficial.

The essential point to be made here is that higher education will have an opportunity to contribute in more and varied ways to the nation's productivity through joint training ventures with corporations. Cooperative education could play a significant role in these joint ventures. The principal requirements will be a commitment to such ventures, a creative approach in designing programs collaboratively, and flexibility in determining how to best meet the needs of the worker-students.

Internationalism. For some time now the United States has experienced a series of economic dislocations in particular industries. A few years ago the automotive industry was in crisis. It has since recovered substantially, but now the agricultural, petroleum, and banking industries are experiencing difficulty. Cyclical downturns in the economy are not new to America, but these recent ones are occasioned by different factors than in the past and have called for different solutions (Varty, 1986). The principal causes of these economic woes are international economic conditions and international competition. The United States is experiencing considerable competition for its goods in what have traditionally been its virtually exclusive markets. Clearly, the nation has entered a new era of international competition.

As a consequence and in order to improve its competitiveness, the United States has begun to enter into joint ventures with companies of other countries, linking national economies. According to Naisbitt (1984), for example, "Ford's new world car, the Escort, is being put together in the United States, Britain and Germany from parts made in Spain, Italy, Britain, Japan and Brazil. . . . Volkswagen provides engines for Dodge Omni/Horizon cars and Mitsubishi the engines for Chrysler's Dodge Colt and other models. Many of the components are produced in the Third World" (p. 65). The automotive industry is not the only example of an international joint venture involving the production of components and assembly of final products; among others are the electronic and computer industries.

The purposes of the joint ventures are, of course, to improve the productivity, quality, and cost-effectiveness of participating corporations, all or most of which are already multinational. To further these same purposes, it is likely that American corporations will put new efforts into research and design and, to the fullest extent possible, will use applications of high technology in manufacturing.

This developing internationalism has broad implications for higher education and for cooperative education. It could, for example, stimulate foreign nationals to study in the United States with the intent of returning to their home countries and working for an American multinational corporation. Having these students participate in co-op programs with the multinational, both in the United States and at "home," are distinct possibilities, as discussed by Vozzella and Tillman (see Chapter Twelve). It might also be that employee travel to other countries to confer with foreign colleagues will greatly increase and become commonplace. In this case, overseas co-op placement of American students may become more frequent. Even if graduates never physically travel to another country, the likelihood is that they will interact regularly with their counterparts in other countries by telex, telephone, or computer. The need for students to develop an international perspective so that they will be able to communicate effectively on such issues as design, engineering, manufacturing, and distribution could become critical (Varty, 1986). Cooperative education work experiences and associated seminars could help to provide this perspective and promote necessary cross-cultural understandings.

The recent growth of international communication regarding cooperative education has hardly been a consequence of the rapidly developing international economic links but is surely related to a growing international sensitivity. Brunel University, England, was the site of the first World Conference on Cooperative Education. Since then, four other biennial conferences have been held, in Boston, Melbourne, Edinburgh, and Amsterdam. These conferences have demonstrated, as the report by Turner and Frederick (see Chapter Four) has documented, that cooperative education in a variety of forms is a worldwide instructional method. In 1983, two international organizations were created, the World Council for Cooperative Education and the World Assembly for Cooperative Education. The Council is a body of fifteen persons from eight countries: Australia, Canada, England, Hong Kong, the Netherlands, the Philippines, Singapore, and the United States. The Assembly is a substantially larger group, representing, for the most part, the same countries as the Council. The Council functions as does a board of trustees or directors. It sets goals and agendas for the future direction of worldwide participation in cooperative education. The Assembly is an advisory group to the Council. The work of both bodies is developing slowly, and it is perhaps still too early to know how they will develop and how effective they will be in their effort to coalesce world interest in cooperative education.

Already, the world conferences have spawned a number of cooperative exchange programs as delegates from different countries have met and discussed mutual interests. These have been student exchanges and co-op coordinator exchanges. It is certainly to be expected that, if these conferences continue and delegates from additional countries attend, more of these exchanges will be arranged. Multinational companies could play an important role in this enterprise. It also seems likely that there

could be an exchange of ideas about cooperative education—
ways of better integrating study and work, arrangements with
employers, and means of assessing effectiveness.

There is no doubt that this nation has entered an era of
international competition, international joint ventures, and
international communication. There is, likewise, little doubt
that this internationalism is going to affect all facets of American life, including higher education and, within that, cooperative education. Precisely where that effect will lead is uncertain,
but lead it will.

A Look Ahead

As noted in the beginning of this chapter, the major
strengths of cooperative education that should stand this educational plan in good stead are its soundness as an educational
method, its potential for easing the costs of higher education,
its potential for human resource development, and its adaptability to a wide variety of institutional settings and conditions.
The societal conditions and circumstances that seem likely to
affect the future direction of cooperative education include the
declining pool of traditional college-age students, the continuing increase in the costs of higher education, pressure for educational reform, the demand for ever changing work skills and
competencies precipitated by advances in technologies, and the
rapidly developing interdependence of nations.

These conditions will undoubtedly affect the institution
itself, if not the co-op program. Institutions may choose to re-
trench until such time as the pool of available college-age students increases. They may not choose to market the institution
through the cooperative program, or they may not choose to
recruit foreign nationals or adult workers. Similarly, institutions
may or may not wish to respond to any or all of the other conditions. If an institution chooses to accept the opportunities
proferred by new conditions and rises to the challenges offered,
there are several implications for the future of cooperative
education.

1. Cooperative education programs will become larger

and more comprehensive, have more heterogeneous student populations, and operate in more than a single mode. Institutions will have a greater diversity of students: traditional, foreign nationals, and adult workers in full-time and specialized programs of study. Students will participate in co-op for various reasons and they will enter into it with varying needs and varying constraints upon their participation. Some, for example, will participate in co-op because they see it as an entrée into a career in their home country; others will see it as a bridge between current employment and retraining goals. But, in general, co-op will become more comprehensive, both in regard to institutional coverage and modes of operation.

2. Business and industry will increase their participation in cooperative education and will enter into other joint ventures with colleges and universities that have a co-op component. To achieve greater assurance of a flow of able graduates into their organizations, particularly graduates who have had experience in their operations, business and industry will rely increasingly on cooperative education as a means of identifying, recruiting, and employing full-time, professional employees. They will also enter into training and retraining programs with nearby colleges and look to cooperative education programs to help achieve integration between workers' studies, their current work, and their future work. These activities could lead to very different kinds of cooperative education, which will function concurrently with traditional programming.

3. The number of cooperative programs may increase, but there is considerable uncertainty about it. Certainly, the pressures that will cause existing programs to grow larger will apply, and some institutions may initiate programs to achieve the same kind of results. If federal support for cooperative education continues through Title VIII, even more institutions may explore and implement programs. Should Title VIII be zero-funded, the likelihood of many new programs becomes much less.

4. Cooperative education programs will explore ways of more closely integrating the work experiences into the academic framework of the institutions of which they are a part. Increas-

ingly, learning objectives for cooperative work assignments will be articulated in terms of students' general education. More collaborative efforts between co-op professionals and teaching faculty will be encouraged. There will also be more efforts to develop an appropriate pedagogical rationale for cooperative education, and discussions and debates relating to these efforts will appear in professional journals and be the subject of papers given at forums and conferences.

5. Cooperative education will become more involved in overseas assignments for American students and in the placement of foreign nationals with American multinational companies. These placements will occur both in the United States and in the students' home country. There will also be an increase in the number of cooperative education exchange programs between the colleges and universities in the United States and institutions in other countries. This latter will be stimulated, in part because better and more frequent communication will result from increasing effectiveness and influence of the World Council and the World Assembly and in part because of technological advances in networking.

The challenges and opportunities that face higher education in the United States are substantial. They will have great impact on many parts of the nation's colleges and universities. No unit, however, will be tested more or presented greater opportunity to contribute to meeting these challenges than their programs of cooperative education.

References

Naisbitt, J. *Megatrends.* New York: Warner Books, 1984.

Varty, J. "Cooperative Education: Directions for the 90's and Beyond." *Journal of Cooperative Education,* 1986, *24* (2).

Resource

Organizations, Societies, and Agencies Involved in Cooperative and Experiential Education

The organizations, societies, and agencies listed below are sources of additional information about cooperative and other forms of experiential and work-related education.

Centers of Cooperative Education Training

Each of the following is a cooperative education training center supported by a grant from Title VIII of the Higher Education Act. Each develops and presents its own programs and sets its own calendar of programs.

> Association for International Practical Training
> National Office
> Park View Building, Suite 320
> 10480 Little Patuxent Parkway
> Columbia, MD 21044-3502
> 301/997-2200

> Center for Cooperative Education
> Northeastern University
> 360 Huntington Avenue
> Boston, MA 02115
> 617/437-4213

Mountain and Plains Center for Cooperative Education
Red Rocks Community College
12600 W. 6th Avenue
Golden, CO 80401
303/988-6160

National Commission for Cooperative Education
Training Division
99 Westcliff Road
Weston, MA 02193
617/239-0257

National Community College Training Center
Room 1031
30 E. Lake Street
Chicago, IL 60601

Northwest Cooperative Education Center
Highline Community College
Stop 25-5A
Midway, WA 98031
206/433-8590

Southwest Cooperative Education Training Center
University of Alabama
PO Box 222
University, AL 35486
205/348-6422

University of Cincinnati
Division of Professional Practice
MC 115
Cincinnati, OH 45221
513/475-3061

Western Resource Center for Cooperative Education
California Polytechnic State University at San Luis
Obispo
Chase Hall, Room 108
San Luis Obispo, CA 93407
805/544-5446

Societies and Agencies Involved in
Cooperative and Experiential Education

College Placement Council, Inc.
    62 Highland Avenue
    Bethlehem, PA 18017
    215/868-1421

Coordinates the activities of seven regional college placement associations. Develops and publishes materials to assist college placement staff, including an annual survey of salary offers. Publishes *CPC Annual.*

Cooperative Education Association
    655 Fifteenth Street N.W.
    Washington, DC 20005
    202/639-4770

The principal professional society for persons involved or interested in cooperative education. The CEA holds annual conferences and publishes a professional journal, *Journal of Cooperative Education,* and a newsletter.

Cooperative Education Division of the American Society
for Engineering Education
    One Dupont Circle
    Washington, DC 20036
    202/293-7080

CED is the oldest professional society for cooperative education personnel. It holds an annual meeting in conjunction with the annual conference of ASEE and publishes a newsletter.

Cooperative Education Research Center
    Northeastern University
    360 Huntington Avenue
    Boston, MA 02115
    617/437-3780

Conducts research into various topics in cooperative education. Maintains a computerized database of cooperative education programs and their characteristics for postsecondary institutions in the United States and Canada and maintains a clearinghouse of articles and reports on cooperative education, which it makes available at cost.

Council for Experiential and Adult Learning
American City Building, Suite 212
Columbia, MD 21044
301/997-3535

An organization for which there are institutional memberships. It provides a network of consulting services and conducts forums on organizing and operating experiential programs and on the assessment of experience-based learning.

Cooperative Work Experience Education Association
Reporters Building, Room 615
400 Maryland Avenue S.W.
Washington, DC 20202
202/732-2433

A professional society for persons interested or involved in secondary and/or vocational education. It holds an annual conference in conjunction with that of the American Vocational Association.

National Association of Student Employment Administrators
Care of: Student Employment Service
The University of Texas at Arlington
Arlington, TX 76019
817/273-2895

A professional society of institution administrators of student employment services. It holds annual meetings. In 1985 NASEA published a report entitled *Education at Work*.

National Commission for Cooperative Education
360 Huntington Avenue
Boston, MA 02115
617/437-3465

An agency for advocacy of cooperative education with institutional memberships. It provides consultancy and training programs for the cooperative education community and undertakes projects to promote the growth of cooperative education.

The National Center for Research in Vocational Education
    The Ohio State University
    1960 Kenny Road
    Columbus, OH 43210
    614/486-3655 or 800/848-4815

Provides technical assistance, leadership development, training, and information services to vocational, adult, and other educators.

National Institute for Work Learning
    1200 18th Street N.W.
    Washington, DC 20036
    202/887-6800

Seeks to improve the relationship between institutions of work and of learning and to facilitate linkages between them. Provides technical assistance, conducts research and policy studies, and undertakes pilot projects in information networking.

National Society for Internships and Experiential Education
    122 St. Mary's Street
    Raleigh, NC 27605
    919/834-7536

A professional association for persons involved with internships, service learning, cooperative education, intercultural learning, and other forms of experiential education. Holds annual conferences and publishes a newsletter.

U.S. Department of Education
    Office of Postsecondary Education
    Cooperative Education
    ROB #3, Room 3514
    400 Maryland Avenue S.W.
    Washington, DC 20202
    202/245-3253

Responsible for the administration of Title VIII (Cooperative Education) of the Higher Education Act of 1965, as amended. It can supply a list of current federally supported cooperative education training programs.

Office of Vocational and Adult Education
   Cooperative Education, Work Study and Work Experience Programs
   Reporters Building, Room 615
   400 Maryland Avenue S.W.
   Washington, DC 20202
   202/732-2433

Responsible for postsecondary and adult education occupational programs. Provides technical assistance and guidance on funding through vocational education acts.

Index